EARLY FAMILIES OF
YORK COUNTY
PENNSYLVANIA

Volume 2

Keith A. Dull

HERITAGE BOOKS
2006

HERITAGE BOOKS

AN IMPRINT OF HERITAGE BOOKS, INC.

Books, CDs, and more—Worldwide

For our listing of thousands of titles see our website
at
www.HeritageBooks.com

Published 2006 by
HERITAGE BOOKS, INC.
Publishing Division
65 East Main Street
Westminster, Maryland 21157-5026

Other books by the author:

Early Families of York County, Pennsylvania, Volume 1
Early Families of Somerset and Fayette Counties, Pennsylvania
Early Families of Berks, Bucks and Montgomery Counties, Pennsylvania
Early Families of Lancaster, Lebanon and Dauphin Counties, Pennsylvania
Early German Settlers of York County, Pennsylvania

International Standard Book Number: 978-1-58549-312-0

This book is dedicated to my Grandmother
Dorothy Viola (Shock) Dull

with special thanks to
my wife Karen for her support

and the following researchers
whose work contributed to portions of this book

David L. Bailey
Caral Mechling Bennett
Darleen Berens
Harry A. Diehl

TABLE OF CONTENTS

UNCONNECTED YORK COUNTY LINES

INTRODUCTION

Compilation of these genealogies was based on research conducted at the Allen County Public Library, Fort Wayne, Indiana; Huntington County Public Library, Huntington, Indiana; and the York County Historical Society, York, Pennsylvania.

Church records for the following churches were consulted:
Christ's Evangelical Lutheran Church, York, Pennsylvania.
Emmanuel Lutheran Church.
First Reformed Church of Lancaster, Pennsylvania.
Fissel's (Jerusalem) Union Church, near Shrewsbury, Pennsylvania.
Friedensaal (Schuster's, White) Church.
Glade Reformed Church.
Rader's Lutheran Church, Timberville, Virginia.
Rocky Hill (Grace) Lutheran Church, Woodsboro, Maryland.
Saddler's (St. John's) Lutheran Church, Stewartstown, Pennsylvania.
St. Jacob's (Stone) Union Church, near Brodbecks, Pennsylvania.
St. Jacobus Lutheran Church.
St. Paul's (Zeigler's) Evangelical Lutheran Church.
St. Peter's (Yellow) Reformed Church.
Seltenreich Reformed Lutheran Church.
Sponagle Lutheran Church, Suger Grove, Ohio.
Steltz Union (Bethlehem) Church, New Freedom, Pennsylvania.
Strayer's (Salem) Lutheran Church.
Strayer's (Salem) Reformed Church.
The First Reformed Church of York, York, Pennsylvania.
The Private Pastoral Records of Reverend Jacob Lischy.
The Private Pastoral Records of Johan Casper Stoever.
The White Oaks Congregation.

The following court records were consulted:
Fairfield County, Ohio Deeds, Tax Records, and Wills.
Frederick County, Maryland Deeds, Tax Records, and Wills.
Hocking County, Ohio Deeds, Tax Records, and Wills.
Lancaster County, Pennsylvania Deeds, Tax Records, and Wills.
Rockingham County, Virginia Deeds, Tax Records, and Wills.
Warren County, Ohio Deeds, Tax Records, and Wills.
York County, Pennsylvania Deeds, Tax Records, and Wills.

The following census records were consulted:
Fairfield County, Ohio 1820-1920.
Hocking County, Ohio 1830-1920.
Montgomery County, Virginia 1850

Rockingham County, Virginia 1800-1850.
York County, Pennsylvania 1790-1860.

Information on the European Origins of some of families has been
taken from Annette K. Burgert's *Eighteenth Century Emigrants
from the Northern Alsace to America.* (Camden, ME: Picton Press,
1992).

THE KULL FAMILY (1)

Johann Phillip,[1] progenitor, b. March 7, 1699/1700, and m. Anna Maria[1.5n], dau. of Matthias[1n] and Anna Catharina Kroeller, at Neusatz, Neuenbuerg, Wuerttemburg, Germany in 1722. Johann Phillip d. at Neusatz Sept. 28, 1753. Phillip and Anna Maria had the following children in Neusatz: Gottfried[1.1], b. March 27, 1723; Elisabetha[1.2], b. March 23, 1723/24; Johann Adam[1.3], b. Nov. 12, 1725; Egedius[1.4], b. Feb. 22, 1728/29; Christoph[1.5], b. Jan. 29, 1730/31; Jacob Friedrich[1.6], b. Nov. 7, 1733; Anna Martha[1.7], b. Sept. 18, 1737; Ludwig[1.8], b. Feb. 9, 1739/40.

Christoph[1.5] Kull, son of Johann Phillip and Anna Maria, b. Jan. 29, 1730/31, and m. Regina Barbara[1.1.1.1o], dau. of Johann Michael[1.1.1o] and Anna Maria[1.3.3q] (Hamann) Ragg. They had the following children in Neusatz, Neuenbuerg, Wuerttemburg, Germany: Johann Christoph[1.5.1], b. Oct. 6, 1761; Jacob Friedrich[1.5.2], b. July 6, 1763; Johann Michael[1.5.3], b. May 10, 1765; Johann Phillip[1.5.4], b. Jan. 9, 1770; Gottfried[1.5.5], b. Jan. 20, 1773.

Johann Christoph[1.5.1] Kull, son of Christoph and Regina Barbara, m. Christina[1.1.2.3r], dau. of Jakob Bernhard[1.1.2r] and Agatha[1.5.1s] (Oechner) Arechtler, at Neusatz on April 30, 1793. She was b. at Neusatz on Nov. 25, 1773, and d. there on Dec. 7, 1844. Christoph d. at Neusatz on June 6, 1818. Johann Christoph and Christina had the following children at Neusatz, Neuenbuerg, Wuerttemburg: Christina[1.5.1.1], b. May 22, 1794; Gottfried[1.5.1.2], b. July 27, 1796; Jacob Friedrich[1.5.1.3], b. June 18, 1799; Elisabetha[1.5.1.4], b. Sept. 23, 1801; Regina[1.5.1.5], b. Sept. 6, 1803; Gottlieben[1.5.1.6], b. Oct. 11, 1806; Justina[1.5.1.7], b. Jan. 6, 1809; Catharina[1.5.1.8], b. Jan. 29, 1811, and d. Aug. 29, 1811; Andreas[1.5.1.9], b. July 8, 1812; Christoph[1.5.1.10], b. Sept. 15, 1815, and d. Jan. 4, 1818; Christoph[1.5.1.11], b. Aug. 17, 1818.

Johann Michael[1.5.3] Kull, son of Christoph and Regina Barbara, m. Catharina Guentner in Doebel, Neuenbuerg on April 30, 1793 and Anna Maria Michel (Mitschelen) at Neusatz on Oct. 4, 1802. Catharina was b. at Doebel on Oct. 22, 1773, and d. there on May 11, 1802. Johann Michael had the following children in Neusatz: Christina[1.5.3.1], b. in 1793; George Friedrich[1.5.3.2], b. March 3, 1795; Johann Michael[1.5.3.3], b. in 1797, and d. Aug. 27, 1807; Elisabetha[1.5.3.4], b. Nov. 11, 1800; Christoph Friedrich[1.5.3.5], b. Nov. 10, 1804; Johann Michael[1.5.3.6], b. Nov. 23, 1807.

Johann Phillip[1.5.4] Kull, son of Christoph and Regina Barbara, m.

Elisabetha Dreser at Neusatz on Nov. 5, 1793, and d. there on July 4, 1809. She was b. at Neusatz on April 12, 1774. They had the following children at Neusatz: Johann Friedrich$^{1.5.4.1}$, b. Oct. 16, 1795, and d. Oct. 18, 1811; Regina Elisabetha$^{1.5.4.2}$, b. Dec. 27, 1798; Johann Phillip$^{1.5.4.3}$, b. Jan. 9, 1802; Johann Matthaus$^{1.5.4.4}$, b. April 9, 1805, and d. Nov. 1, 1811; Gottfried$^{1.5.4.5}$, b. Feb. 24, 1808, and d. March 8, 1808.

Gottfried$^{1.5.5}$ Kull, son of Christoph and Regina Barbara, m. Christina Maritza Becker at Neusatz on May 13, 1794 and Elisabetha Schuler at Neusatz on May 26, 1812. Christina was b. at Rotenfol, Neuenbuerg June 16, 1776, and d. at Neusatz on Nov. 8, 1811. Elisabetha was b. at Neusatz on April 12, 1774, and d. there on Nov. 19, 1831. Gottfried d. at Neusatz on Feb. 12, 1825. Gottfried had the following children at Neusatz: Maria Barbara$^{1.5.5.1}$, b. March 28, 1796, and d. Aug. 4, 1796; Christina Maritza$^{1.5.5.2}$, b. Aug. 11, 1797; Johann Phillip$^{1.5.5.3}$, b. June 17, 1800; Gottfried$^{1.5.5.4}$, b. Aug. 18, 1803; Johann Friedrich$^{1.5.5.5}$, b. Dec. 9, 1806; Johann Matthaus$^{1.5.5.6}$, b. March 27, 1810, and d. Aug. 15, 1812; Johann Matthaus$^{1.5.5.7}$, b. Dec. 1, 1814.

Gottfried$^{1.5.1.2}$ Kull, son of Johann Christoph and Christina, m. Margaretha, dau. of Georg Friedrich and Justina (Karcher) Duerr, at Neusatz on Jan. 10, 1826. She was b. in Neusatz Nov. 1, 1800. In 1835/36, Gottfried and his brother, Andreas, immigrated to America. Gottfried was a farmer, and resided in Hocking Co., Marion Twp., Ohio in 1850. He d. in Marion Twp. on Sept. 20, 1876. His death is recorded in the Emmanuel Evangelical Lutheran Church Archives. They had the following children (b. in Neusatz before 1835 and Hocking Co., Ohio after 1835):

Georg Friedrich$^{1.5.1.2.1}$, b. Jan. 12, 1827, m. Mary Ann Greiner in Hocking Co., Ohio, March 4, 1858, and d. in Hocking Co., Ohio in 1905.

Jacobina$^{1.5.1.2.2}$, b. March 26, 1829. She may be the Jacobina Kull that m. Christian Zettner in Franklin Co., Ohio on Jan. 18, 1853. She was not on the 1850 census.

Gottfried$^{1.5.1.2.3}$, b. Oct. 13, 1831. He was not on the 1850 census.

Elisabetha$^{1.5.1.2.4}$, b. Jan. 31, 1834, and d. May 8, 1834.

Johann Friedrich$^{1.5.1.2.5}$, b. Oct. 1, 1835, m. Christine, dau. of Peter and Susanna Daubenmeier, in Hocking Co., Ohio on Feb. 24, 1868, and d. in Hocking Co., Marion Twp., Ohio on Jan. 5, 1874. He is buried in Sponagle cemetery. Christine was b. in Hocking Co., Marion Twp., Ohio June 1, 1843.

Catharina$^{1.5.1.2.6}$, b. May 16, 1839, bapt. at St. Jacobus Lutheran Church June 2, 1839, and sponsored by her parents. She m.

Seth Wilhelm, son of Michael H. and Salma Sarah (Grove) Sollenbarger, in Hocking Co., Ohio on Sept. 26, 1862. She d. in Fairfield Co., Sugar Grove, Ohio on May 26, 1930. Seth was b. in Hocking Co., Ohio on April 12, 1838, and d. in Sugar Grove on Feb. 20, 1913.

    Phillip[1.5.1.2.7], b. Sept. 20, 1845 (42), m. Susanna, dau. of Peter and Susanna Daubenmeier, and d. in Fairfield Co., Carroll Twp., Ohio on March 7, 1877. Susanna was b. in Hocking Co., Ohio in 1852.

    Mary[1.5.1.2.8], b. in 1845, and m. Gottfried Pifer in Hocking Co., Ohio on April 13, 1858.

Jacob Friedrich[1.5.1.3] Kull, son of Johann Christoph and Christina, is probably the Jacob Friedrich Kull that m. Ustinia Walker, and had a son born in Wuerttemberg: Gottfried[1.5.1.3.1], b. Aug. 2, 1828, and probably immigrated to America with his uncles, Gottfried and Andreas Kull, around 1835. His death certificate names his parents as Jacob Friedrich Kull and Ustinia Walker. Presumably, his parents d. young, and Gottfried was taken in by Gottfried and or Andreas Kull. Clearly, there was a close kinship between these families, because Gottfried and his wife, Caroline, sponsored two of Gottfried and Margaretha's grandchildren at their baptism. Gottfried m. Caroline, dau. of Johann Georg and Regina Carolina (Schmied) Schweigert, in Fairfield Co., Ohio on Sept. 4, 1856. She was b. in Baden, Baden in March, 1834, and d. in Fairfield Co., Madison Twp., Stoutsville, Ohio in 1910. Gottfried d. in Stoutsville on March 30, 1915. They are buried in Maple Hill cemetery.

Andreas[1.5.1.9] Kull, son of Johann Christoph and Christina, was confirmed in 1826, and immigrated to America with his brother, Gottfried, in 1835/36. Andreas m. Elisabetha Magdalene Roth in 1836. She was b. in (Voldeck?) Baden-Wuerttemberg, Germany on June 22, 1808, and d. in Fairfield Co., Berne Twp., Ohio on Jan. 24, 1886. She was buried Jan. 26, 1886. They were said to have been m. in Fairfield Co., Ohio, but no evidence has been uncovered that the Kull families were in Fairfield Co., Ohio before 1837. Magdalene immigrated to America in 1834. She had an illegitimate son named James Roth before her marriage to Andreas. Andreas was a farmer, and had 100 acres in Section 1 of Berne Twp., and 58 acres in Section 36. He d. in Berne Twp. on April 12, 1882. Andreas and Magdalene are buried in Sponagle cemetery.

Andreas and Magdalene had the following children:
    Christoph Friedrich[1.5.1.9.1], b. May 9, 1837, bapt. at St. Jacobus Lutheran Church in Hocking Co., Marion Twp., Ohio on June

11, 1837, and sponsored by Friedrich and Catharina Scholl. He
m. Lydia[1.6.4.5.3a], dau. of Daniel[1.6.4.5a] and Susanna
(Friesner) Swartz, in Fairfield Co., on Nov. 20, 1862 (Daniel
Swartz officiated), and Laura LaMunyon, widow of William
Rider, and Saul Friesner, sometime between 1900 and 1910.
Laura was b. in Kentucky in 1837. Frederich was a farmer and
wagon maker. He resided in Fairfield Co., Berne Twp. in 1860
(he is listed with his father, and as an assistant carriage maker
living with Anthony Zeick); Greenfield Twp., in 1880; Mercer
Co., Black Creek Twp., Ohio in 1900, and in Mercer Co., Union
Twp., Mendon, Ohio in 1920. Lydia d. in Fairfield Co.,
Greenfield Twp., Ohio Aug. 24, 1892, and is buried in Mt.
Tabor cemetery. Frederich d. at the home of his dau., Sarah,
in Dublin Twp. April 29, 1931. He was buried in Fairfield Co.,
Baltimore, Ohio.

Eduard[1.5.1.9.2], b. March 31, 1839, bapt. at St. Jacobus Lutheran
Church May 19, 1839, and sponsored by Friedrich and
Catharina Scholl. He m. Mary[1.6.4.5.6a], dau. of Daniel[1.6.4.5a]
and Susanna (Friesner) Swartz, in Fairfield Co., Ohio on Dec.
18, 1862. Eduard was a farmer in Greenfield Twp. in 1880.
He d. 1919, and she d. in 1898. They are buried in Mt. Tabor
cemetery.

Christina[1.5.1.9.3], b. Jan. 14, 1842, and m. Louis Emde in Fairfield
Co., Ohio on May 23, 1867. He was b. Nov. 6, 1826, and d. in
Berne Twp. on Feb. 16, 1888. Christina d. in Berne Twp. on
June 24, 1927. They are buried in the Evangelical cemetery.

Georg[1.5.1.9.4], b. in April, 1844, and m. Nancy J., dau. of Eliza J.
Lichfield, in Kosciusko Co., Indiana on June 6, 1880 (and may
be the Georg Kull that m. Elisabeth Engel in Emmanuel
Lutheran Church, Hocking Co., Ohio on Jan. 14, 1867). Nancy
J. was b. in Indiana July, 1860. Georg sold 300 acres in
Kosciusko Co., Indiana to Jep Grimes on June 23, 1877. Georg
and Nancy were on the 1880 and 1900 census of Kosciusko Co.,
Wayne Twp., Indiana and the 1920 census of Elkhart Co.,
Goshen, Indiana. Magdalena[1.5.1.9.5], b. in 1847, and m.
Salomon Engel in Emmanuel Lutheran Church, Hocking Co.,
Ohio on April 4, 1868. He was b. in Hocking Co., Marion Twp.,
Ohio on Nov. 3, 1836.

Mary A.[1.5.1.9.6], b. April 30, 1849, m. Noah Snoke, a stone mason.
He was b. in Ohio Feb. 8, 1848, and d. Nov. 10, 1894. Mary A.
Snoke d. in Fairfield Co., Berne Twp., Ohio Nov. 8, 1932. They
are buried in Crawfis-Emery cemetery.

Elizabeth[1.5.1.9.7], b. 1851, and m. Johannes Henry. He was b. in
Ohio in 1852. They resided with Andreas in 1880.

****

4

Jacob Friedrich[2], no known relation to the above family, was b. at
Koenigreich, Wuerttemberg, Germany Nov. 7, 1772. He m. Maria
Magdalena Benkiser at Schwarzwaldkreis, Herranalb, Wuerttemberg
Oct. 10, 1792. She was b. Jan. 20, 1775. They immigrated to America,
and arrived at Baltimore Sept. 30, 1830. They were residing in
Baltimore in Feb., 1831, and moved to Marion Co. (Richland Twp.),
Ohio before Sept., 1831, and to Fairfield Co., Ohio between March,
1837 and 1838. In 1838, Jacob Friedrich had 80 acres in Berne Twp.
R/T/S-18/13/12. He d. in Fairfield Co., Berne Twp. Dec. 7, 1839, and
Maria Magdalena d. Oct. 10, 1851. They are buried in Sponagle
Cemetery. They had the following children in Herrenalb (unless
otherwise noted):

(son[2·1]), b. about 1793 (this has not been confirmed)
Eva Christine[2·2], b. at Vonster Hezzulp, Nueneburg Dec. 12, 1794.
   She m. Johan Georg Volz at Herranalb June 11, 1816, and
   Johan Baumann in Fairfield Co., Ohio in 1840. She d. in
   Fairfield Co., Berne Twp. March 19, 1871, and is buried in
   Sponagle cemetery. Johan Georg Volz d. 1837. Johan Georg
   and Eva had 10 children, and in 1871, four of these children
   were dead. Eva and Georg immigrated to America in 1830.
Jacob Friedrich[2·3], b. Dec. 14, 1796.
Maria Magdalena[2·4], b. July 10, 1800.
Eberhardine/Evaline Elisabeth[2·5], b. April 10, 1802.
Christoff Frederich[2·6], b. Dec. 19, 1803.
Carl L./ F.[2·7], b. in 1809 (06). He is presumed to be the Charles
   that m. Margaret Keil in Marion Co., Ohio on March 5, 1837.
   Carl F. Kull d. in Marion Co., Richland Twp., Ohio on Aug. 17,
   1843, aged 37 years, and is buried in Klingel Cemetery.
   According to the immigration manifests list Charles L. Kull, son
   of Jacob Friedrich and Maria Magdalena, was b. 1809.
Carolina Philippina[2·8], b. Aug. 23, 1812, m. Adam Conrad in
   Fairfield Co., Ohio on June 5, 1835, and Charles Waggonhals.

(son[2·1]) KULL, son of Jacob Friedrich and Maria Magdalena
(Benkiser) Kull: his existence is suspected because of the presence of a
parent-less child on the immigration lists with Jacob Friedrich's family.
The unidentified son of Jacob Friedrich may have d. before leaving
Germany, or enroute. The following child immigrated to America in
1830, possibly a son of this unidentified son was Jacob Friedrich[2·1·1],
b. in 1820.

JACOB FRIEDRICH KULL[2·3], son of Jacob Friedrich and Maria
Magdalena (Benkiser) Kull, was b. Dec. 14, 1796. He m. Katharine

5

Elisabeth Kaz in Herranalb Feb. 25, 1827. Katharine was b. at
Pforzheiam, Wuerttemberg July 23, 1806, and d. in Hocking Co.,
Marion Twp., Ohio July 22, 1889. Jacob Friedrich Kull was naturalized
Sept. 18, 1840, and d. of pneumonia in Marion Twp. July 23, 1846.
They are buried in Sponagle cemetery. Jacob Frederich had the fol-
lowing children:

Catherine Frederiche[2.3.1], b. in Herranalb April 8, 1827, and m.
Johan Philip Diesch in Hocking Co., Ohio June 22, 1845. He
was b. in Wuerttemberg in 1812. They were residing in Miami
Co., Indiana in 1860. Catherine d. in Miami Co., Peru, Indiana
March 8, 1893.

Lene[2.3.2], b. March, 1830.

Caroline Elisabeth[2.3.3], bapt. in Baltimore Co., Baltimore,
Maryland, Gay Street and Court House Plaza on Feb. 13, 1831.
She m. John Ruff in Hocking Co. May 9, 1861.

Ludwig F.[2.3.4], b. Aug. 19, 1833, and d. in Fairfield Co., Berne
Twp., Ohio Jan. 12, 1913. He m. Mary Ann, dau. of Frederick
and Catharine Sholl, in Fairfield Co. June 3, 1855. She was b.
in Ohio Jan. 4, 1837, and d. Feb. 3, 1908.

Jacob Friedrich[2.3.5], bapt. at St. Jacobus Lutheran Church on April
15, 1835, sponsored by Ludwig and Elisabeth Consear. He m.
Caroline Leffler in Hocking Co., Ohio Nov. 8, 1863.

Emma[2.3.6], b. Dec. 12, 1839, and m. Phillip Baumann in Fairfield
Co., Ohio Sept. 17, 1861. He was b. in Ohio April 6, 1839, and
d. in Ohio Feb. 1, 1901. Emma d. June 12, 1908, and is buried
in Forest Rose Cemetery in Fairfield Co., Lancaster, Ohio.

(dau.).[2.3.7], b. in 1842.

Johannes Philipp[2.3.8], b. Sept. 16, 1843, and bapt. at Sponagle
Lutheran Church, and d. Dec. 20, 1860. He is buried in
Sponagle cemetery.

Amanda[2.3.9], b. in 1845, and m. Joseph Grim. He was b. in Ohio in
1845.Jacob Friedrich[2.3] m. Katharine Elisabeth Kaz in Herranalb Feb. 25, 1827. Katharine was b. at Pforzheiam,
Wuerttemberg July 23, 1806, and d. in Hocking Co., Marion
Twp., Ohio July 22, 1889. He was naturalized Sept. 18, 1840,
and d. of pneumonia in Marion Twp. July 23, 1846. They are
buried in Sponagle cemetery.

MARIA MAGDALENA KULL,[2.4] dau. of Jacob Friedrich and Maria
Magdalena (Benkiser), was b. July 10, 1800, and is presumed to be the
Magdalena that m. Frederick Kull, in Marion Co., Ohio on Sept. 3,
1831. He was b. in Wuerttemberg, Germany on Oct. 13, 1801. The
baptismal registers for Jacob Friedrich and Maria Magdalena's dau.
state the birth date as 1800; the immigration manifest says 1813; the
1850 census says 1810; and the 1860 census says 1808. Frederick d. in

6

Marion Co., Richland Twp., Ohio June 8, 1862, and is buried in Klingel cemetery. They resided in Marion Co., Richland Twp., Ohio in 1860, and had the following children there: William[2.4.1], a wagon maker, b. 1832, and m. Elizabeth Kauffman (b. 1836) in Marion Co. July 6, 1854; Margaret[2.4.2], b. c.1834, m. Jacob Kauffman in Marion Co. Sept. 19, 1850; Jacob[2.4.3], b. 1837, m. Caroline Fies in Marion Co., Ohio April 30, 1868; Christina[2.4.4], b. 1839, m. John Baringer in Marion Co. March 24, 1859; Mary C.[2.4.5], b. 1841, m. Cline J. Wolf in Marion Co. Oct. 19, 1868; Elizabeth[2.4.6], b. 1843, m. George Wiswisser in Marion Co. Sept. 5, 1865; Caroline[2.4.7], b. 1849, m. Samuel Kraner in Marion Co. Oct. 8, 1868.

EBERHARDINE/EVALINE ELISABETH KULL[2.5], dau. of Jacob Friedrich and Maria Magdalena (Benkiser), b. April 10, 1802, m. Ludwig Frederich Baumann in 1825. She d. in Hocking Co., Goodhope Twp. April 16, 1876, and is buried in Fairfield Co., Sponagle cemetery. Ludwig was b. in Gerrebb, Neuenbuerg, Wuerttemberg, Germany Jan. 23, 1803, and d. April 16, 1875. They immigrated to America in 1830. They had the following children in Goodhope Twp.: Magdalena[2.5.1], b. in Ohio 1831; Christina[2.5.2], b. 1833; Adam[2.5.3], b. 1836; William[2.5.4], b. 1838; Caroline[2.5.5], b. 1840; Willhelmina[2.5.6], b. 1842; Emanuel[2.5.7], b. 1846.

Christoff Frederich Kull[2.6], son of Jacob Friedrich and Maria Magdalena (Benkiser), b. Dec. 19, 1803. He m. Johanna Maria in Germany before 1830. She was b. in Germany in 1811. Frederich d. in Shelby Co., Strasburg, Illinois Sept. 16, 1874. Christoff and Maria had the following children in Hocking Co., Goodhope Twp., Ohio:

Christian[2.6.1], b. in Ohio Jan. 13, 1832, m. Rosanna Walker, dau. of Bernhard and Barbara (Bauer) Walker, in Fairfield Co., Ohio Feb. 12, 1856, and d. in Shelby Co., Illinois Oct. 8, 1881. She was b. in Wuerttemberg June 20, 1833. They moved to Illinois in 1864.

Carl Friedrich[2.6.2], b. Feb. 16, 1834, bapt. at St. Jacobus Lutheran Church June 15, 1834, and sponsored by C. F. and Magdalina Spannage. He m. Margaret, dau. of Adam Lower, in Shelby Co., Rose Twp., Illinois in 1857, and d. in Shelby Co., Illinois on Oct. 12, 1908.

Frederick[2.6.3], b. in 1836, and m. Elizabeth Kneller in Fairfield Co., Ohio April 13, 1858.

Anna Maria[2.6.4], b. Oct. 6, 1837, bapt. at St. Jacobus Lutheran Church May 12, 1838, and sponsored by Christ. and Maria Magd. Spanngel.

Caroline[2.6.5], b. 1840.

Wilhelmina[2.6.6], b. 1841, m. George M. Strong in Hocking Co., Ohio

Feb. 11, 1858.

A son[2.6.7], b. c.1843, and d. c.1845.

Amelia[2.6.8], b. 1845, and m. Christian Bronne in Hocking Co. Dec. 6, 1863.

Adolph Frederich[2.6.9], b. Dec. 9, 1846, d. Feb. 5, 1847.

Matilda[2.6.10], b. Nov. 29, 1847, m. Johannes Friedrich Mauz, d. in Shelby Co., Illinois Nov. 10, 1919. He was b. in Nellingen, Necker, Wuerttemberg April 3, 1840, d. in Shelby Co., Illinois Feb. 5, 1920. They were residing in Illinois in 1869.

Emanuel[2.6.11], b. 1849.

JACOB FRIEDRICH KULL[2.1.1], possibly a grandson of Jacob Friedrich and Maria Magdalena (Benkiser) through an unidentified son, was naturalized in Fairfield Co., Ohio Sept. 19, 1840. He m. Margaret Strohl in Fairfield Co. Sept. 21, 1840. Margaret is presumed to have been may have been the Margaret (b. in 1823) in Hocking Co., Marion Twp., Ohio in 1850 residing with Michael and Christina Watter.

Margaret was the mother of the following children:

William A.[2.1.1.1], b. in 1842, and resided with his mother in 1850. He m. Elizabeth Primer in Hocking Co., Ohio Oct. 14, 1863.

Phillip[2.1.1.2], b. 1843, and resided Emanuel and Elizabeth Crook and John and Rachel Hamilton in Hocking Co., Marion Twp. in 1850.

Georg Henry Yorick[2.1.1.3], b. Nov. 8, 1846, and resided with William and Henrietta Plummer in Hocking Co., Marion Twp. in 1850. He m. Caroline C. Onstott in Warren Co., Iowa on Dec. 17, 1879. Georg d. in Hobart, Oklahoma March 22, 1930. Caroline was b. in Iowa March 29, 1856

****

THE KROELLER FAMILY

MATTHIAS KROELLER[1n], b. in Neusatz, Neuenbuerg, Wuerttemberg on March 22, 1663, m. Anna Catharina, d. in Neusatz Feb. 28, 1737. Anna Catharina, b. Sept., 1674, d. Dec. 26, 1723.

Matthias and Anna Catharina had the following children in Neusatz: Elisabetha[1.1n], b. April 2, 1695; Johann Jacob[1.2n], b. Oct. 25, 1697; Anna Catharina[1.3n], b. March 10, 1699; Anna Maria[1.4n], b. March 10, 1700; Anna Maria[1.5n], b. Sept. 26, 1702, and m. Johann Phillip Kull[1].

****

THE RAGG FAMILY

GEORG RAGG[1o] had a son, Johann Peter[1.1o]. JOHANN PETER RAGG[1.1o], son of Georg, m. Anna Barbara[1.4p], dau. of Jacob[1p] and

Maria Agnes Schonhaler, in Schwann, Wuerttemberg Sept. 16, 1714, and had the following son in Schwann named Johann Michael$^{1 \cdot 1 \cdot 1o}$, b. Sept. 2, 1720.

JOHANN MICHAEL RAGG$^{1 \cdot 1 \cdot 1o}$, son of Johann Peter and Anna Barbara, was b. Sept. 2, 1720. He m. Anna Maria$^{1 \cdot 3 \cdot 3q}$, dau. of Christoph$^{1 \cdot 3q}$ and Anna Maria (Hammols) Hamann, in Conweiler, Wuerttemberg on Aug. 7, 1742. They had the following children in Conweiler: Regina Barbara$^{1 \cdot 1 \cdot 1o}$, b. April 2, 1743, m. Christoph Kull$^{1 \cdot 5}$; Anna Maria$^{1 \cdot 1 \cdot 1 \cdot 2o}$, b. July 16, 1746; Maria Eva$^{1 \cdot 1 \cdot 1 \cdot 3o}$, b. March 31, 1751, d. March 2, 1751/52; Johann Michael$^{1 \cdot 1 \cdot 1 \cdot 4o}$, b. Sept. 1, 1752, d. in Conweiler in 1818.

****

THE SCHONHALER FAMILY

JACOB SCHONHALER^{1p} m. Maria Agnes, and had the following children, b. Schwann, Wuerttemberg: Margaretha$^{1 \cdot 1p}$, b. March 6, 1667; Conrad$^{1 \cdot 2p}$, b. Feb. 24, 1669; Anna Maria$^{1 \cdot 3p}$, b. March 12, 1671; Anna Barbara$^{1 \cdot 4p}$, b. June 12, 1673, m. Johann Peter Ragg$^{1 \cdot 1o}$; Agnes$^{1 \cdot 5p}$, b. March 10, 1675; Christina$^{1 \cdot 6p}$, b. March 6, 1678; Anna Veronica$^{1 \cdot 7p}$, b. Jan. 12, 1680.

****

THE HAMANN FAMILY

HANS HAMANN^{1q} m. Anna Maria, and had the following children, b. Conweiler, Wuerttemburg: Anna Catharina$^{1 \cdot 1q}$, b. Jan. 21, 1676; Hans Martin$^{1 \cdot 2q}$, b. March 6, 1677; Christoph$^{1 \cdot 3q}$, b. Jan. 8, 1679; infant$^{1 \cdot 4q}$, b. and d. June 29, 1680; Hans Jacob$^{1 \cdot 5q}$, b. July 18, 1682; Anna Maria$^{1 \cdot 6q}$, b. Sept. 10, 1684; Hans Jakob$^{1 \cdot 7q}$, b. Jan. 25, 1686; Ursula$^{1 \cdot 8q}$, b. May 10, 1688.

Christoph Hamann

Christoph$^{1 \cdot 3q}$ m. Anna Maria, dau. of Phillip Hammols, in Conweiler July 28, 1705, and had the following children: Anna Margaretha$^{1 \cdot 3 \cdot 1q}$, b. Sept. 1, 1706; Maria Margaretha$^{1 \cdot 3 \cdot 2q}$, b. March 4, 1708; Anna Maria$^{1 \cdot 3 \cdot 3q}$, b. Oct. 20, 1710, and m. Johann Michael Ragg$^{1 \cdot 1 \cdot 1o}$; Maria Elisabetha$^{1 \cdot 3 \cdot 4q}$, b. March 21, 1713; Christina Catharina$^{1 \cdot 3 \cdot 5q}$, b. Oct. 29, 1715; Maria Susanna$^{1 \cdot 3 \cdot 6q}$, b. Aug. 1, 1718; Regina$^{1 \cdot 3 \cdot 7q}$, b. March 31, 1721.

****

Juergen Arechtler

Juergen^{1r} had a son in Shielburg, Baden, Germany, named Michael$^{1.1r}$. Michael m. Maria Magdalena, dau. of Andreas Karcher of Wildbad, Wuerttemberg, at Neusatz, Neuenbuerg, Wuerttemberg on Feb. 10, 1722, and d. at Neusatz on May 12, 1760. They had the following children at Neusatz: Margaretha$^{1.1.1r}$, b. April 18, 1723; Jakob Bernhard$^{1.1.2r}$, b. Nov. 21, 1727; Christina Magdalena$^{1.1.3r}$, b. June 15, 1730, d. at Neusatz Jan. 18, 1818; Hans Michael$^{1.1.4r}$, b. and d. Dec. 28, 1732; Hans Michael$^{1.1.5r}$, b. April 20, 1736; Anna Barbara$^{1.1.6r}$, b. Dec. 8, 1738.

Jakob Bernhard$^{1.1.2r}$ m. Agatha$^{1.5.1s}$, dau. of Johann Friedrich$^{1.5s}$ and Anna Catharina (Klunder) Oechner, in Neusatz on Jan. 30, 1755, and had the following children: Matthaus$^{1.1.2.1r}$, b. in 1758; Maria Magdalena$^{1.1.2.2r}$, b. in 1764; Christina$^{1.1.2.3r}$, b. Nov. 25, 1773, and m. Johann Christoph Kull$^{1.5.1}$.

****

Matthaus Oechner

Matthaus^{1s} m. Anna Margaretha. She d. in Dennach, Wuerttemberg May 18, 1742. They had the following children in Dennach: Matthaus$^{1.1s}$; Johannes$^{1.2s}$, b. June 21, 1697; Catharina$^{1.3s}$, b. Feb. 26, 1699; Johann Adam$^{1.4s}$, b. Aug. 9, 1701; Johann Friedrich$^{1.5s}$, b. March 27, 1703; Agatha$^{1.6s}$, b. Jan. 25, 1705; Rosina$^{1.7s}$, b. March 22, 1707; Christianus$^{1.8s}$, b. Oct. 14, 1708; Antonius$^{1.9s}$, b. Oct. 27, 1710; Adam Georg$^{1.10s}$, b. May 22, 1712; Anna Margaretha$^{1.11s}$, b. March 17, 1716;

Matthaus$^{1.1s}$ had the following children in Dennach: Johann Adam$^{1.1.1s}$, b. Sept. 3, 1719; Matthaus$^{1.1.2s}$, b. April 10, 1722; Johann Georg$^{1.1.3s}$, b. May 16, 1724.

Johann Friedrich$^{1.5s}$ m. Anna Catharina, dau. of Hans Juergen Klunder, in Dennach on June 17, 1727, and had a dau. Agatha$^{1.5.1s}$, b. March 26, 1735, and m. Jakob Bernhard Arechtler$^{1.1.2r}$.

****

Andreas Swartz

Andreas^{1a} was b. in Europe about 1720, m. Anna Margaretha c.1743. Andreas was a Yeoman in York Co., Shrewsbury Twp., Pennsylvania as of 1745. He was Supervisor of Highways in 1759, and 1760, and Constable in 1768. He took the Sacrament on April 4, 1763, and was naturalized on April 11, 1763. Andreas or his son, Andreas, purchased 50 acres from Charles Diehl in Shrewsbury Twp. on Nov. 5, 1773. In 1783, he had 200 acres in Shrewsbury Twp. Andreas d. May, 1789,

and Anna Margaretha d. sometime between 1786 and 1789. The will of
Andreas Swartz mentioned his son Abraham, and the following
children: Conrad, Jacob, Mary Margaret, m. to Dewalt Schneider,
Henry Swartz, Andrew Swartz, and Catharina Swartz and dau.
Catharine.

Andreas and Anna Margaretha had the following children:
> Conrad[1.1a], b. Dec. 4, 1744.
> Catharina[1.2a], bapt. by Reverend Jacob Lischy at the First
> Reformed Church of York on March 17, 1744/45, sponsored by
> Mathies and Catharine Ness, and d. sometime before 1761.
> Jacob[1.3a], b. in 1747; Anna Maria Margaretha[1.4a], b. Dec. 27, 1748;
> Henrich[1.5a], b. July 22, 1751.
> Andreas[1.6a], b. about 1740, and d. in Shrewsbury Twp. in Jan.,
> 1804. He served in the Revolutionary War in 1780-81. He
> named his siblings, and the children of his deceased brother,
> Henrich, as his beneficiaries. Theobald Schneider was granted
> administration on Jan. 30, 1804.
> Abraham[1.7a], b. June 26, 1758, and d. in Shrewsbury Twp. on Feb.
> 8, 1806. He is buried in St. Paul's Cemetery. He m. Anna
> Maria. He named his siblings and the children of his deceased
> brother, Henrich, as his beneficiaries. On June 21, 1800,
> Abraham and his wife, deeded 210 acres 34 perches in
> Shrewsbury Twp. to Bernhard Bope. The land had been given
> to Abraham by his father, and released by his siblings in 1798.
> His will was written on Jan. 15, 1805, and probated on Feb. 12,
> 1806. Anna Maria's will written on March 21, 1818, and
> probated on Feb. 12, 1821. It named her sister, Eve
> (deceased), and her (Eve's?) dau.s, Elizabeth, wife of Josophine
> Young, Catharina, Eve, Barbara, and Christina Bop. Anna
> Maria was b. Oct. 28, 1759, d. May 3, 1821, and is buried in
> Friedensaal cemetery. Abraham served in the Revolutionary
> War, the following is a record of his service: Abraham
> Schwartz of Shrewsbury Twp., fines 13.10 pounds by warrant
> dated May 10, 1777, while a resident of Hellam Twp., for
> failure to "meet and exercise in order to learn the art of
> military," as was required in an Act of Assembly of Feb. 14,
> 1777. Private in Sixth (Captain George Geiselman) Company,
> Seventh Battalion, York Co., Militia according to an undated
> return assigned to the year 1778; he remained a member of
> this unit when (in 1779) it became the Seventh (Captain
> George Geiselman) Company, Fifth Battalion, York Co., Militia
> and in 1782 was listed in the Seventh Class of this company.
> From Dec. 7, 1781 to Feb. 7, 1782 he saw actual service in a
> detachment of the Seventh Class of the York Co. Militia under

the command of Captain Geiselman, guarding prisoners of war
at Camp Security in York Co. Abraham is buried in St. Paul's
cemetery in North Codorus Twp.

Anna Catharina[1.8a], b. Jan. 19, 1761

Johan Peter[1.9a], b. Jan. 19, 1761, and d. sometime before 1789. He
was bapt. at Christ's Lutheran Church of York on Jan. 20,
1761, and sponsored by Henry and Dorothea Walter, and
Catharine, dau. of Conrad Mueller.

Conrad Swartz

Conrad[1.1a] m. Dorothea Stein about 1767. She d. sometime after
1790, and he m. Elizabeth Raus. In the Revolutionary War, Conrad
was a Private in the Fifth (Captain John Ehrman) Company, Seventh
Battalion, York Co., Militia in 1778. He remained with this unit when
it became the Fifth (Captain Henry Ferree) Company, Fifth Battalion
in 1781. During the period Oct. 5-Dec. 5, 1781 he was in the detachment of the Sixth Class of the previous Company under the command
of Captain William Dodds guarding prisoners at Camp Security in York.
He served until Dec. 28, 1782. In 1783, Conrad had 80 acres in
Shrewsbury Twp. He d. in Shrewsbury Twp. March 11, 1831.
Conrad's will was written on April 21, 1826, had a codicil added on
June 7, 1830, and probated on March 14, 1831. His beneficiaries were
his siblings Margaret Schneider, Catharina Heinrich, and the children
of his deceased brother Henrich. His nephew, Henrich Swartz Jr., was
made executer and trustee of the inheritance of the children of
Henrich Swartz and the children of Henrich's deceased son Georg.
Conrad and Dorothea had the following dau.:

Anna Margaretha[1.1.1a], bapt. at Friedensaal Lutheran Church on
June 25, 1768, and sponsored by her aunt, Anna Margaretha
Swartz, and Felix Kladfelter. She d. sometime before 1826.

Jacob Swartz

Jacob[1.3a] m. Dorothea[1.2m], dau. of Johannes and Anna Barbara
(Glatfelder) Hildebrand about 1771. She was b. June 21, 1751, and is
buried in Stines cemetery. In the Revolutionary War, Jacob served as
a Sergeant in the Seventh (Captain George Geiselman) Company, Fifth
Battalion York Co., Militia in 1780, and in 1782, he was a Private in
the Second Class of the same Company. In 1783, he had 100 acres in
Shrewsbury Twp. Jacob d. in Shrewsbury Twp. Nov. 20, 1804, and he
is buried in Bupp's cemetery. His will was written on Feb. 21, 1804,
and probated on Dec. 19, 1804. Jacob and Dorothea had the following
children:

Dorothea[1.3.1a], b. May 31, 1772, bapt. at Friedensaal June 7, 1772,
and sponsored by her uncle and aunt, Conrad and Dorothea
Swartz. She d. before 1780.

Johan Jacob[1.3.2a], b. March 28, 1774, bapt. at Friedensaal April 24, 1774, and sponsored by his grandparents, Andreas and Anna Margaretha Swartz. He d. sometime before 1783.

Johan[1.3.3a], b. about 1776; Anna Maria[1.3.4a], b. Oct. 3, 1778, bapt. Nov. 8, 1778, and sponsored by Anna Maria Hildebrand. She d. before 1788.

Anna Dorothea[1.3.5a], b. June 3, 1780, bapt. July 9, 1780, and sponsored by her grandparents, Andreas and Margaretha Swartz. She m. John, son of John Glattfelter in Christ's Lutheran Church of York April 8, 1803.

Jacob[1.3.6a], b. Oct. 18, 1783, bapt. at St. Peter's (Yellow) Reformed Church, and sponsored by Felix and Elisabeth Klatfelter.

Peter[1.3.7a], b. Aug. 14, 1785, bapt. at St. Peter's Oct. 8, 1785, and sponsored by Casper and Barbara Hildebrand.

Anna Maria[1.3.8a], b. Jan. 26, 1788, bapt. at St. Peter's April 2, 1788, and sponsored by Johannes and Anna Maria Sheurer. She m. George Walter.

Philip[1.3.9a], b. May 3, 1791, bapt. at St. Peter's, and sponsored by his uncle and aunt, Henrich and Magdalena Swartz.

Catharina[1.3.10a], b. March 9, 1793, bapt. at St. Peter's, and sponsored by Catharina Swartz (single).

Johan Swartz

Johan[1.3.3a] m. Rosina, and Christina about 1814. He is probably the John Swartz of Springfield Twp., whose letters of administration were granted on Jan. 17, 1838 to Frederick Bahn, and for which an inventory was filed on Feb. 17, 1838. Christina was b. April 25, 1776, d. Oct. 5, 1852, and is buried in Friedensaal cemetery. John had the following children bapt. at Friedensaal: Justina[1.3.3.1a], b. Dec. 14, 1801, bapt. Dec. 19, 1801; Dorothea[1.3.3.2a], b. Dec. 18, 1803; Jacob[1.3.3.3a], b. Jan. 1, 1805, bapt. March 2, 1805; Daniel[1.3.3.4a], b. April 17, 1806, bapt. May 24, 1806; Rosina[1.3.3.5a], b. June 11, 1807, bapt. July 18, 1807; Catharina[1.3.3.6a], b. Oct. 2, 1808, bapt. Dec. 18, 1808; Eva[1.3.3.7a], b. Jan. 31, 1810, bapt. on May 18, 1810; Salome[1.3.3.8a], b. May 24, 1811, bapt. July 7, 1811; Eva[1.3.3.9a], b. Aug. 26, 1812, bapt. Sept. 27, 1812; Charles[1.3.3.10a], b. March 14, 1815, bapt. April 12, 1815; John Peter[1.3.3.11a], b. Oct. 11, 1816, bapt. Oct. 11, 1816; George[1.3.3.12a], b. Sept. 3, 1817, bapt. Oct. 19, 1817.

John Peter Swartz

Peter[1.3.3.11a] m. Adalina. She was b. Sept. 1, 1823, d. April 22, 1896. Peter d. March 15, 1893. They are buried in Bupp's cemetery in Springfield Twp., along with the following children: Henry[1.3.3.11.1a], d. 1857; Jacob[1.3.3.11.2a], d. 1852; Mary[1.3.3.11.3a], d. 1844.

Jacob Swartz

Jacob[1.3.6a] received 105 acres 20 perches warranted to Andreas Swartz for the use of his son Jacob on Nov. 20, 1771, and 31 acres 50 perches warranted to Jacob Swartz Sr. on Dec. 10, 1789, through a release by his siblings on Feb. 6, 1808. He m. Magdalena, dau. of Michael Geiselman, in Christ's Lutheran Church of York March 9, 1805, and had a son bapt. at Friedensaal named Michael[1.3.6.1a], b. Dec. 14, 1806, bapt. Jan. 24, 1807.

Anna Maria Margaretha Swartz

Margaretha[1.4a] was bapt. at Christ's Lutheran Church of York Jan. 22, 1749, and sponsored by Rebecca Hamspacker. She m. Dewalt Schneider, and resided in York Co., Codorus Twp., Pennsylvania. They had the following children:

> Georg[1.4.1a], b. July 10, 1783, bapt. at Fissel's (Jerusalem) Union Church Aug. 17, 1783, sponsored by John Gantz.
>
> Elisabeth Margaretha[1.4.2a], b. 19 July, 1787, bapt. at Sherman's Union Church Aug. 26, 1787, and sponsored by Georg and Margaretha Bortner.
>
> Magdalena[1.4.3a], b. Nov. 18, 1791, and bapt. at St. Jacob's (Stone) Union Church Jan. 29, 1792.

Henrich Swartz

Henrich[1.5a] was bapt. at Christ's Lutheran Church of York Nov. 17, 1751, and sponsored by Henry and Catharine Brehm. He m. Anna Magdalena[1.4.5b], dau. of Johan David[1.4b] and Anna Catharina (Simon) Schaffer, c.1773. She was bapt. in Shrewsbury Twp. Oct. 19, 1751, and d. sometime after March, 1801, when guardians were appointed for Henrich's minor children. Henrich lived in Shrewsbury Twp., and served from 1778-1782 as a Private during the Revolutionary War. He served in Captain George Geiselman's Company, Seventh Battalion, York Co. Militia in 1778, and remained a member of this unit in 1779, when it became the Seventh Company, Fifth Battalion under Captain Geiselman. He was listed in the Seventh Class of this company in 1780 and 1782. He was a Private in a detachment of the Seventh Class under Capt. Geiselman, in service guarding prisoners at Camp Security in York from Dec. 7, 1781 to Feb. 7, 1782. He was a member of the Sixth Class on Jan. 30, 1781. In 1783, he had 80 acres in Shrewsbury Twp. Henrich d. in Shrewsbury Twp. Dec., 1799. Henrich and Magdalena had the following children:

> Henrich[1.5.1a], b. April 23, 1774.
>
> Justina[1.5.2a], b. Sept., 1776, bapt. at Friedensaal Sept. 10, 1776, sponsored by her grandmother, Catharina Schaffer. She is not mentioned in her father's will.
>
> Elisabeth[1.5.3a], b. Feb. 5, 1779, bapt. at Friedensaal, and sponsored

14

by Elisabeth, dau. of Georg Kleinfelter. She d. sometime before 1795.

Georg Henrich[1.5.4a], b. May 30, 1781.

Anna Margaretha[1.5.5a], b. March 2, 1783, bapt. March 23, 1783, sponsored by her uncle and aunt, Conrad and Dorothea Swartz. She m. Francis Groff in Christ's Lutheran Church of York April 28, 1803. She was mentioned in the orphan's court docket on March 24, 1801.

Catharina[1.5.6a], b. April 2, 1786, bapt. at Friedensaal on April 9, 1786, sponsored by her aunt, Catharina Swartz. She may have m. Samuel Keyser at Christ's Lutheran Church of York in 1812, and d. July 13, 1846. She was mentioned in the orphan's court docket on March 24, 1801.

Maria Magdalena[1.5.7a], b. July 9, 1788, bapt. at Ziegler's (St. Paul's) Lutheran Church Aug. 9, 1788, sponsored by her uncle and aunt, Abraham Swartz and wife. She was mentioned on the orphan's court docket on March 24, 1801.

Elisabeth[1.5.8a], b. March 13, 1795, bapt. at Friedensaal on April 26, 1795, sponsored by John and Anna Maria Heinrich. She may have m. Uriah Matson on June 2, 1821. She was listed on the orphan's court docket on March 24, 1801.

Henrich Swartz

Henrich[1.5.1a] was bapt. at Friedensaal April 30, 1774, sponsored by his grandparents, Andreas and Margaretha Swartz. He m. Anna Maria Catharina, dau. of Michael and Dorothea Zech. She was b. April 30, 1778, bapt. at Friedensaal June 8, 1778, sponsored by Jacob and Maria Catharina Zech. She d. Sept. 18, 1852, and buried in Fissel's cemetery. On March 25, 1835, Henrich received 3 tracts in Shrewsbury Twp. from the estate of Michael Zech, that he assigned to Mathias Ness on the same day. Henry Swartz Jr. and William Swartz were granted letters of administration on June 7, 1844, and filed an inventory on July 31, 1844. Henrich resided in Shrewsbury (now Springfield) Twp., and d. May 27, 1844. He is buried in Friedensaal cemetery. Heinrich and Anna Maria had the following children bapt. at Friedensaal:

Michael[1.5.1.1a], b. c.1796, and mentioned in the orphans court docket on Aug. 6, 1844.

Henry[1.5.1.2a], b. Sept. 15, 1798, sponsored by Jacob and Catherine at his baptism. He resided in Paradise Twp. in 1844. He may have m. Catherine, dau. of Frederick Giselman of Shrewsbury Twp. Jan. 22, 1834.

Maria Magdalena (Polly)[1.5.1.3a], b. May 5, 1800, bapt. at Friedensaal June 29, 1800, sponsored by her grandmother, Magdalena Swartz. She m. John Bahn.

Dorothea[1.5.1.4a], b. c.1802, m. Frederick Glatfelter. She is mentioned on the orphans court docket on Aug. 6, 1844.

Mary[1.5.1.5a], b. c.1804. She m. George Taylor, and appeared on the orphans court docket on Aug. 6, 1844.

Anna[1.5.1.6a], b. Dec. 22, 1805, bapt. Jan. 5, 1806, sponsored by Anna Maria. She d. before Aug., 1844.

Catherine[1.5.1.7a], b. July 30, 1807, bapt. Aug. 16, 1807, sponsored by Frederick and Catherine Bahn. She m. _____ Bechley. She was a widow in 1844.

John[1.5.1.8a], b. Oct. 26, 1808, bapt. Nov. 20, 1808, sponsored by John and Rosina Swartz. He was mentioned on the orphans court docket on Aug., 1844.

William[1.5.1.9a], b. Sept. 10, 1811, bapt. Oct. 27, 1811, sponsored by Michael and Dorothea Zech. He resided in Springfield Twp. 1844. He m. Mary, and d. Jan. 19, 1877. Mary was b. Oct. 18, 1808, d. Dec. 28, 1891. They are buried in St. Jacob's Union cemetery in North Codorus Twp.

Elizabeth[1.5.1.10a], b. Sept. 12, 1812, bapt. Oct. 25, 1812, sponsored by Conrad and Elizabeth Swartz. She was unmarried in Aug., 1844.

Christine[1.5.1.11a], b. Dec. 20, 1814, bapt. April 2, 1815, sponsored by Jacob and Christine Zeller. She d. before Aug., 1844.

Leah[1.5.1.12a], b. May 17, 1818, bapt. July 26, 1818, sponsored by George and Anna Maria Walter. She was unmarried in Aug., 1844.

Rachel[1.5.1.13a], b. Nov. 24, 1819, bapt. March 20, 1820, sponsored by Eva Zech. She m. Jeremiah Krebs.

Georg Henrich Swartz

Georg[1.5.4a] was bapt. at Friedensaal June 10, 1781, sponsored by his uncle and aunt, Jacob and Dorothea Swartz. He m. Elenora[1.1.1.5.4d], dau. of Johannes[1.1.1.5d] and Anna Catharina (Ripp) Seitz, at York Co., Glen Rock, Pennsylvania in 1799. Georg purchased 34 acres and 146 perches in Shrewsbury Twp. from George Moor on May 17, 1798, and Georg and Elenora sold this land to Frederick Myers on Aug. 9, 1805. They moved to Fairfield Co., Berne Twp., Ohio in 1805. Georg was a cooper and miller. He operated a grist mill called Swartz Mill, which was connected to the Swartz Post Office. Swartz Mill Bridge was named for this mill. It was removed in 1962. He received a land grant in the East 1/2 of Section 36 of Berne Twp. on Feb. 3, 1807. This land was situated on Rush Creek. He d. April 6, 1821, and Elenora d. Dec. 29, 1847. They are buried in Delapp cemetery, and had the following children: Elizabeth[1.5.4.1a], b. Dec. 11, 1800, bapt. at Friedensaal Feb. 7, 1801, d. in Fairfield Co., Berne Twp., Ohio June 7, 1868, buried in Mt. Tabor cemetery; Joseph[1.5.4.2a], b. Feb. 2, 1802; Lydia[1.5.4.3a], b. March 17, 1803; Benjamin[1.5.4.4a], b. in 1805, and d.

before 1821; Daniel[1.5.4.5a], b. June 13, 1806; George[1.5.4.6a], b. June 29, 1807; Henry[1.5.4.7a], b. Dec. 7, 1809; John[1.5.4.8a], b. Dec. 7, 1809; Catherine[1.5.4.9a], b. Oct. 8, 1811; Mary Magdalena[1.5.4.10a], b. April 5, 1812; Elenora[1.5.4.11a], b. April 5, 1812.

Joseph Swartz

Joseph[1.5.4.2a] m. Catherine, dau. of Abraham and Catherine (Fast) Beery, in Fairfield Co., Ohio Nov. 3, 1826. Joseph d. in Fairfield Co., Ohio April 10, 1882, and Catherine on Oct. 24, 1892. They are buried in Mt, Tabor cemetery. They had the following children in Fairfield Co., Pleasant Twp.:

Sarah[1.5.4.2.1a], b. in 1828, and d. in Berne Twp. on Aug. 27, 1888. She never married, but had a dau. Samantha in 1865.

Noah[1.5.4.2.2a], b. March 14, 1829, and d. in Berne Twp. on March 4, 1849.

Joel B.[1.5.4.2.3a], b. in 1831, and m. Emma Hunter in Fairfield Co. on Oct. 25, 1855. She was b. in 1836 in Ohio.

Andrew S.[1.5.4.2.4a], b. in 1833. He was converted in a Mennonite church in 1857, and held services as the minister at the Mt. Tabor Church. Mt. Tabor was built in 1852, and Andrew became it's superintendent. He m. Rachel Roby in Fairfield Co. on March 13, 1855.

Catherine[1.5.4.2.5a], b. 1839, m. Noah Sheldon Miesse (1834-1879) in Fairfield Co. March 13, 1856. She d. in Berne Twp. in 1919.

Lydia Swartz

Lydia[1.5.4.3a] m. David Wolf in Fairfield Co., in Oct., 1823. He was b. in Dauphin Co., Pennsylvania. They moved to Hancock Co., Ohio, and were the parents of the following children: Christian[1.5.4.3.1a], m. J. Fisher; Levi[1.5.4.3.2a], m. M. Davis; George[1.5.4.3.3a]; Joseph[1.5.4.3.4a], John[1.5.4.3.5a], m. M. Mills; Daniel[1.5.4.3.6a], m. M. Brand; Samuel[1.5.4.3.7a]; Jacob[1.5.4.3.8a]; Susan[1.5.4.3.9a], m. W. Richie; Mary[1.5.4.3.10a], m. Samuel Crites.

Daniel Swartz

Daniel[1.5.4.5a] m. Susanna, dau. of Johan Frederick and Magdalena (Ehrhardt) Friesner, at Fairfield Co., Lancaster, Ohio Sept. 20, 1827. Daniel was a farmer and an Evangelical Lutheran minister (for 60 years) in Berne Twp. Susanna d. in Berne Twp. July 19, 1884, and Daniel d. March 7, 1891. They are buried in Mt. Tabor cemetery. Daniel had 204 acres in Section 36 of Berne Twp., near Sugar Grove, Ohio, which was his father's old homestead on Rush Creek. After Susanna's death, Daniel m. Susan Rife. Daniel and Susanna had the following children in Berne Twp.: Louis[1.5.4.5.1a], b. 1828, m. Priscilla

(b. in Ohio 1835), dau. of (Samuel) and Sarah Engel; Benjamin[1.5.4.5.2a], b. 1832, a blacksmith, m. Sophia (b. in 1836), dau. of (Samuel) and Sarah Engel; Lydia[1.5.4.5.3a], b. April 2, 1834, m. Christoph Friedrich Kull[1.5.1.9.1]; Magdalene[1.5.4.5.4a], b. 1835, m. Henry Hite in Fairfield Co., Ohio March 23, 1851, and S. J. Carpenter c.1863; David[1.5.4.5.5a], b. Nov., 1836, m. Esther Engel in Fairfield Co., Ohio Nov. 5, 1857; Mary[1.5.4.5.6a], b. 1838, m. Eduard Kull[1.5.1.9.2]; Samuel[1.5.4.5.7a], b. 1840, m. Katie Brown; Lear[1.5.4.5.8a], b. 1843, m. D. Miesse; Susanna[1.5.4.5.9a], b. 1845, and m. George Stroll; Noah[1.5.4.5.10a], b. 1847, and d. Jan. 28, 1928, m. Jennie Roby; Elenora[1.5.4.5.11a], b. June, 1850, m. Amos Miller, they resided in Fairfield Co., Liberty Twp. in 1900; Elizabeth[1.5.4.5.12a], b. 1853, m. _____ Friesner.

George Swartz

George[1.5.4.6a] m. Mary, dau. of Abraham and Catherine (Fast) Beery, in Fairfield Co., Ohio Oct. 6, 1831. She was b. in Fairfield Co., Ohio on Aug. 25, 1812, and d. in Hancock Co., Findlay, Ohio in 1868. George d. in Fairfield Co., Berne Twp., Ohio in (Jan. 20) 1860. They had the following children in Fairfield Co., Berne Twp.:

Simeon[1.5.4.6.1a], b. Dec. 21, 1832, a minister, d. in Berne Twp. Jan. 7, 1910, m. Sarah Kring.

Joseph[1.5.4.6.2a], b. May 8, 1834, m. Barbara, dau. of Abraham and Barbara (Tussing) Keller, and granddau. of Jacob and Anna (Miller) Keller, in Fairfield Co., Ohio on April 6, 1857. She was b. in Licking Co., Kirkersville, Ohio July 8, 1840, d. in Woodford Co., El Paso, Illinois May 11, 1914. Abraham and Barbara Keller d. 1840/41; their dau. was raised by Joseph Keller, and one of Barbara (Tussing) Keller's sisters. Joseph Swartz d. in El Paso April 6, 1895.

Solomon B.[1.5.4.6.3a], b. May 1, 1836, m. Sarah A. Radabaugh.

George H.[1.5.4.6.4a], b. 1838, m. Lovina Downing.

Daniel[1.5.4.6.5a], b. 1841, and killed in 1863, at the battle of Stone River during the Civil War.

Rebecca[1.5.4.6.6a], b. in 1844, m. Jeremiah Ewing.

William[1.5.4.6.7a], b. in 1846, d. 1850.

David[1.5.4.6.8a], b. about 1848, d. c.1849.

Henry Swartz

Henry[1.5.4.7a] m. Sarah, dau. of Abraham and Catherine (Fast) Beery, in Fairfield Co., Ohio Dec. 31, 1829. She was b. in Fairfield Co. July 2, 1807, d. in Berne Twp. June 12, 1852. After Sarah's death, Henry m. Rebecca Hufford. She was b. 1821. Henry d. in Shelby Co., Pickaway Twp., Illinois Feb. 4, 1882. Henry had the following children in Berne Twp.:

Abraham[1.5.4.7.1a], b. 1829, m. Catherine Hamilton.

Mary[1.5.4.7.2a], b. July 21, 1832, d. in Fairfield Co. March 18, 1874, m. Lewis (Jan 1827 - Dec 21, 1908), son of Abraham Beery, in Fairfield Co. April 19, 1855.

Elizabeth[1.5.4.7.3a], b. July 21, 1832, m. Jacob Bruner.

Catherine[1.5.4.7.4a], b. 1833, m. Jacob M. Eversole in Fairfield Co., March 20, 1856.

Sophia[1.5.4.7.5a], b. 1835, m. Reuben, son of Joseph (1798), and grandson of Nicholas Beery. After Reuben's death, she m. Thomas Wagoner.

John[1.5.4.7.6a], b. Jan. 2, 1837, d. in Shelby Co., Pickaway Twp., Illinois Sept. 28, 1883. He m. Rachel, dau. of Henry and Rebecca (Seitz) Friesner in Fairfield Co. Feb. 18, 1858. She was b. Feb. 20, 1838, d. in Shelby Co., Illinois 1899. John served in the Civil War in Company F, 46th Ohio Regiment as a Sgt. under General Sherman from Feb. 5, 1861 to July 8, 1865.

Eli[1.5.4.7.7a], b. 1838, and was killed in 1862, at the Battle of Shiloh during the Civil War. He m. Elizabeth Jackson (b. in Ohio in 1839).

Henry C.[1.5.4.7.8a], b. 1842, and m. Susanna[1.5.4.8.8a], dau. of John[1.5.4.8a] and Mary (Bright) Swartz.

Sarah[1.5.4.7.9a], b. 1844, d. in Fairfield Co. 1899, m. W. Miller.

Rebecca[1.5.4.7.10a], b. Feb. 22, 1847, m. John W. Beery (b. 1844), descendent of Abraham Beery.

Hannah[1.5.4.7.11a], b. 1849, m. H. Downs.

Nancy[1.5.4.7.12a], b. 1851, m. J. L. Magenbach.

Elijah[1.5.4.7.13a], b. 1853.

Reuben[1.5.4.7.14a], b. 1855.

Rachel Jane[1.5.4.7.15a], b. Dec. 26, 1856, m. Henry, son of Abraham Friesner. She d. Jan. 25, 1937.

Emily/Emma[1.5.4.7.16a], b. 1859, m. G. Natkins, had children, an infant, Alice, Nancy, Josie, Brom, Omma, and Jesse.

Daniel[1.5.4.7.17a], b. c.1861, m. _____ Croucher.

Lincoln[1.5.4.7.18a], b. c.1863.

Charles[1.5.4.7.19a], b. c.1865, m. _____ Logenback.

Fannie[1.5.4.7.20a], b. c.1867, m. W. Croucher, had children, Ora, M., W., Alfy, and Ollie.

John Swartz

John[1.5.4.8a] m. Mary, dau. of John Bright, in Fairfield Co. March 20, 1836. She was b. 1814, and d. in Fairfield Co., Liberty Twp. in 1873. John d. in Liberty Twp. in 1866. They had the following children in Liberty Twp.: Eleanor[1.5.4.8.1a], b. 1837, m. John Y. Crites in Fairfield Co. Sept. 15, 1859; Elizabeth[1.5.4.8.2a], b. 1841, m. H. Knelpper;

Hannah$^{1.5.4.8.3a}$, b. 1843, m. S. Smith; Susanna$^{1.5.4.8.4a}$, b. 1846, m. Henry C.$^{1.5.4.7.8a}$, son of Henry$^{1.5.4.7a}$ and Sarah (Beery) Swartz; John B.$^{1.5.4.8.5a}$, b. 1848; George$^{1.5.4.8.6a}$, b. 1851, m. S. Skank; Amos$^{1.5.4.8.7a}$, b. 1853; Noah$^{1.5.4.8.8a}$, b. 1855; Mary$^{1.5.4.8.9a}$, b. 1858; Dora$^{1.5.4.8.10a}$, b. c.1861, m. ____ Burne; Ida$^{1.5.4.8.11a}$, b. c.1863, m. J. Fletcher; Ora$^{1.5.4.8.12a}$, b. c.1865, m. ____ Boyer.

Catherine Swartz

Catherine$^{1.5.4.9a}$ m. William Laney in Fairfield Co. in 1834. He was b. in Ohio March 6, 1813, d. in Fairfield Co., Berne Twp. March 6, 1864. She d. in Berne Twp. in 1893. They had the following children in Berne Twp.: Henry$^{1.5.4.9.1a}$; Joseph C.$^{1.5.4.9.2a}$, m. L. Evans, was in the sewing machine business in Springfield; John S.$^{1.5.4.9.3a}$, m. R. Codington, and resided in Dakota; Elnora$^{1.5.4.9.4a}$, m. Thomas J. Kirk, and resided in Baltimore (Ohio); Sarah$^{1.5.4.9.5a}$, m. Moses Kepper, and resided in Violet Twp. (she may also be the Sarah who m. Jonas Miperly in 1854); Susan$^{1.5.4.9.6a}$, residing with her sister, Elizabeth in 1883; Elizabeth$^{1.5.4.9.7a}$, m. Henry Lamb, and resided in Walnut Twp; Catherine$^{1.5.4.9.8a}$, m. G. W. Gardner; William$^{1.5.4.9.9a}$, m. ____ Lehman, and ____ Baughman, and resided in Baltimore (Ohio); Franklin$^{1.5.4.9.10a}$, served in the Civil War in the 1st Ohio Cavalry in 1861, d. in Indianapolis, Indiana in 1871.

Mary Magdalena Swartz

Mary Magdalena$^{1.5.4.10a}$ m. Abraham Leonard in Fairfield Co. Nov. 29, 1832, d. in Benton Co., Blairstown, Iowa. He was b. March 28, 1812, and d. in Fairfield Co., Berne Twp., Ohio on Sept. 29, 1849. He is buried in Mt Tabor cemetery. They had the following children: Mollie$^{1.5.4.10.1a}$, b. Feb. 8, 1837; Edward$^{1.5.4.10.2a}$; Susanna$^{1.5.4.10.3a}$; Christian$^{1.5.4.10.4a}$; Ellen$^{1.5.4.10.5a}$; Catherine$^{1.5.4.10.6a}$; John$^{1.5.4.10.7a}$, m. C. Mell, and C. Grable; Abraham$^{1.5.4.10.8a}$; Lenus$^{1.5.4.10.9a}$, m. ____ Hildebrand; Noah$^{1.5.4.10.10a}$, m. A. Crowl, and ____ Hilbesh.

Elenora Swartz

Elenora$^{1.5.4.11a}$ m. John Strayer (b. 1817). They resided in Fairfield Co., Berne Twp., Ohio in 1850. She d. in Franklin Co., Rocky Fork, Ohio. They had the following children: George$^{1.5.4.11.1a}$; John$^{1.5.4.11.2a}$; Catherine$^{1.5.4.11.3a}$, m. S. Baughman; Precilla$^{1.5.4.11.4a}$, m. Levi Kring; Abraham$^{1.5.4.11.5a}$, m. J. Mitchel.

Anna Catharina Swartz

Anna Catharina$^{1.8a}$ was bapt. at Christ's Lutheran Church of York Jan. 20, 1761, and sponsored by Henry and Dorothea Walter, and Catharine, dau. of Conrad Mueller. She m. Jacob, son of Nicolus and

Margarethe Heinrich. He was b. Dec. 18, 1755, bapt. at Friedensaal, and sponsored by Jacob Heinrich, and Anna Maria Bremm. Jacob and Catharina had the following children: Jacob[1.8.1a], b. Jan. 7, 1796, bapt. at Ziegler's (St. Paul's) Lutheran Church on Feb. 21, 1796, and sponsored by his uncle and aunt, Jacob and Dorothy Swartz; Catherine[1.8.2a], b. Feb. 11, 1799, bapt. at Ziegler's on March 17, 1799, and sponsored by Catherine Schneider; John[1.8.3a], b. Dec. 29, 1800, bapt. at Ziegler's on Feb. 15, 1801, and sponsored by John Swartz.

****

Johan Jacob Schaffer

Johan Jacob[1b], son of the dairy farmer, m. Anna Maria Biber in Hirschland Lutheran Church, Hirschland, Northern Alsace France on Jan. 10, 1708, and Maria Catharina, dau. of Theobald Biber on July 20, 1723. Anna Maria was b. in 1684, and d. at Hirschland on Dec. 3, 1722. Johan Jacob and Anna Maria bapt. the following children in Hirschland Lutheran Church: Catharina[1.1b], bapt. Nov. 22, 1708; Johan Petrus[1.2b], bapt. Jan. 6, 1710; Johan Henrich[1.3b], bapt. Oct. 20, 1711, and confirmed in 1724; Johann David[1.4b], bapt. Jan. 22, 1713, and sponsored by David Schmith, weaver of Hirschland, Martinus Biber, and Eva Schmid; Anna Maria[1.5b], bapt. May 12, 1715; Anna Christina[1.6a], bapt. Feb. 21, 1717; Anna Magdalena[1.7a], bapt. July 6, 1719; Anna Catharina[1.8a], bapt. March 15, 1722.

Johann David Schaffer

Johann David[1.4b] immigrated to America, and arrived at Philadelphia in the ship *Robert and Alice* in 1739. David m. Anna Catharina[1.1.6c], dau. of Johann Nickel[1.1c] and Maria Margaretha (Von Marxheim) Simon, in York Co., Codorus Twp., Pennsylvania on March 13, 1742/43. David took the Sacrament on Sept. 18, 1763, and was naturalized on Sept. 24, 1763. He was the constable for Shrewsbury Twp. in 1754, and supervisor of the highways in 1761. On June 15, 1762, he sold the 50 acre tract in Shrewsbury Twp. that he purchased on Sept. 10, 1750 to George Kleinfelter. David was a farmer in Shrewsbury Twp., and d. Jan., 1770 (his will was written on Dec. 29, 1769, and probated on Jan. 9, 1770). In 1783, Catharina had 200 acres in Shrewsbury Twp. Catharina d. Jan., 1797. They had the following children in Shrewsbury Twp.: Maria Elisabeth[1.4.1b], b. Jan. 16, 1743/44; Johan Philip[1.4.2b], b. April 5, 1745; Catharina[1.4.3b], b. c.1747; Charles[1.4.4b], b. c.1749, d. before Jan. 1786; Anna Magdalena[1.4.5b], bapt. by Reverend Jacob Lischy Oct. 19, 1751, sponsored by Joseph and Magdalena Welschans, m. Henrich Swartz[1.5a]; Elisabetha[1.4.6b], b. about 1753; Anna Maria[1.4.7b], b. c.1755; Margaretha[1.4.8b], b. c.1757, m. Johannes Ehrhardt[1.4g(a)]; David[1.4.9b], b. June 15, 1759, had a guardian appointed for him on Nov. 27, 1771.

Maria Elisabeth Schaffer

Maria Elisabeth[1.4.1b], was bapt. at Christ's Lutheran Church of York March 17, 1743/44, sponsored by Johan Adam and Maria Elisabeth Simon. She m. Baltzer Kohler/Koller who was possibly the son of Andreas and Magdalena Kohler, bapt. by Reverend Jacob Lischy on June 18, 1749. Baltzer was a tailor, received a farm in Shrewsbury Twp. from David Schaffer on Nov. 27, 1762. Baltzer and Maria Elisabeth resided in Shrewsbury Twp., and had the following children: Johannes[1.4.1.1b], b. Aug. 25, 1763, bapt. at Friedensaal on the 19th Sunday after Trinity, and sponsored by Lorentz and Margareta Kleinfelter; Johan Jacob[1.4.1.2b], b. c.1764; Johann Georg[1.4.1.3b], b. Oct. 7, 1766, bapt. at Friedensaal Nov. 9, 1766, sponsored by Georg and Anna Barbara Kleinfelter; a dau.[1.4.1.4b], b. about 1769, and m. Henry Rieman; Margareta[1.4.1.5b], b. c.1772; Adam[1.4.1.6b], b. c.1775.

Johannes Koller

Johannes[1.4.1.1b] m. Maria Elisabeth, dau. of Peter Gerberich, c.1776. They had the following children in Shrewsbury Twp.: Johannes[1.4.1.1.1b], b. April 3, 1777; Jacob[1.4.1.1.2b], b. Jan. 6, 1781, bapt. at Friedensaal Jan. 21, 1781, sponsored by his grandfather, Baltzer Koller; Johan Peter[1.4.1.1.3b], b. Jan. 31, 1788, bapt. at Fissel's Feb. 24, 1788, sponsored by Peter and Margaretha Gerberich; Magdalena[1.4.1.1.4b], b. Oct., 1791, bapt. at Fissel's Nov. 20, 1792, sponsored by Johannes and Margaretha Gerberich.

Johannes Koller

Johannes[1.4.1.1.1b] m. Catharina, dau. of Carl and Christina (Stabler) Diehl. She was b. Dec. 6, 1780, d. May 20, 1863. He was a farmer and blacksmith in Shrewsbury Twp., d. Jan. 28, 1847. They had the following children; Elizabeth[1.4.1.1.1.1b], b. c,1799, m. Henry Rieman, resided in Wayne Co., Indiana; Christina[1.4.1.1.1.2b], b. Oct. 10, 1801, m. Peter Ehrhart, d. Aug. 11, 1862; Daniel[1.4.1.1.1.3b], m. Magdalena Koller; Catherine[1.4.1.1.1.4b], m. David Hoffacker, resided in Wayne Co., Indiana; Mary Ann[1.4.1.1.1.5b], b. March 15, 1817, m. Simon Anstine, d. June 9, 1889; Zachariah[1.4.1.1.1.6b], b. Aug. 9, 1819, m. Cassandra Schaffer, d. June 19, 1892; Susanna[1.4.1.1.1.7b]; Sarah[1.4.1.1.1.8b].

Johan Jacob Koller

Johan Jacob[1.4.1.2b] m. Anna Catharina Miller sometime before 1779, and Barbara c.1797. Jacob's heirs gave a release to their attorney on Nov. 24, 1845. Jacob bapt. the following children at Fissel's: Catherine[1.4.1.2.1b], b. Sept. 28, 1781, and m. Carl Diehl; Eva[1.4.1.2.2b], b. May 3, 1788, bapt. May 12, 1788, sponsored by Georg and Eva Kroph; Michael$^{1.4.1.2.3b}$, b. in June, 1789, bapt. July 11, 1789, sponsored by Philip and Barbara Schaffer; Jacob$^{1.4.1.2.4b}$, b. June 11, 1798, bapt. July 8, 1798, sponsored by Jacob Schaffer; Henrich$^{1.4.1.2.5b}$, b. July 20, 1800, sponsored by Henrich and Elisabeth Kunckel.

Margareta Koller

Margareta$^{1.4.1.5b}$ m. Johannes, son of Johannes Adam and Appolonia Kleinfelter, c.1773. He was b. in Shrewsbury Twp. c.1763. They had the following children in Shrewsbury Twp.; Eva$^{1.4.1.5.1b}$, b. Nov. 6, 1794, bapt. at Fissel's, sponsored by Eva Heiss, m. Jacob Dellinger; Adam$^{1.4.1.5.2b}$, b. May 1, 1796, bapt. at Fissel's, sponsored by his uncle, Adam Koller; Johann$^{1.4.1.5.3b}$, b. Oct. 27, 1799, bapt. at Fissel's, sponsored by his uncle and aunt, Jacob and Barbara Koller; dau.$^{1.4.1.5.4b}$, m. Peter Kohler.

Adam Kleinfelter

Adam$^{1.4.1.5.2b}$ was bapt. at Fissel's on Nov. 10, 1799, sponsored by Adam Koller. He was an Evangelical Minister, d. in 1878. He resided in Fairfield Co., Lancaster, Ohio in 1821, and m. Margaret, dau. of Conrad Dillman, in Summit Co., Greensburg, Ohio in 1825. They had the following children: William$^{1.4.1.5.2.1b}$, was a minister of the church in Iowa; Kate$^{1.4.1.5.2.2b}$.

Johan Philip Schaffer

Johan Philip$^{1.4.2b}$ was bapt. by Reverend Jacob Lischy on May 23, 1745, sponsored by his uncle, Johan Philip Simon. In 1783, Philip had 350 acres in Shrewsbury Twp. He was a Private in the Fifth (Captain John Ehrman) Company, Seventh Battalion, York Co., Militia in 1778, and continued in the same Company, Second Class, when it was reorganized (in 1779) as the Fifth (Captain Henry Ferree) of the Fifth Battalion in 1781, and Dec. 27, 1782. He d. in Shrewsbury Twp. June 21, 1824, buried in Fissel's cemetery. His will was written on Aug. 27, 1821, probated on June 26, 1824. He m. Anna Maria Barbara, dau. of Jacob and Maria Barbara (Keller) Scherer. She was b. Nov. 11, 1755 (1753), d. March 29, 1832. They are buried in Fissel's cemetery. They had the following children in Shrewsbury Twp.:

Anna Maria Barbara$^{1.4.2.1b}$, b. Oct. 8, 1776, bapt. at Friedensaal Nov. 9, 1776, sponsored by her aunt, Anna Maria Schaffer.
Elizabeth$^{1.4.2.2b}$, b. c.1777.
Johann Jacob$^{1.4.2.3b}$, b. Dec. 3, 1778, bapt. at Friedensaal on Jan. 21, 1779, sponsored by his uncle and aunt, Jacob Koller and wife. He m. Catherine E., d. Dec. 19, 1858. She was b. Feb. 26, 1783, d. April 23, 1866. They are buried in Fissel's cemetery. They had a dau. who m. George Hengst in

Shrewsbury Twp. Feb. 25, 1823.

Johannes[1.4.2.4b], b. Dec. 20, 1780, bapt. at Friedensaal on Dec. 25, 1780, sponsored by his uncle and aunt, David and Anna Maria Schaffer. He m. Elizabeth Albrecht in Christ's Lutheran Church of York Jan. 3, 1804.

Johann Peter[1.4.2.5b], b. Feb. 8, 1784, bapt. at Friedensal on April 4, 1784, sponsored by Felix and Elisabetha Hildebrand. He d. before 1821.

Henry[1.4.2.6b], b. July 12, 1786, and was mentioned in his father's will.

Friederich[1.4.2.7b], b. c.Dec. 3, 1786, bapt. at Fissel's c.Dec. 1, 1787, sponsored by Jacob and Susanna Baehli. He was alive in 1821.

dau.[1.4.2.8b], b. c.1789, d. before 1821.

Eva[1.4.2.9b], b. June 1, 1791, bapt. at Fissel's Aug. 14, 1791, sponsored by her cousin, Margaret Koller. She may have been the dau. that m. John Grove. A Justine Schaffer m. a John Graff in the First Reformed Church of York on May 13, 1794.

Johann Philip[1.4.2.10b], b. Oct. 30, 1794, bapt. at Fissel's, sponsored by his cousin, Jacob Koller, and his wife Catharina.

Anna Maria Barbara Schaffer

Anna Maria Barbara[1.4.2.1b] never married. Her will was dated Aug. 14, 1848, and probated on Oct. 25, 1848. She d. in Springfield Twp. Oct. 2, 1848, buried in Fissel's cemetery. She had a dau., Polly[1.4.2.1.1b].

Polly (Schaffer)

Polly[1.4.2.1.1b] m. ____ Sechrist and ____ Gantz, and had the following children (the first two by ____ Sechrist) all before 1848: Daniel[1.4.2.1.1.1b], assigned the interest to the estate of his grandmother, Barbara Schaffer on March 17, 1849; Leah[1.4.2.1.1.2b], m. Jacob Foust; Lucy[1.4.2.1.1.3b], m. Jacob Caslow; Barbara[1.4.2.1.1.4b]; Polly[1.4.2.1.1.5b]; William[1.4.2.1.1.6b].

Elizabeth Schaffer

Elizabeth[1.4.2.2b] m. Henry Rockey, and had a son bapt. at Fissel's named Jacob[1.4.2.2.1b], b. April 11, 1798, bapt. May 19, 1798, sponsored by David and Anna Maria Schaffer.

Henry Schaffer

Henry[1.4.2.6b] d. in Shrewsbury Twp. July 15, 1826. He had 82 acres in Shrewsbury, and left a wife and six children at his death. Henry m. Eva, and had the following children: Magdalena[1.4.2.6.1b], b. Aug. 1, 1809, d. Dec. 22, 1826, buried in Fissel's cemetery; Henry[1.4.2.6.2b], b.

April 25, 1823, d. March 10, 1825, buried in Fissel's cemetery.

dau. Schaffer
dau.[1.4.2.8b] m. _____ Faust, d. before 1821, and had the following children: John[1.4.2.8.1b], b. c.1810, signed a release in 1834 similar to his brother's to his uncle Philip Schaffer, Jr.; Henry[1.4.2.8.2b], b. in 1812, residing in Somerset Co., Connemaugh Twp. in 1834; Elizabeth[1.4.2.8.3b], b. c.1814.

Johann Philip Schaffer
Johann Philip[1.4.2.10b] d. July 25, 1870. He m. Elizabeth, and Christina c.1863. Elizabeth was b. July 11, 1795, d. Nov. 29, 1862. Christina was b. Jan. 9, 1821, d. April 26, 1865. They were buried in Fissel's cemetery. Philip and Elizabeth had the following children: Jacob[1.4.2.10.1b], b. March 19, 1819, d. Dec. 26, 1834, buried in Fissel's cemetery; infant[1.4.2.10.2b], b. Aug. 29, 1833, d. Sept. 1, 1833, buried in Fissel's cemetery; Philip[1.4.2.10.3b], b. July 2, 1835, d. March 1, 1836, buried in Fissel's cemetery.

Catharina Schaffer
Catharina[1.4.3b] m. Johan Georg Ehrman before Dec., 1769. He received 220 1/2 acres called "Broad Spring," in Shrewsbury Twp., from her father, David, on Sept. 23, 1769. They had the following children in Shrewsbury Twp.: Maria Magdalena[1.4.3.1b], b. Sept. 23, 1770, bapt. at Friedensaal; Michael[1.4.3.2b], b. April 12, 1780, bapt. at Friedensaal June 4, 1780, sponsored by Georg and Catharina Hamspacher; David[1.4.3.3b], b. Sept. 1781, bapt. at Friedensaal Dec. 2, 1781, sponsored by his uncle and aunt, David and Anna Maria Schaffer; Catharina[1.4.3.4b], b. April 17, 1783, bapt. at Friedensaal on July 6, 1783, sponsored by her grandmother, Catharina Schaffer; Wilhelm[1.4.3.5b], b. Jan. 26, 1787, bapt. at Friedensaal on April 29, 1787, sponsored by his uncle and aunt, David and Anna Maria Schaffer; Peter[1.4.3.6b], bapt. at Friedensaal on June 15, 1789, sponsored by John and Elizabeth Schneider.

Elisabetha Schaffer
Elisabetha[1.4.6b] m. Peter Long. This is presumed to be the Johan Peter, son of Michael and Maria Barbara Lang, that was bapt. at Christ's Lutheran Church of York on March 26, 1749. Peter and Elisabetha Lang bapt. the following children at Christ's Lutheran Church of York: Regina[1.4.6.1b], bapt. Dec. 4, 1774; Elisabeth[1.4.6.2b], bapt. Oct. 20, 1776; Peter[1.4.6.3b], bapt. Aug. 23, 1778; Friedrich[1.4.6.4b], bapt. July 30, 1780; Catharina[1.4.6.5b], bapt. Nov. 17, 1782.

Anna Maria Schaffer

Anna Maria[1.4.7b] m. Michael Ehrman, and had the following children in Shrewsbury Twp.: Johannes[1.4.7.1b], b. 1782, bapt. at Friedensaal, sponsored by Johannes Schneider.

David Schaffer

David[1.4.9b] m. Anna Maria Venus, and Christina after 1808. David was a Private in the Fifth (captain John Ehrman) Company, Seventh Battalion, York Co., Militia in 1778, and a Private under Captain Henry Moore, assigned to guard prisoners at Camp Security in York from Aug. 20 to Sept. 20, 1781, and performed the same duty under Captain William Lindsay from Dec. 8, 1781 to Feb. 8, 1782. He d. in Shrewsbury Twp. on Dec. 23, 1823, and is buried in Keeny's cemetery. His will was written on Feb. 23, 1820, and probated on Sept. 30, 1823. He deeded 25 acres in Shrewsbury Twp. to Adam Shaffer on Nov. 24, 1787. On Jan. 5, 1786, David's siblings; Philip; Marilis wife of Baltzer Kohler; Margaret, wife of John Ehrhard; Catharina, wife of George Ehrman; Magdalena, wife of Henry Schwartz; Elizabeth, wife of Peter Long; and Anna Maria, wife of Michael Ehrman, signed a release to David. Anna Maria was b. Dec. 25, 1757, d. Aug. 30, 1808. Christina was b. Aug. 22, 1790, d. Nov. 18, 1872. Christina petitioned for guardians to be appointed for Mary, George, Samuel, Rebecca, and Benjamin, minor children of David on April 6, 1825. David had the following children in Shrewsbury Twp.:

Johann Philipp[1.4.9.1b], b. June 11, 1780, bapt. at Friedensaal July 9, 1780, sponsored by his uncle and aunt, Johann Philipp and Barbara Schaffer. He d. Dec. 21, 1849, buried in Keeny's cemetery in Shrewsbury Twp.

Daniel[1.4.9.2b], b. Aug. 7, 1783, bapt. at Friedensaal Aug. 31, 1783, sponsored by her uncle and aunt, Henrich and Magdalena Swartz. He d. before 1820.

Elizabeth[1.4.9.3b], b. Sept. 10, 1785, bapt. at Friedensaal Sept. 18, 1785, sponsored by Peter and Elizabeth Leiss. She d. before 1820.

Magdalena[1.4.9.4b], b. Aug. 17, 1787, bapt. at Friedensaal on Aug. 19, 1787, sponsored by Johan Adam and Elisabetha (Kleinfelter) Schaffer. She d. before 1820.

David[1.4.9.5b], b. Feb. 13, 1790, bapt. at Friedensaal on April 25, 1790, sponsored by Conrad and Dorothea Swartz. He m. Margaretha (b. Aug. 20, 1800, d. Sept. 20, 1863). David d. Dec. 10, 1858, buried in Fissel's cemetery.

Eva[1.4.9.6b], b. Sept. 24, 1792, bapt. at Friedensaal Jan. 13, 1793, sponsored by Justina Schaffer. She d. before 1820.

Johannes[1.4.9.7b], b. May 22, 1795, bapt. at Friedensaal, sponsored by Johannes Ehrman. He d. before 1802.

Moses$^{1\cdot4\cdot9\cdot8b}$, b. July 31, 1797, bapt. at Saddler's Oct. 15, 1797, sponsored by Andreas Berkebeil. His mother is not named. He d. before 1820.

Christina$^{1\cdot4\cdot9\cdot9b}$, b. March 25, 1799, bapt. at Friedensaal April 5, 1799, sponsored by Barbara Schaffer.

Johannes$^{1\cdot4\cdot9\cdot10b}$, b. Jan. 31, 1802, bapt. at Saddler's, sponsored by Andreas Berckebeil and wife.

Barbara$^{1\cdot4\cdot9\cdot11b}$, b. c.1804.

Joscht$^{1\cdot4\cdot9\cdot12b}$, b. Sept. 16, 1809, and bapt. at Saddler's on Nov. 26, 1809. His mother is named as Chaderina. He d. before 1820.

Mary$^{1\cdot4\cdot9\cdot13b}$, b. in 1812.

Johan George$^{1\cdot4\cdot9\cdot14b}$, b. Feb. 13, 1813, bapt. at Friedensaal May 8, 1813, sponsored by George and Elizabeth Kleinfelter. On April 2, 1834, he resided in Shrewsbury Twp., and signed a release to his guardian, George Kleinfelter on the estate of his father, David Schaffer.

Samuel$^{1\cdot4\cdot9\cdot15b}$, b. Jan. 6, 1815, bapt. April 2, 1815, sponsored by Henry and Anna Maria Swartz.

Rebecca$^{1\cdot4\cdot9\cdot16b}$, b. Feb. 6, 1817, bapt. May 24, 1817, sponsored by John and Margaret Zeller.

Benjamin$^{1\cdot4\cdot9\cdot17b}$, b. Aug. 4, 1818, d. Nov. 15, 1898. He m. Anna. She was b. June 13, 1816, d. Jan. 8, 1889. They are buried in the Lutheran cemetery in Shrewsbury Twp.

****

Adam Simon/Simonis

Adam^{1c} m. Eva Straus at Rheinland, Herran-Sulzbach, Germany on Oct. 23, 1644. They had the following children: Johan Peter$^{1\cdot1c}$, bapt. Nov. 2, 1645; Anna Catharina$^{1\cdot2c}$, bapt. Jan. 6, 1650.

Johan Peter Simon

Johan Peter$^{1\cdot1c}$ m. Maria Agnes Meyer on Aug. 9, 1676, and had the following children at Rheinland, Herran-Sulzbach, Germany: Johann Nickel$^{1\cdot1\cdot1c}$, bapt. Oct. 3, 1677; Johann Stephen$^{1\cdot1\cdot2c}$, bapt. July 16, 1679; Johann Peter$^{1\cdot1\cdot3c}$, bapt. March 12, 1683, and m. Anna Juliana Jung at Herran-Sulzbach on Nov. 24, 1711.

Johann Nickel Simon

Johann Nickel$^{1\cdot1\cdot1c}$ m. Maria Margaretha Von Marxheim at Herran-Sulzbach on Nov. 17, 1705. He followed his sons, Jacob and Adam, to America, and arrived at Philadelphia in the ship *Samuel* on Aug. 27, 1739. Johann Nickel d. in Lancaster Co., Warwick Twp., Pennsylvania sometime after Aug. 1739. Nickel and Maria Margaretha had the following children in Herran-Sulzbach: Johann Niclass$^{1\cdot1\cdot1\cdot1c}$, b. March 6, 1706/7; Johann Jacob$^{1\cdot1\cdot1\cdot2c}$, b. Sept. 4, 1709, immigrated to America with his brother, Adam in the ship *Charming Nancy* Nov. 9, 1738, resided in Lancaster Co., Pennsylvania in 1760; Johan Adam[1.1.1.3c], b. 1716; Maria Elisabeth[1.1.1.4c], b. c.1720, and m. Johan Daniel Diehl[1.1.1.11]; Johann Philipp[1.1.1.5c], b. March 3, 1722/23; Anna Catharina[1.1.1.6c], b. Aug. 30, 1725, and m. Johan David Schaffer[1.4b].

Johan Adam Simon

Johan Adam[1.1.1.3c] m. Maria Elisabeth, dau. of Johan Adam and Maria Catharina (Kreischer) Diehl, in Lancaster Co., Warwick Twp., Pennsylvania on Dec. 26, 1740. Johan Adam Diehl was b. in Unden Cappeln, Germany Sept. 12, 1690, d. April, 1755. He m. Maria Catharina Kreischer on Dec. 4, 1712. Adam Simon arrived at Philadelphia on the ship *Charming Nancy* with his brother on Nov. 8, 1738. He was granted 100 acres on a branch of the Codorus adjoining his brother-in-law, Carl Adam Diehl's land in Shrewsbury Twp. On March 6, 1760, Abraham Welty purchased Adam's land, and Adam moved to Franklin Co., Lurgen/Letterkenny Twp., Pennsylvania, nine miles southeast of Shippensburg. He moved to Washington Co., in 1776/77, and took out a land warrant in West Bethlehem Twp. in 1787, for 343 and 3/4 acres named *Despair*. The land was patented on March 19, 1788. Maria Elisabeth was b. in Homberg Germany April 4, 1715, d. in Washington Co., Bethlehem Twp., Pennsylvania Feb. 12, 1806. Adam d. intestate in Bethlehem Twp. March 28, 1788. They are buried in Dutch Glory cemetery. They had the following children in York Co., Shrewsbury Twp., Pennsylvania:

Michael[1.1.1.3.1c], b. Jan. 25, 1742.

Liese Catherine[1.1.1.3.2c], b. Jan. 6, 1744, d. after 1797. She m. Philip Stark/Strong.

Angelica Elizabeth "Agnes"[1.1.1.3.3c], b. July 28, 1745, d. after 1797. She m. Michael Beltz.

Catharine[1.1.1.3.4c], b. c.1748, d. in Washington Co., Pennsylvania on Dec. 18, 1815. She m. George Densor in Cumberland Co., Pennsylvania on April 6, 1769.

Andreas[1.1.1.3.5c], b. Nov. 16, 1751, bapt. Nov. 25, 1751, sponsored by Andreas and Dorothea Kuertzel. He d. in Ohio on July 9, 1828. He m. Maria Elisabeth Geckler. On March 19, 1764, He was taken captive by Indians, adopted by them, and returned to his family eight months later, after being freed when Col. Henry Bouquet defeated the Indians at Bushy Run. He received a tract in West Bethlehem Twp. called *The Addition* in 1787. He d. in Columbiana Co., Ohio in 1828.

Margaret[1.1.1.3.6c], b. c.1753, and resided in Franklin Co., Pennsylvania in 1800. She m. George Wright.

Jacob[1.1.1.3.7c], b. c.1755, d. in Mahoning Co., Ohio in March, 1845. He m. Catharine.

Adam[1.1.1.3.8c], b. c.1756, d. before 1788.

Anna Maria[1.1.1.3.9c], b. c.1758, and resided in Trumbull Co., Ohio in 1828. She m. James Stall, and Abraham Moser.

Nicholas[1.1.1.3.10c], b. in 1761, d. in Portage Co., Ohio on Jan. 14, 1834. He m. Susan Geckler.

Michael Simon

Michael[1.1.1.3.1c] d. in Mahoning Co., Boardman Twp., Ohio (buried in Washington Co., Bethlehem Twp., Pennsylvania) on May 20, 1839. He m. Anna Ottillia, dau. of Valentine and Gertrude Schmeltzer, in York Co., Pennsylvania on Sept. 2, 1766, Anna Margaretha Rhoda Mohr, widow of ____ Althaus in Washington Co., Pennsylvania on Oct. 9, 1791, and Gertrude Schmidt, widow of John Dice. Anna Ottillia was b. Feb. 2, 1741, immigrated to America on the ship *Royal Union* on Aug. 15, 1750, d. July 25, 1791. Anna Margaretha d. in childbirth c.1792. Gertrude was b. in 1750, d. in 1837. Michael resided in Franklin Co., Pennsylvania near the Maryland line (he had some children bapt. in Maryland) until 1776/77, when he moved to Washington Co., Pennsylvania. He received a warrant for a tract called *Blackberry* in West Bethlehem Twp. in 1787. He moved to Ohio and purchased 1200 acres in 1800. During the Revolutionary War, he was a Frontier Ranger under Captain Abner Howell, in the Third Battalion, Washington Co., Militia. Michael had the following children:

Elisabeth[1.1.1.3.1.1c], b. Aug. 2, 1767, bapt. at Friedensaal on Aug. 30, 1767, sponsored by Valentin and Gertraut Schmeltzer. She m. Andrew Ginter/Kinter, d. in Ohio c.1807.

Anna Margaretha[1.1.1.3.1.2c], b. Sept. 21, 1768, m. George Kinter/Ginter and Henry Harsh, d. Sept. 7, 1844.

Catherine Barbara[1.1.1.3.1.3c], b. Feb. 28, 1770, m. ____ Fisher and George Zedaker, d. Feb. 2, 1827.

Michael[1.1.1.3.1.4c], b. May 4, 1771, m. Barbara Dice and Elizabeth Crottinger, d. April 10, 1838.

Anna Maria[1.1.1.3.1.5c], b. Dec. 16, 1772, m. George Macherman, and resided in Wood Co., Ohio in 1849.

Ester[1.1.1.3.1.6c], b. Feb. 2, 1774, m. J. Henry Hewitt, d. June 15, 1856.

Maria Catharina[1.1.1.3.1.7c], b. Nov. 28, 1775, m. John N. Phister, d. Dec. 28, 1841.

Johan Adam[1.1.1.3.1.8c], b. April 26, 1777, m. Rebecca Reinhart, d. before 1846.

George[1.1.1.3.1.9c], b. June 2, 1779, d. in Columbiana Co., Ohio c.1804.

Peter[1.1.1.3.1.10c], b. May 29, 1781, and m. Margaret.

Andrew[1.1.1.3.1.11c], b. Dec. 18, 1783, d. in Crawford Co., Hutsonville, Illinois on Sept. 23, 1857.

Jacob[1.1.1.3.1.12c], b. Jan. 12, 1786, m. Elizabeth Stemple on Jan. 13, 1811, d. Sept. 14, 1861.
dau.[1.1.1.3.1.13c], b. and d. c.1792.
Abraham[1.1.1.3.1.14c], b. Dec. 3, 1794, m. Mary Catherine Crouse on Nov. 4, 1819, d. in Mahoning Co., Ohio on Dec. 16, 1873.
Henry[1.1.1.3.1.15c], b. June 7, 1796, m. Anna Catherine Stemple and Elizabeth Miner, d. in Eaton, Michigan on May 17, 1872.

Johann Philipp Simon

Johann Philipp[1.1.1.5c] m. Anna Gertrude, dau. of Peter Schneider, in the First Reformed Church of Lancaster, Pennsylvania on Feb. 2, 1745/46. Philipp received a land warrant in York Co., Shrewsbury Twp. March 9, 1753. Philipp d. intestate in 1760. Gertrude m. John Gable, in 1761; she d. in Shrewsbury Twp. in 1770. Philipp and Gertrude had the following children: Maria Elisabeth[1.1.1.5.1c], b. Dec. 3, 1746, m. Felix Hildebrand[1.1m]; Hans Adam[1.1.1.5.2c], b. c.1749; Elisabeth Catharina[1.1.1.5.3c], bapt. by Reverend Jacob Lischy on Oct. 19, 1751, sponsored by Jacob Pfluger and Elisabeth Catharina Schneiderin; Anna Maria[1.1.1.5.4c], bapt. by Reverend Jacob Lischy on Oct. 5, 1755, sponsored by Paul Schneider and Anna Maria Diehl.

****

Franz Seitz

Franz[1d] m. Anna Brichstuhl of Switzerland, and had a son at Adelshofen, Eppingen, Bavaria, Germany, named Hans Andreas[1.1d], b. in 1669.

Hans Andreas Seitz

Hans Andreas[1.1d] m. Anna Maria (1672-1722), dau. of Hans Elias Schlauch, in 1697. Hans Andreas d. in 1744. Hans Andreas and Anna Maria had a son at Adelshofen named Johann Andreas[1.1.1d], b. 1700.

Johann Andreas Seitz

Johann Andreas[1.1.1d], m. Anna Dorothea, dau. of Johan and Anna Dorothea Welk, at Adelshofen Feb. 8, 1728/29. She was b. in Dammhof, Bavaria, in 1710. Johann Andreas d. in 1745. They had the following children at Adelshofen: Johannes Andreas[1.1.1.1d], b. 1731; Susanna Barbara[1.1.1.2d], b. 1733; Johann Peter[1.1.1.3d], b. 1736; Johann David[1.1.1.4d], b. 1738; Johannes[1.1.1.5d], b. Jan. 30, 1739/40; Anna Barbara[1.1.1.6d], b. 1742.

Johannes Seitz

Johannes[1.1.1.5d] m. Anna Catharina, dau. of Johannes and Anna Maria Ripp/Reub, at Adelshofen May 8, 1764. Johannes Ripp was a citizen and bricklayer of Adelshofen. Anna Catharina was b. Oct. 21, 1741, bapt. at Adelshofen Oct. 22, 1741. Johannes, Anna Catharina, and their adopted son, Ludwig Von Gemmingen aka Seitz, arrived at Philadelphia on the ship *Richmond* on Oct. 20, 1764. They settled in York Co., Shrewsbury Twp. sometime prior to 1784. He purchased 636 acres near Glen Rock on April 28, 1786. Johannes was taxed in Shrewsbury Twp. in 1773, and served during the Revolutionary War in 1777/78 in Captain John Erman's Company, Seventh Battalion, Fifth Company, York Co. Militia. Johannes d. April, 1793, buried at St. Peter's (Yellow) Reformed Church. Anna Catharina d. in Shrewsbury Twp. Feb. 20, 1820, buried in Mt. Zion Evangelical Church cemetery. Johannes and Anna Catharina had the following children:

Catharina$^{1.1.1.5.1d}$, b. Jan. 5, 1765, m. Heinrich Keller.

Anna Maria$^{1.1.1.5.2d}$, b. Dec. 12, 1766, m. Christian, son of Christian and Anna Stabler, in York Co. April 11, 1812 (he was b. July 21, 1764, d. in Baltimore Co., Stablerville, Maryland on Dec. 6, 1846). Anna Maria d. at Stablerville on March 19, 1845. They are buried in Stablersville cemetery.

Elisabeth$^{1.1.1.5.3d}$, b. Dec. 10, 1769.

Elenora$^{1.1.1.5.4d}$, b. in 1771.

Barbara$^{1.1.1.5.5d}$, b. Nov. 20, 1774.

Margaretha$^{1.1.1.5.6d}$, b. March 11, 1776.

Johannes$^{1.1.1.5.7d}$, b. March 22, 1778.

Andreas$^{1.1.1.5.8d}$, b. Dec. 21, 1779.

infant$^{1.1.1.5.9d}$, b. c.1782, d. in infancy.

Michael$^{1.1.1.5.10d}$, b. Feb. 3, 1787, bapt. at Friedensaal on March 18, 1787, sponsored by Michael and Elisabeth Meyer. He d. sometime before 1792.

Elisabeth Seitz

Elisabeth$^{1.1.1.5.3d}$ m. Josef, son of Ulrich, and Elisabeth (dau. of John Huber) Leib, and grandson of Ulrich and Veronica Leib. Ulrich and Veronica immigrated to America on the ship *Molley* on Sept. 30, 1727. Josef was b. Sept. 13, 1766, d. in Fairfield Co., Rush Creek Twp., Ohio Aug. 26, 1839. Elisabeth d. in Rush Creek Twp. March 4, 1841, buried beside her husband in Grandview cemetery. They moved to Fairfield Co. in 1801, and Josef built the second mill on Rush Creek. Josef purchased 300 acres in Rush Creek Twp. Aug. 1817. They had the following children (not all children have been confirmed (they were said to have four sons and seven daus.):

Elizabeth$^{1.1.1.5.3.1d}$, b. Feb. 15, 1794, d. Dec. 11, 1805. She is buried in St. Peter's cemetery, and hasn't been confirmed as a dau.

Daniel$^{1.1.1.5.3.2d}$, b. April 1, 1795.

Susannah$^{1.1.1.5.3.3d}$, b. Nov. 8, 1796, m. Amos Davis in 1817, d. in LaGrange Co., Indiana on Dec. 5, 1873. She had a dau. who m.

Samuel Doty.

Henry$^{1.1.1.5.3.4d}$, b. c.1798, m. Catherine "Kate," dau. of Frederick Seitz of Fairfield Co., Pleasant Twp., Ohio, and resided in Oberlin, Kansas.

Joseph$^{1.1.1.5.3.5d}$, b. Oct. 1, 1799.

John Henry$^{1.1.1.5.3.6d}$, b. Oct. 15, 1800.

Catharine$^{1.1.1.5.3.7d}$, b. c.1801.

David$^{1.1.1.5.3.8d}$, b. c.1802 (not confirmed).

Moses$^{1.1.1.5.3.9d}$, b. April 25, 1802, d. Oct. 3. He is buried in St. Peter's cemetery, and has not been confirmed as a son.

Benjamin$^{1.1.1.5.3.10d}$, b. c.1804 (not confirmed).

Margaret/Mahala/Rebecca$^{1.1.1.5.3.11d}$, b. c.1806, m. William Black/Block/Blake, and resided in Perry Co., Ohio.

Barbara$^{1.1.1.5.3.12d}$, b. c.1807, m. Frederick Fisher, and resided in Fairfield Co., Bremen, Ohio.

Elizabeth$^{1.1.1.5.3.13d}$, b. c.1807.

Sarah A. "Sally"$^{1.1.1.5.3.14d}$, b. Oct. 25, 1809, m. Samuel Mains on May 1, 1828, d. June 7, 1863. Samuel was b. Feb. 14, 1807, d. in Greenfield, Ohio on Jan. 11, 1897.

Jane$^{1.1.1.5.3.15d}$, b. c.1810, and resided with her brother, John in Crawford Co., Illinois.

James$^{1.1.1.5.3.16d}$, b. c.1811 (not confirmed).

Amos$^{1.1.1.5.3.17d}$, b. c.1813, m. Elizabeth Pope, d. in Millersport, Ohio in 1892 (not confirmed).

Elias$^{1.1.1.5.3.18d}$, b. c.1815, and m. Delilah Hill in Fairfield Co. on Jan. 24, 1836.

Daniel Leib

Daniel$^{1.1.1.5.3.2d}$ m. Barbara Leslie June 30, 1818, d. in Highland Co., Ohio Oct. 16, 1854. He moved to Westerville, Ohio, and in 1839 moved to Highland Co., Ohio. They had the following children: Joseph$^{1.1.1.5.3.2.1d}$; David$^{1.1.1.5.3.2.2d}$; Enos/Amos$^{1.1.1.5.3.2.3d}$; Clarissa$^{1.1.1.5.3.2.4d}$.

Joseph Leib

Joseph$^{1.1.1.5.3.5d}$ m. Clarissa, dau. of Levi and Sarah Allen, d. in Fairfield Co. on March 31, 1880. She was b. in Waterford, Connecticut on Dec. 6, 1803, d. Feb. 6, 1864. She was a school teacher. Joseph inherited his father's mill and homestead. Joseph and Clarissa had the following children: Samuel$^{1.1.1.5.3.5.1d}$, was a distinguished, wealthy lawyer in California, and a trustee of Stanford University of California in Palo Alto; Joseph$^{1.1.1.5.3.5.2d}$, was a horse breeder in Champaign Co., Illinois; Hamilton$^{1.1.1.5.3.5.3d}$, d. of a disease he contracted in the army; dau.$^{1.1.1.5.3.5.4d}$, m. Mason Fauley; dau.$^{1.1.1.5.3.5.5d}$, m. Sheriff Barbee of Grove City, Ohio; dau.$^{1.1.1.5.3.5.6d}$, resided in

California.

John Henry Leib
John Henry[1.1.1.5.3.6d] m. Elizabeth Ann Williams on Nov. 29, 1823, d. in Crawford Co., Illinois in Nov., 1883. She was b. in Rush Creek Twp. May 27, 1800. They had the following children; James[1.1.1.5.3.6.1d], b. Oct. 15, 1824; Lidia[1.1.1.5.3.6.2d], b. Sept. 23, 1826; John Augustus[1.1.1.5.3.6.3d], b. Aug. 20, 1828; Benjamin[1.1.1.5.3.6.4d], b. May 3, 1830; Joseph Hamilton[1.1.1.5.3.6.5d], b. Nov. 3, 1832, m. Mary Lent of Missouri; Annie Elizabeth[1.1.1.5.3.6.6d], b. Dec. 3, 1834; John Henry[1.1.1.5.3.6.7d], b. Nov. 13, 1836, and served as a Captain in the military; Isaac A.[1.1.1.5.3.6.8d], b. Oct. 3, 1838; George Washington[1.1.1.5.3.6.9d], b. Dec. 23, 1840, m. Amelia Ann, dau. of James Richard, d. in Lawrence Co., Illinois 1880; Mary Jane[1.1.1.5.3.6.10d], b. Dec. 22, 1843, m. ____ Evans, and Bill Poindexter.

Catherine Leib
Catharine[1.1.1.5.3.7d] m. John Frey, and had the following children in Fairfield Co., Rush Creek Twp., Ohio: M.[1.1.1.5.3.7.1d], was a doctor in Hocking Co., Logan, Ohio; Henry[1.1.1.5.3.7.2d], m. a dau. of John Shaw; dau.[1.1.1.5.3.7.3d], m. Thomas Paden; Benjamin[1.1.1.5.3.7.4d], m. Mary Leib, and resided in Rush Creek Twp.

Elizabeth Leib
Elizabeth[1.1.1.5.3.13d] m. Ralph/Randolph Cherry, moved to Hancock Co., Ohio, and later moved to Illinois. They had a son, Joseph[1.1.1.5.3.13.1d].

Barbara Seitz
Barbara[1.1.1.5.5d] m. Heinrich Einsel in York Co., Pennsylvania on March 11, 1798. He was b. in Germany Jan. 29, 1775, and may have d. in Seneca Co., Ohio. Barbara d. in Fairfield Co., Berne Twp., Ohio Aug. 1851, buried in Delapp cemetery. They moved to Ohio in 1801, and were the parents of the following children: Johannes[1.1.1.5.5.1d], b. Feb. 3, 1799, bapt. at Saddler's, sponsored by his uncle, Johannes Seitz; Catherine[1.1.1.5.5.2d], b. May 23, 1800, bapt. at Saddler's, sponsored by Catherine Ruhl (single); Henry[1.1.1.5.5.3d], b. 1801, m. Sallie Keller, d. in Seneca Co., Ohio Nov. 12, 1884; George[1.1.1.5.5.4d], b. c.1803, m. Elizabeth Snyder; Jacob[1.1.1.5.5.5d], b. c.1805, m. Rose Ann Gail and Elizabeth Stoneburner; Joseph[1.1.1.5.5.6d]; Elizabeth[1.1.1.5.5.7d], b. c.1807; Lewis[1.1.1.5.5.8d], b. c.1809.

Johannes Einsel
Johannes[1.1.1.5.5.1d] m. Elizabeth Welty, moved to Seneca Co., Ohio,

d. April 1, 1865. They had the following children: Sarah$^{1.1.1.5.5.1.1d}$, b. in Fairfield Co., Ohio Dec. 11, 1826, and m. Robert McClellan in Seneca Co., Ohio Jan. 21, 1848; Henry$^{1.1.1.5.5.1.2d}$, b. in Seneca Co., Ohio Oct. 6, 1834, m. Emily Spitler in Seneca Co. on Dec. 25, 1854.

Lewis Einsel

Lewis$^{1.1.1.5.5.8d}$ m. Catherine Driesbach, and resided in Battleground, Indiana and Nebraska. He was a Lutheran minister and in the banking business. They had a son: Edward$^{1.1.1.5.5.8.1d}$.

Margaretha Seitz

Margaretha$^{1.1.1.5.6d}$ m. John Zeller, d. in York Co., Pennsylvania on Aug. 26, 1822. She was buried in St. Peter's (Yellow) Reformed Church cemetery. He was murdered in York Co., Pennsylvania sometime after 1817. They had the following children in Shrewsbury Twp.: John$^{1.1.1.5.6.1d}$, b. Oct. 28, 1800, d. Jan. 28, 1810, buried in St. Peter's cemetery; Heinrich$^{1.1.1.5.6.2d}$, b. in 1805; Carl$^{1.1.1.5.6.3d}$, b. in 1808; Catharina$^{1.1.1.5.6.4d}$, b. in 1809; Eleanor$^{1.1.1.5.6.5d}$, b. c.1811.

Johannes Seitz

Johannes$^{1.1.1.5.7d}$ m. Eva, dau. of Adam and Christina Stabler, in York Co., Pennsylvania March 10, 1801. She was b. March 18 (15), 1785, bapt. at Friedensaal on April 17, 1785, sponsored by Eva, dau. of Michael Kleinfelter. She d. Oct. 3, 1856. Johannes was a Evangelical minister, d. in Shrewsbury Twp. on July 4, 1856, and is buried in Mt. Zion Evangelical Lutheran cemetery. They had the following children in Shrewsbury Twp.: Samuel$^{1.1.1.5.7.1d}$, b. Jan. 30, 1802; Daniel$^{1.1.1.5.7.1d}$, b. April 26, 1803, d. in York Co. Jan. 16, 1853, m. Annie Dice; Jacob$^{1.1.1.5.7.3d}$, b. Feb. 21, 1805; Catherine$^{1.1.1.5.7.4d}$, b. July 4, 1806, d. before 1821; Elizabeth$^{1.1.1.5.7.5d}$, b. Sept. 14, 1808; George$^{1.1.1.5.7.6d}$, b. Oct. 20, 1810, m. Anna Mary Knisely. George d. in York Co., Fairview Twp., Pennsylvania c.1840; Samuel$^{1.1.1.5.7.7d}$, b. Dec. 28, 1811; Christina$^{1.1.1.5.7.8d}$, b. July 4, 1813; John$^{1.1.1.5.7.9d}$, b. Sept. 24, 1814; Joseph$^{1.1.1.5.7.10d}$, b. March 16, 1816; Noah$^{1.1.1.5.7.11d}$, b. May 22, 1817; Magdalena$^{1.1.1.5.7.12d}$, b. June 16, 1819; Catherine$^{1.1.1.5.7.13d}$, b. Aug. 24, 1821; Adam$^{1.1.1.5.7.14d}$, b. Feb. 5, 1826, d. in Shrewsbury Twp. on Feb. 12, 1905; Benjamin$^{1.1.1.5.7.15d}$, b. May 15, 1827.

Andreas Seitz

Andreas$^{1.1.1.5.8d}$ d. in West Liberty, Maryland on April 19, 1835, buried in West Liberty M. E. cemetery. He m. Anna Catherine, dau. of Peter and Elisabetha (Schaffer) Kleinfelter. She was b. Aug. 25, 1784, bapt. at Friedensaal Sept. 5, 1784, sponsored by Johan Jacob and

Catherine Koller. Andreas was a miller and farmer at Gorsuch Mills, Baltimore Co., Maryland. Andreas and Anna Catherine had twelve children, all b. in Baltimore Co., Maryland. Anna Catherine d. Aug. 21, 1859, buried in Gooding's School House cemetery, near Glen Rock, Pennsylvania. Andreas and Catherine had the following children: Elizabeth[1.1.1.5.8.1d], b. April 2, 1805, m. Edward Norris (b. Harford Co., Maryland, Oct 15, 1792, d. Norrisville, Maryland, June 17, 1875); she d. Nov. 6, 1884; Samuel[1.1.1.5.8.2d], b. Feb. 28, 1808; Michael Kleinfelter[1.1.1.5.8.3d], b. Nov. 30, 1809; Catharine[1.1.1.5.8.4d], b. Feb. 2, 1812, m. Jacob Ludwig, d. Jan. 23, 1878; He d. in York Co., Shrewsbury Twp., Pennsylvania on March 5, 1883; Joseph[1.1.1.5.8.5d], b. in 1814; Nicholas[1.1.1.5.8.6d], b. April 12, 1816, m. Barbara Kleinfelter and Otilda Elizabeth Messinger, d. May 9, 1875; John[1.1.1.5.8.7d], b. c.1818, and moved to Ohio in 1835; William[1.1.1.5.8.8d], b. Dec. 16, 1821, m. Magdalena Zeigler, d. Jan. 11, 1871; Andrew[1.1.1.5.8.9d], b. Jan. 1, 1823, m. Amanda Yakey, d. July 7, 1888; Henry[1.1.1.5.8.10d], b. Aug. 1, 1824, m. Hannah Heathcote, d. in 1899; Mary Ann[1.1.1.5.8.11d], b. July 1, 1827, m. Charles Allison, d. March 11, 1869.

Samuel Seitz

Samuel[1.1.1.5.8.2d] m. Elizabeth Giesey in York Co., Pennsylvania on Jan. 12, 1832, and Martha Jeffries. Elizabeth was b. in Shrewsbury Twp. April 3, 1814, d. 1870. In 1850, Samuel resided in Shrewsbury Boro, and in 1870, resided in Glen Rock. Samuel and Elizabeth had the following children: William[1.1.1.5.8.2.1d], b. c.1832; Noah K.[1.1.1.5.8.2.2d], b. 1833, d. in York Co. 1920; John W. C.[1.1.1.5.8.2.3d], b. c.1839; Sarah J.[1.1.1.5.8.2.4d], b. c.1841; Susan[1.1.1.5.8.2.5d], b. c.1843; Andrew[1.1.1.5.8.2.6d], b. c.1845; Hester A.[1.1.1.5.8.2.7d], b. c.1847; Penfield[1.1.1.5.8.2.8d], b. c.1850; Emma[1.1.1.5.8.2.9d], b. c.1852; Witella/Velletta[1.1.1.5.8.2.10d], b. c.1855.

Michael Kleinfelter Seitz

Michael Kleinfelter[1.1.1.5.8.3d] m. Anna Maria Zeigler, d. in York Co., Seitzland, Pennsylvania on March 28, 1892. Anna Maria was b. in Shrewsbury Twp. Jan. 8, 1813, d. Sept. 22, 1896. They are buried in Kleinfelter-Seitz cemetery. Michael was a farmer, and worked at Seitzland Grist Mill in Codorus Twp. In 1842, he bought a farm one mile south of Seitzland. Michael and Anna Maria had the following children:

Levi Z.[1.1.1.5.8.3.1d], b. Dec. 24, 1833, and m. Lucinda, d. in York Co., Pennsylvania on Aug. 16, 1908. She was b. Aug. 15, 1835, d. Feb. 14, 1882.

Elizabeth Ann[1.1.1.5.8.3.2d], b. Oct. 20, 1837, d. Nov. 20, 1902.

Emanuel[1.1.1.5.8.3.3d], b. Aug. 16, 1837, d. Aug. 21, 1837.

George Washington$^{1.1.1.5.8.3.4d}$, b. in 1840, and m. Anna Elizabeth (Kraft), d. in York Co., Pennsylvania on Feb. 28, 1929. She was b. in 1845, d. in 1911.

Nathaniel Z.$^{1.1.1.5.8.3.5d}$, b. in 1843.

Michael$^{1.1.1.5.8.3.6d}$, b. Feb. 6, 1845, d. Aug. 22, 1860.

William H. H.$^{1.1.1.5.8.3.7d}$, b. c.1847.

Elmira$^{1.1.1.5.8.3.8d}$, b. c.1849.

Edgar Monroe$^{1.1.1.5.8.3.9d}$, b. Jan. 25, 1853, d. Feb. 14, 1870.

Magdalene$^{1.1.1.5.8.3.10d}$, b. Aug. 1, 1859, d. Dec. 28, 1859.

Joseph Seitz

Joseph$^{1.1.1.5.8.5d}$ m. Elizabeth Gorsuch on Feb. 24, 1843 and Jane Bell. Jane and Joseph d. of typhoid fever in the fall of 1873. They are buried in Hopewell Church cemetery in York Co., Pennsylvania. Joseph and Jane had the following children: William Nicholas$^{1.1.1.5.8.5.1d}$; John W.$^{1.1.1.5.8.5.2d}$; Lucretia L.$^{1.1.1.5.8.5.3d}$, b. July 3, 1847, and m. B. Franklin Hershner; Hannah A.$^{1.1.1.5.8.5.4d}$, b. July 17, 1848, m. Arthur S. Carmen, d. of typhoid fever in the fall of 1873; Joseph O.$^{1.1.1.5.8.5.5d}$, b. Aug. 20, 1849, and m. Rachel Emma, dau. of Isaac and Jemima (Curtis) King, on Jan. 20, 1878 (she was b. Dec. 8, 1855, d. in York Co., Hopewell Twp., Pennsylvania Sept. 25, 1916; Beulah Ella$^{1.1.1.5.8.5.6d}$, b. May 22, 1851, d. of typhoid fever in the fall of 1873; Pleasant$^{1.1.1.5.8.5.7d}$, b. Nov. 18, 1853, m. Kate A. Evans; Charles William$^{1.1.1.5.8.5.8d}$, b. July 18, 1854, m. Lucinda Eaton and Anna Sophia Orwig; Perry$^{1.1.1.5.8.5.9d}$, b. July 8, 1855; Jane$^{1.1.1.5.8.5.10d}$, b. Feb. 4, 1856, m. Benjamin F. Krout; Rachel Alice$^{1.1.1.5.8.5.11d}$, b. July 24, 1858, and m. Emanuel Hendrix.

****

Joseph Seitz

Joseph$^{1d(b)}$ has no known relationship to the previous Seitz Line, but is placed here for clarity. Joseph m. Elisabeth. They were sponsors at the baptism of Elisabeth, dau. of Adam and Elisabeth Streher, at Friedensaal on Sept. 11, 1773. Joseph and Elizabeth had the following children: Johannes$^{1.1d(b)}$, b. c.1765; Adam$^{1.2d(b)}$, b. c.1767.

Johannes Seitz

Johannes$^{1.1d(b)}$ m. Eva Elisabetha, dau. of Johannes Michael and Appolonia Kleinfelter, c.1786. She was bapt. at St. Jacob's on Dec. 13, 1766, sponsored by her uncle and aunt, Jacob and Eva Elisabetha Baehli. She d. in Indiana Co., Pennsylvania Nov. 1832. Johannes and Eva Elisabetha had the following children in Shrewsbury Twp.:

Adam$^{1.1.1d(b)}$, b. March 26, 1787, bapt. at Friedensaal on April 29, 1787, sponsored by his uncle and aunt, Adam Seitz and wife.

Christina$^{1.1.2d(b)}$, b. March 26, 1787, bapt. at Friedensaal on April

29, 1787, sponsored by Adam and Christina Stabler.

Henry[1.1.3d(b)], b. July 12, 1793, bapt. at Friedensaal, sponsored by Johannes Kleinfelter and wife.

Joseph[1.1.4d(b)], b. Nov. 17, 1795, bapt. at Friedensaal on Dec. 6, 1795, sponsored by his grandparents, Joseph and Elisabeth Seitz.

Michael[1.1.5d(b)], b. April 25, 1799, bapt. at Friedensaal on June 2, 1799, sponsored by Peter and Barbara Gudling.

Adam Seitz

Adam[1.1.1d(b)] m. Christina, dau. of Carl and Christina (Stabler) Diehl. She was b. Feb. 26, 1789. Adam d. in Springfield Twp., York Co. in Nov., 1870. They had the following children:
Charles[1.1.1.1d(b)], d. before 1867, m. Lydia; Levi[1.1.1.2d(b)], b. Dec. 22, 1811, d. Jan. 21, 1850, m. Magdalena Dice; John[1.1.1.3d(b)], b. Sept. 21, 1814, d. Aug. 25, 1866, m. Sarah Schnell; Lydia[1.1.1.4d(b)], m. Nathaniel Gilespie May 15, 1851; Elizabeth[1.1.1.5d(b)];
Catherine[1.1.1.6d(b)], b. 1820, d. before 1867; Adam[1.1.1.7d(b)], b. in 1826, d. in Kansas on Dec. 28, 1896, m. Carolina, dau. of Peter and Rosina (Ruhl) Kleinfelter; Magdalena[1.1.1.8d(b)],

Adam Seitz

Adam[1.2d(b)] m. Anna Elisabeth, dau. of Casper Hildebrand, and had the following children in Shrewsbury Twp.: Josephus[1.2.1d(b)], b. June 22, 1786, bapt. at Friedensaal on July 23, 1786, sponsored by his grandparents, Joseph and Elisabeth Seitz; Johannes[1.2.2d(b)], b. July 13, 1793, bapt. at Saddler's on Aug. 4, 1793, sponsored by Andrew Miller and wife.

****

Johan Welk

Johan[1e] was a dairy farmer/dairymaster at Dammhof, Bavaria. He m. Anna Dorothea, and had the following children: Anna Dorothea[1.1e], b. in 1710, and m. Johan Andreas Seitz[1.1.1d]; Johan Michael[1.2e].

Johan Michael Welk

Johan Michael[1.2e] was a tailor at Adelshofen, and had a dau. Dorothea[1.2.1e], b. c.1742.

Dorothea Welk

Dorothea[1.2.1e] had a child out of wedlock with Johann Philipp, son of Freidrich Von Gemmingen. Freidrich Von Gemmingen was b. at Neckarzimmerin, Baden, Germany on June 6, 1691, d. Nov. 2, 1738 at Hornburg of consumption. Friedrich m. Maria Flandrina Thumb of Neuburg in 1718 (they had a son, Wilhelm Ludwig, on May 27, 1727).

She d. in 1727, and Friedrich m. Wilhelmine Leopoldine Ruedt of
Collenberg on Dec. 6, 1727. She d. at Boedigheim in 1763. Philipp was
b. Dec. 5, 1729, d. Feb. 2, 1766. He m. Regina Eleanora Von Stein
zum Rechtenstein on Nov. 8, 1764. She was b. 1744, d. 1799. Philipp
and Regina had a son, Ludwig Friedrich, at Wimpfen Dec. 3, 1765.
Ludwig Friedrich d. Feb. 14, 1816. Philipp and Dorothea had a son at
Dammhof named Ludwig[1.2.1.1e], b. Jan. 5, 1763.

Ludwig Von Gemmingen aka Seitz

Ludwig[1.2.1.1e] was presumed to have been adopted by his first cousin
once removed, Johannes Seitz, and his wife Anna Catharina, and
assumed the name Ludwig Seitz (it has not been confirmed that
Ludwig Seitz and Ludwig Von Gemmingen are the same person). If
they are the same person, the adoption may have been done to insure
he had the chance to grow up without the stigma surrounding his
birth. The family immigrated to Pennsylvania when Ludwig was about
two years old on Oct. 20, 1764, in the ship *Richmond*. Ludwig m.
Anna, dau. of John and Catharina (Hunsaker) Beery, in York Co.,
Pennsylvania in 1789. She was b. in York Co., Pennsylvania on Jan.
30, 1768, d. in Fairfield Co., Rush Creek Twp., Ohio on Sept. 30, 1831.
Ludwig was a farmer and a predestinarian minister in the Baptist
church. After their marriage, they moved to Rockingham Co., Linnville
District, Virginia c.1789/90. In 1801, Ludwig moved to Fairfield Co.,
Ohio, and purchased land from the government. In 1802, he returned
to Virginia, sold some of his household effects, placed the rest in
wagons, and moved his family to Ohio. He received land from the
government, located on the east side of the present location of Mt.
Tabor Evangelical Lutheran Church. While in Virginia, Ludwig was an
elder in the Whitehouse congregation, and in 1806, helped establish
Pleasant Run Church, near Lancaster, Ohio. He was an ordained
Baptist minister, and the first minister of Pleasant Run. In 1804, he
was a Judge in Rush Creek Twp. He died while on a trip in
Washington Co. Pennsylvania in 1824. Ludwig and Anna had the
following children (surname Seitz):
> John[1.2.1.1.1e], b. Oct. 28, 1790, d. in 1874. He m. Magdalen Spitler
> in Fairfield Co. on June 11, 1811.
> Daniel[1.2.1.1.2e], b. Dec. 17, 1791, d. in Fairfield Co. in 1864. He m.
> Elizabeth Hite in Fairfield Co. on June 13, 1813, and Catharine
> Beery in Fairfield Co. on April 15, 1832.
> Catherine[1.2.1.1.3e], b. Feb. 3, 1792, d. in Seneca Co., Ohio on Jan.
> 21, 1863. She m. Jacob, son of Jacob and Nancy (Henry)
> Spitler, in Fairfield Co. on Aug. 22, 1809. He was b. in
> Shenandoah Co., Virginia on Aug. 6, 1784, d. in Seneca Co.,
> Ohio on July 7, 1865. They are buried in the Honey Creek
> Baptist cemetery.

38

Elizabeth[1.2.1.1.4e], b. March 20, 1794, d. sometime after 1843. She
m. John Hite in Fairfield Co. on Nov. 26, 1811.

Mary[1.2.1.1.5e], b. May 3, 1795, and m. Niclas Beery in Fairfield Co.
on April 4, 1811, and Henry, son of Jacob and Nancy (Henry)
Spitler.

Abraham[1.2.1.1.6e], b. June 25, 1796, d. in 1882. He m. Rebecca
Huddle on Dec. 17, 1817.

Jacob[1.2.1.1.7e], b. Sept. 6, 1797.

Noah[1.2.1.1.8e], b. Dec. 29, 1798, d. in 1867. He m. Polly
Stoneburner on Aug. 15, 1819.

Lydia[1.2.1.1.9e], b. March 20, 1800, d. in 1866. She m. John Bretz.

Susanna[1.2.1.1.10e], b. July 21, 1801, d. 1875, m. John Staly Oct. 26,
1817.

Lewis[1.2.1.1.11e], b. Oct. 21, 1802, d. 1890, m. Barbara Kagy and
Martha Hershberger.

Anna[1.2.1.1.12e], b. July 21, 1805, d. 1863, m. Benjamin Huddle
(1803-60) in Fairfield Co. Aug. 17, 1823.

Rebecca[1.2.1.1.13e], b. April 18, 1807, m. Henry Friesner.

Peter[1.2.1.1.14e], b. 1810, m. Rebecca Spitler in Fairfield Co. June
17, 1832.

Jacob Seitz

Jacob[1.2.1.1.7e] m. Catherine Meyer (b. in Pennsylvania in 1800), and
had the following children in Berne Twp.: John A.[1.2.1.1.7.1e], b. in
1827, m. Elizabeth (b. 1832 in Ohio), and had a child, Lafayette in
1849; Absalom[1.2.1.1.7.2e], b. in 1830; Emanuel[1.2.1.1.7.3e], b. in 1834.

****

Johannes Friesner

Johannes[1f] m. Susanna Margaret, dau. of Peter Grimm, at Lancaster
Co., Lancaster, First Reformed Church, Pennsylvania on April 13, 1773.
Johannes may have been the Johannes that arrived at Philadelphia on
the ship *Brothers* on Aug. 24, 1750, or it may have been his father.
Johannes was a freeman in Lancaster Co., Earl Twp., Pennsylvania in
1770, and a tailor in 1772. In 1782, he resided in Lancaster Co.,
Warwick Twp. In 1783, he was residing in York, Pennsylvania, as a
tailor, and in 1790 he was residing in Rockingham Co., Linneville
District, Virginia. In 1792, he was taxed at Linneville Creek, the west
portion of Linneville District (Captain Jacob Lincoln's Company). He d.
in July, 1801, and his wife d. sometime before that date. Johannes
son, Johan, chose Peter Kring (Krim) as his guardian. Johannes and
Susanna were the parents of the following children: Johan Henrich[1.1f],
b. March 12, 1774; Johan Frederick[1.2f], b. Dec. 1, 1775; Marie[1.3f], b.
in 1780, m. James Cahon in Rockingham Co., Virginia on Aug. 18,
1807; Jacob[1.4f], b. c.1782; Johan Michael[1.5f], b. Sept. 29, 1785.

Johan Henrich Friesner

Johan Henrich[1.1f] was bapt. at Seltenreich Reformed Lutheran
Church Dec. 18, 1774, sponsored by his uncle and aunt, Johan Henrich
and Christina Grimm. He was confirmed at Rader's Lutheran Church
on Oct. 23, 1801. He m. Barbara, dau. of Jacob Cook/Koch in
Rockingham Co. March 20, 1803. Henrich moved to Fairfield Co., Ohio
c.1806, d. 1847. They are buried in Colfax cemetery. Henrich and
Barbara had the following children: Andrew[1.1.1f], b. 1804; John[1.1.2f],
b. Oct. 8, 1805; Jacob[1.1.3f], b. c.1808; Susanna[1.1.4f], b. c.1811, d. in
Hancock Co., Illinois, m. Isaac Swigert; Samuel[1.1.5f], b. May 4, 1812;
Elizabeth[1.1.6f], b. in 1813, m. Samuel Barr in Fairfield Co. March 8,
1835; Henry[1.1.7f], b. in 1818; Lewis[1.1.8f], b. 1819; Anna
Elizabeth[1.1.9f], b. 1822, m. George W. Warner in Fairfield Co. in 1843;
Levi[1.1.10f], b. 1824, m. Catherine Friesner[1.5.7f] in Fairfield Co. May
17, 1846, and Lucy Ann Macklin in Fairfield Co. Aug. 17, 1856 (b. in
Ohio in 1836), resided in Pleasant Twp. in 1850.

Andrew Friesner

Andrew[1.1.1f] d. in Fairfield Co. 1895. He m. an unknown woman
c.1826, Elizabeth Mufser in Fairfield Co. on Oct. 31, 1834, and Sarah
Rugh in Fairfield Co. Jan. 25, 1849. Elizabeth d. sometime before
1849. Sarah was b. in Ohio in 1824. Andrew had the following
children in Berne Twp.: Sarah[1.1.1.1f] (not confirmed as a dau. of
Andrew), b. c.1826, m. Joseph Hish in Fairfield Co., Lancaster Aug. 3,
1848; Mary[1.1.1.2f], b. in 1828, may have m. David Engle in Fairfield
Co. Sept. 12, 1850; Isabell[1.1.1.3f], b. in 1832, m. Peter Harmon in
Fairfield Co. on Aug. 7, 1855; Martha M.[1.1.1.4f], b. in 1834, m. Lewis
Friesner[1.2.4.4.f]; Andrew Jackson[1.1.1.5f], b. in 1837, m. Sarah
Elizabeth Bowman in Perry Co., Ohio March 6, 1856 (in 1868, they
resided in Coffey Co., Leroy, Kansas).

John Friesner

John[1.1.2f] d. in Fairfield Co. Jan. 12, 1876. He m. Emily Dean in
Fairfield Co. March 4, 1829. She was b. Nov. 3, 1807, d. Feb. 10, 1895.
They had the following children in Pleasant Twp.:
Samuel Edward[1.1.2.1f], b. March 13, 1831, m. Hannah Hamilton in
Fairfield Co. Feb. 27, 1853; Barbara Jane[1.1.2.2f], b. Feb. 7, 1834, m.
Elias H. Cupp in Fairfield Co. May 13, 1855; John D.[1.1.2.3f], b. Dec.
27, 1836, m. Mary Arnold in Fairfield Co., Lancaster Feb. 14 (11?),
1861; Allen D.[1.1.2.4f], b. Dec. 6(8?), 1838, m. Mary Ann Weaver in
Fairfield Co. June 5, 1864; Emily[1.1.2.5f], b. Feb. 9, 1841, m. Isaac W.
Keller in Fairfield Co. March 19, 1861; Richard Henry[1.1.2.6f], b. Feb.
8, 1844, m. Nancy N. Kiger in Fairfield Co. Jan. 19, 1871; Emanuel
D.[1.1.2.7f], b. Feb. 17, 1847, m. Elizabeth Brown July 14, 1859 and

Sadie J. Miller in Fairfield Co. March 19, 1876; Benavel D.$^{1.1.2.8f}$, b. July 20, 1849, m. Sarah Meipe in Fairfield Co. on Jan. 1, 1874.

Jacob Friesner

Jacob$^{1.1.3f}$ d. in Coles Co., Charleston, Illinois sometime before 1878, m. Mary Wheel. She was b. May 14, 1806, d. in Effingham Co., Mocassin Creek Twp., Illinois on Nov. 5, 1878. They had the following children: Leah Grace$^{1.1.3.1f}$, b. 1843 at Coles Co., Illinois, m. William Ezekiel Ensign Nov. 25, 1861; Elizabeth$^{1.1.3.2f}$, m. _____ Bader; Herman$^{1.1.3.3f}$; Levi$^{1.1.3.4f}$; Noah$^{1.1.3.5f}$; Barbara$^{1.1.3.6f}$, m. _____ Letner; Nancy$^{1.1.3.7f}$, m. _____ Moore, d. before 1878.

Samuel Friesner

Samuel$^{1.1.5f}$ d. in Champaign Co., Thomasboro, Illinois on Oct. 24, 1891. He m. Mary, dau. of David and Catherine (Spitler) Kauffman, in Fairfield Co. on Jan. 28, 1836. She was b. in Fairfield Co., Ohio May 3, 1818, d. in Story Co., Nevada, Iowa Sept. 24, 1900. Samuel moved to Pratt Co., Illinois in 1852. They had the following children: David K.$^{1.1.5.1f}$, m. Elsie Ann Burriff in Fairfield Co. Dec. 23, 1858, and Cal Wilson; Henry C.$^{1.1.5.2f}$, m. Sarah C. Morain; Anna Elizabeth$^{1.1.5.3f}$; Susan Catherine$^{1.1.5.4f}$; Mary Jane$^{1.1.5.5f}$.

Henry Friesner

Henry$^{1.1.7f}$ probably m. Lavina Kemper in Fairfield Co. March 9, 1846. He was unmarried and residing with his brother, Andrew, in 1850. He m. Jane Farier (b. in Pennsylvania in 1840) in Fairfield Co. Aug. 28, 1859, and had a dau. Sarah E.$^{1.1.7.1f}$, b. in 1860.

Lewis Friesner

Lewis$^{1.1.8f}$ m. Martha Ann Warner in Fairfield Co. on April 1, 1847. She was b. in Ohio in 1829. They had a son Thomas J.$^{1.1.8.1f}$, b. 1852.

Johan Frederick Friesner

Johan Frederick$^{1.2f}$ was bapt. at Seltenreich Reformed Lutheran Church March 10, 1776, sponsored by his uncle and aunt, Johan Frederick and Eva Schuetz. He was confirmed at Rader's Lutheran Church Oct. 23, 1801. He m. Magdalena, dau. of Georg and Elisabetha Ehrhardt, in Rockingham Co., Rader's Lutheran Church, Virginia June 21, 1796. She was b. in Frederick Co., Woodsboro, Maryland March 1, 1776, d. in Fairfield Co., Rush Creek Twp., Ohio Aug. 23, 1843. Frederick purchased land in Rush Creek Twp., Fairfield Co., Ohio on Nov. 6, 1805, and in 1827, he had 91 acres in section 29 of Rush Creek Twp. Frederick resided with his son, Noah, in Auburn Twp. in 1850, d. Dec. 28, 1857. Frederick and Magdalena are buried in Friesner cemetery. They had the following children: Elizabeth[1.2.1f], b. June 22, 1797, bapt. at Rader's Lutheran Church Aug. 26, 1798, sponsored by her grandparents, Georg and Elisabetha Ehrhardt, m. James McFradtion in Fairfield Co. April 27, 1817; John[1.2.2f], b. April 5, 1799, bapt. at Rader's Lutheran Church June 9, 1799, sponsored by Jacob and Dorothea Stautenmayer; Frederick[1.2.3f], b. 1801; Henry[1.2.4f], b. Feb. 22, 1803; David [1.2.5f], b. Oct. 26, 1805; Susanna[1.2.6f], b. Oct. 10, 1808, m. Daniel Swartz[1.6.4.5a]; Lydia[1.2.7f], b. c.1812, m. Isaac Bloper/Blokes in Fairfield Co. Jan. 28, 1836; Noah[1.2.8f], b. Oct. 10, 1813; Rebecca[1.2.9f], b. c.1815, m. George Lutz in Fairfield Co. Jan. 26(28), 1836; Polly[1.2.10f], b. c.1817, m. John Shoemaker in Fairfield Co. Feb. 23, 1839.

John Friesner

John[1.2.2f] may have m. Anna M., d. in Hocking Co., Marion Twp. before 1850. Anna M. was b. in Pennsylvania 1806, resided in Marion Twp. in 1850.

Henry Friesner

Henry[1.2.4f] m. Rebecca, dau. of Ludwig and Anna (Beery) Seitz, in Fairfield Co., Ohio March 6, 1825. She d. in Shelby Co., Illinois on Sept. 28, 1887. Henry d. in Fairfield Co., Rush Creek Twp., Ohio Sept. 26, 1855. He is buried in Beery-Miller cemetery. They had the following children in Rush Creek Twp.:

Abraham Seitz[1.2.4.1f], b. Jan. 9, 1826, and m. Eliza Jane Miller (b. in 1829) in Fairfield Co., Lancaster March 9, 1848.

Elizabeth[1.2.4.2f], b. July 1, 1827.

Frederick[1.2.4.3f], b. Oct. 4 (July 28), 1828, m. Elizabeth Geil in Fairfield Co. Aug. 1, 1850, d. Feb. 16, 1862. He is buried in Beery-Miller cemetery.

Lewis[1.2.4.4f], b. Nov. 4, 1829, m. Martha M. Friesner[1.1.1.4f] in Fairfield Co. Sept. 4, 1851, d. Oct. 1, 1855. He is buried in Beery-Miller cemetery.

Catherine[1.2.4.5f], b. Dec. 12, 1831, m. Noah Syphert in Fairfield Co. Aug. 4, 1849. They resided in Allen Co., Lima, Ohio in 1852, and Shelby Co., Shelbyville, Illinois in 1867.

Noah[1.2.4.6f], b. Aug. 18, 1833, d. April 5, 1859. He is buried in Beery Miller cemetery.

Anna[1.2.4.7f], b. Dec. 31, 1834, d. before 1850.

Leah[1.2.4.8f], b. 1837.

Rachel[1.2.4.9f], b. Feb. 20, 1838, m. John Swartz in Fairfield Co. on Feb. 16, 1858.

Daniel[1.2.4.10f], b. in 1839.

Henry[1.2.4.11f], b. 1841, and m. Maria Stuckey in Fairfield Co. on Aug. 25, 1860.

Jacob$^{1.2.4.12f}$, b. 1843.

Rebecca$^{1.2.4.13f}$, b. Feb. 10, 1846, d. Sept. 21, 1855. She is buried in Beery-Miller cemetery.

John$^{1.2.4.14f}$, b. 1847. He may be the John that m. Harriet C. Gallagher in Hocking Co. on Sept. 8, 1870.

George W.$^{1.2.4.15f}$, b. Feb. 16, 1849, d. June 19, 1866. He is buried in Beery Miller cemetery.

Anne$^{1.2.4.16f}$, b. in Aug. 1850.

David Friesner

David$^{1.2.5f}$ m. Elizabeth Spear in Fairfield Co. on Dec. 13, 1826, and Rebecca, dau. of Daniel and Elizabeth (Hite) Seitz, in Fairfield Co. on Dec. 22, 1844. Elizabeth was b. Jan. 14, 1800, d. July 14, 1844. David d. in Fairfield Co., Rush Creek/Auburn Twp. on July 31, 1889. They are buried in Friesner cemetery. In 1850, David resided in Auburn Twp., and in 1860, he resided in Rush Creek Twp. He had the following children: Eli$^{1.2.5.1f}$, b. Aug. 22, 1827, m. Christina Hoffert in Fairfield Co. Dec. 11, 1851; Ephraim$^{1.2.5.2f}$, b. 1828; Catherine$^{1.2.5.3f}$, b. 1831, m. John Geckler in Fairfield Co. Aug. 7, 1851; David J.$^{1.2.5.4f}$, b. 1833, m. Rebecca Hoffert in Fairfield Co. Oct. 27, 1859; Samuel$^{1.2.5.5f}$, b. 1835, m. Catherine Rhinehart (1836-1874) in Fairfield Co. March 23, 1856;; Lydia$^{1.2.5.6f}$, b. 1837; Isaac$^{1.2.5.7f}$, b. 1839, m. Mary Stoneburner in Hocking Co. on Sept. 22, 1861; Joseph$^{1.2.5.8f}$, b. 1843, m. Emma/Emily Barnes in Hocking Co., Ohio Nov. 1, 1860; Eliza$^{1.2.5.9f}$, b. 1846; Lewis$^{1.2.5.10f}$, b. Nov. 8, 1847, d. March 14, 1849, buried in Friesner cemetery; Absalom$^{1.2.5.11f}$, b. in 1849, m. Mahala Beery in Hocking Co. Sept. 27, 1870; Daniel$^{1.2.5.12f}$, b. Aug. 1, 1852, d. Sept. 8, 1870, buried in Friesner cemetery; Bartlett$^{1.2.5.13f}$, b. Dec. 27, 1853 in Auburn Twp., m. Mary Hoffert in Fairfield Co. on April 14, 1877; Mary A.$^{1.2.5.14f}$, b. 1856 in Auburn Twp.

Ephraim Friesner

Ephraim$^{1.2.5.2f}$ m. Diana (b. in Ohio in 1826) Sept. 20, 1849, and had a son, Simeon$^{1.2.5.2.1f}$, b. in 1850.

Noah Friesner

Noah$^{1.2.8f}$ m. Lydia Meucle in Fairfield Co. April 10, 1834. She was b. in Ohio on Jan. 1, 1816, d. Nov. 7, 1862. In 1850 he resided in Auburn Twp., and in 1860, he resided in Rush Creek Twp. Noah d. April 17, 1869. They are buried in Friesner cemetery. They had the following children in Auburn Twp.:

Melinda$^{1.2.8.1f}$, b. in 1835, m. Thomas J. Derr in Fairfield Co. on Aug. 25, 1853; John$^{1.2.8.2f}$, b. Sept. 30, 1838, d. Oct. 24, 1873, buried in Friesner cemetery; Diana$^{1.2.8.3f}$, b. 1847; William A.$^{1.2.8.4f}$, b. Aug.

16, 1849, d. Sept. 22, 1854, buried in Friesner cemetery; Sarah Salome[1.2.8.5f], b. 1858.

Jacob Friesner

Jacob[1.4f], m. Catherine, dau. of Martin Snider, in Rockingham Co., Virginia in 1802. They had a son in Rockingham Co., McGaheysville, Virginia, Joseph[1.4.1f], b. Dec. 23, 1803.

Johan Michael Friesner

Johan[1.5f] was bapt. at the First Reformed Church of York on Jan. 23, 1786. He m. Catherine, dau. of Casper and Catherine (Stihli) Hufford, in Fairfield Co., Ohio Feb. 11, 1812. She was b. in Frederick Co., Woodsboro, Maryland Oct. 7, 1792, d. in Fairfield Co., Pleasant Twp. Jan. 4, 1853. Johan d. in Fairfield Co. sometime after 1850. They had the following children: Barbara[1.5.1f], b. c.1813, m. Joseph Simpson in Fairfield Co. Dec. 7, 1834, resided in Fairfield Co., Bremen, Ohio; Daniel[1.5.2f], b. 1815; Benjamin[1.5.3f], b. 1818; Sarah/Sally[1.5.4f], b. c.1820, and m. Isaac Hunsaker in Fairfield Co., Lancaster Oct. 1835; Casper[1.5.5f], b. 1823, m. Sarah Graves in Fairfield Co., Lancaster March 29, 1846; Michael[1.5.6f], b. Oct. 6, 1824, d. in Fairfield Co. Feb. 14, 1850; Catherine[1.5.7f], b. in 1828, m. Levi Friesner[1.1.10f], residing in Pleasant Twp. in 1850.

Daniel Friesner

Daniel[1.5.2f] d. in Fairfield Co. on Nov. 24, 1859. He m. Elizabeth Shields (b. in Maryland in 1815) in Fairfield Co. Sept. 7, 1837, and had the following children in Hocking Co., Logan Twp., Ohio: William[1.5.2.1f], b. 1838; Catherine[1.5.2.2f], b. 1840. She may be the Kitty A., that m. Charles A. Barker in Hocking Co., Logan Twp. on Oct. 27, 1859; Joseph[1.5.2.3f], b. 1842; Sarah[1.5.2.4f], b. 1845; John[1.5.2.5f], b. 1848.

Benjamin Friesner

Benjamin[1.5.3f] m. Lydia Stemen (b. in Ohio in 1822) in Fairfield Co. on Aug. 29, 1844, and had the following children in Pleasant Twp.: Benton[1.5.3.1f], b. 1846; Ellen[1.5.3.2f], b. 1848; Allen[1.5.3.3f], b. 1850; Franklin[1.5.3.4f], b. 1851; Mary[1.5.3.5f], b. 1853; Amy[1.5.3.6f], b. 1855; Sarah[1.5.3.7f], b. 1857.

****

Christian Ehrhardt

Christian[1g] was the son of Daniel Ehrhardt, and confirmed at Hunspach, Northern Alsace, France in 1730. Daniel d. sometime after 1730 in Retschwiller, Soultz-Sous-Forets, France. Christian m. Anna Barbara, dau. of Jacob Clor, at Hunspach on Oct. 1, 1734, and

Susanna, dau. of Jacob and Susanna Muller of Oberkutzenhausen, at Rittershoffen on May 5, 1738. Anna Barbara was b. at Hunspach, d. at Rittershofen in 1738. Christian arrived at Philadelphia on the ship *Robert and Alice* in 1739, and settled in Lancaster Co., Rapho Twp., Pennsylvania. He was taxed in Rapho Twp. in 1757. He had 100 acres in 1758/59, and 150 acres in 1771. He d. c.1783, and Susanna d. sometime after 1750. They had the following children:

Daniel[1.1g], b. c.1735.

Georg[1.2g], b. c.1736.

Nicholas[1.3g], b. c.1737, d. in Lancaster Co., Hanover Twp. in 1776(?). He took the Oath of Allegiance at Hanover on July 12, 1777. He was taxed in Rapho Twp. in 1758 and 1759, and he was taxed in East Hanover Twp. in 1769 and 1771.

Martin[1.4g], b. c.1738.

Susanna[1.5g], b. May 17, 1741.

Anna Eva[1.6g], b. Dec. 25, 1744.

Jacob[1.7g], b. c.1746. He was taxed as a freeman in Rapho Twp. in 1769. He m. Susanna. Jacob d. Rapho Twp. in July, 1804.

Christian[1.7g], b. May 18, 1748, d. in Lancaster Co., Rapho Twp. Nov. 1793.

Anna Catharina[1.8g], b. April 17, 1750.

Daniel Ehrhardt

Daniel[1.1g] m. Margaret Grau in Lancaster Co. on Sept. 30, 1757. He was taxed in Rapho Twp. in 1777-1783. He was a laborer paying rent to John Miller in Manor Twp., Millerstown, in 1770 and 1771. He took the Oath of Allegiance at Donegal on Nov. 22, 1777. He d. in Lancaster Co., Rapho Twp. in Nov., 1810. Daniel had the following children: Jacob[1.1.1g], b. c.1760; Elizabeth[1.1.2g], b. April 5, 1767, m. Abraham Gerber.

Georg Ehrhardt

Georg[1.2g] was taxed in Lancaster Co., Rapho Twp., Pennsylvania in 1756-59 (in 1759, he had 50 acres). He m. Elisabetha c.1762, and Molly, dau. of David Smith, in Rockingham Co., Virginia in 1798. Georg moved to Frederick Co., Woodsboro, Maryland, c.1766, and Rockingham Co., Timberville, Virginia in 1782. George sold his 200 acres in Woodsboro to George Murdoch for 2,050 pounds in 1781. He had one dwelling and two other buildings in 1784. He was taxed for six horses, and paid taxes for his son John in 1788 (Captain Trumboe's Company number 10). In 1792, he and his sons, Jacob and John were taxed (George with seven people) in Captain Ezekiel Harrison's Company, East Plains District/West Portion of Plains District that included the area of Timberville (aka Rader's Church, The Plains, The Forest). Georg d. in Feb., 1801. Georg's son, Philip, chose Mathias Mil

Georg and Elisabetha gave consent for their dau., Magdalena's, marriage in June, 1796, sponsored her dau.'s baptism in August, 1798. Elisabetha probably d. soon after this because a Georg Ehrhardt m. Molly Smith in Rockingham Co. in 1798. This is presumed to be the elder Georg Ehrhardt, because no other records have indicated that he had a son, Georg Jr. If Georg did remarry, the widow predeceased him. Georg and Elisabetha had the following children:

Andrew[1.2.1g], b. c.1763, and taxed in Rockingham Co., Virginia in 1787 and for one horse in 1788 (Captain George Chrisman's Company number 12).

Catherine[1.2.2g], b. c.1765, d. in Fairfield Co., Lancaster, Ohio. She m. George, son of George Springer, in Rockingham Co. Nov. 11, 1786.

Christian[1.2.3g], b. c.1767.

Johan[1.2.4g], bapt. at Rocky Hill (Grace) Lutheran Church on June 4, 1769.

Anna Elisabetha[1.2.5g], bapt. at Rocky Hill (Grace) Lutheran Church Jan. 25, 1772.

Georg Jacob[1.2.6g], bapt. at Rocky Hill (Grace) Lutheran Church April 30, 1775.

Magdalena[1.2.7g], bapt. at Rocky Hill (Grace) Lutheran Church May 26, 1776, confirmed in Rader's Lutheran Church Oct. 23, 1801, m. Johan Frederick Friesner[1.2f].

Henrich[1.2.8g], bapt. at Rocky Hill (Grace) Lutheran Church Sept. 13, 1778, d. in Rockingham Co., Virginia May 6, 1851, m. Elisabeth, dau. of Jacob Stoutmire, in Rockingham Co. June 9, 1801. They had a son, John, who was b. March 9, 1802, m. - Mary Branner, d. Dec. 13, 1873.

Mary[1.2.9g], b. c.1780, m. Barrett Stoutmire in Rockingham Co. in 1798.

Philip[1.2.10g], bapt. at Rader's Lutheran Church Feb. 16, 1788.

Christian Ehrhardt

Christian[1.2.3g] had his taxes paid for by his father in Rockingham Co. in 1787. He m. Elizabeth, and had a dau. in Shenandoah Co., Virginia; she was Eva[1.2.3.1g], b. April 7, 1793, sponsored by her grandmother, Elisabeth Ehrhardt, at her baptism.

Johann Ehrhardt

Johann[1.2.4g] m. Margaret, dau. of Adam Painter, in Rockingham Co., Virginia in 1790. He moved to Montgomery Co., Christianburg, Virginia between 1792 and 1797. They had the following children: John[1.2.4.1g], b. Sept. 24, 1791; George[1.2.4.2g], b. April 5, 1792; Henry[1.2.4.3g], b. May 13, 1797; Adam[1.2.4.4g], b. Sept. 30, 1801; Margaret[1.2.4.5g], b. April 12, 1806, m. Eli Davis in Montgomery Co.

Jan. 2, 1833; Mary[1.2.4.6g], b. July 17, 1814, m. Andrew Hutsell in Montgomery Co. May 16, 1832.

George Ehrhardt

George[1.2.4.2g] m. Nancy Taylor in Montgomery Co. March 28, 1825. She was b. in Virginia. They had the following children: John[1.2.4.2.1g], b. 1826; William[1.2.4.2.2g], b. 1828; Joseph[1.2.4.2.3g], b. 1831; David[1.2.4.2.4g], b. 1834; Henry[1.2.4.2.5g], b. 1836; Margaret J.[1.2.4.2.6g], b. 1838; Elizabeth[1.2.4.2.7g], b. 1841.

Henry Ehrhardt

Henry[1.2.4.3g] m. Mary Kerby, and had a child in Montgomery Co., Virginia, Rhoda Emily Frances[1.2.4.3.1g], b. July 8, 1834, m. William Davis in Wythe Co., Virginia Oct. 9, 1852.

Adam Ehrhardt

Adam[1.2.4.4g] m. Sarah Lendum Wright (b. in Ireland in 1808), and had the following children in Montgomery Co., 41st District Virginia: Margaret E.[1.2.4.4.1g], b. 1834; Eliza Anne[1.2.4.4.2g], b. 1836; Mary J.[1.2.4.4.3g], b. 1838; Robert B.[1.2.4.4.4g], b. 1840; Emeline[1.2.4.4.5g], b. 1843; Henry J.[1.2.4.4.6g], b. 1845; John[1.2.4.4.7g], b. 1846, d. before 1850.

Anna Elisabetha Ehrhardt

Anna Elisabetha[1.2.5g] m. Philip, son of John and Catharina (Herbine) Brenner, in Shenandoah Co., Virginia Oct. 22, 1794. He was b. in Rockingham Co., Virginia in 1775. They had the following children in Rockingham Co., Virginia: Catharina[1.2.5.1g], b. Jan. 15, 1794; Sarah[1.2.5.2g], b. Dec. 21, 1795; John[1.2.5.3g], b. Aug. 4, 1799; Magdalene[1.2.5.4g], b. 1801; Elizabeth[1.2.5.5g], b. Feb. 2, 1803; Mary[1.2.5.6g], b. Oct. 2, 1804; Jonathan[1.2.5.7g], b. Feb. 2, 1806, m. Margaret Showalter in Rockingham Co. April 5, 1830; Michael[1.2.5.8g], b. Sept. 8, 1807.

Georg Jacob Ehrhardt

Georg Jacob[1.2.6g] m. Catherine, dau. of John Coole, in Rockingham Co., Virginia Feb. 16, 1802. They had the following children in Rockingham Co.: Maria[1.2.6.1g], b. c.1803; John[1.2.6.2g], b. April 5, 1805, m. Mary Ridenouer in Rockingham Co. Jan. 26, 1826; Margaretha[1.2.6.3g], b. Aug. 5, 1805; Solomon[1.2.6.4g], b. Nov. 1, 1811; Jacob[1.2.6.5g], b. Jan. 9, 1813.

Philip Ehrhardt

Philip[1.2.10g] m. Rebecca, dau. of Jacob Mueller, in Rockingham Co., Virginia April 10, 1810. They had the following children in Rockingham

Co., Virginia: Lidia$^{1\cdot2\cdot10\cdot1g}$, b. March 7, 1811; Sarah$^{1\cdot2\cdot10\cdot2g}$, b. June 15, 1812; Michael$^{1\cdot2\cdot10\cdot3g}$, b. Feb. 20, 1814; John$^{1\cdot2\cdot10\cdot4g}$, b. Nov. 2, 1816; Polly$^{1\cdot2\cdot10\cdot5g}$, b. 1818; Katherine$^{1\cdot2\cdot10\cdot6g}$, b. 1820; Philip$^{1\cdot2\cdot10\cdot7g}$, b. Dec., 1821; Rebecca$^{1\cdot2\cdot10\cdot8g}$, b. 1825; Leah Ann$^{1\cdot2\cdot10\cdot9g}$, b. 1826; Abraham$^{1\cdot2\cdot10\cdot10g}$, b. 1828.

Martin Ehrhardt

Martin$^{1\cdot4g}$ m. Anna Maria Kolb in Lancaster Co., Lancaster, Pennsylvania Dec. 13, 1757. He resided in Rapho Twp. in 1770, and took the Oath of Allegiance in Lancaster Co., Donegal on Nov. 22, 1777. He moved to Frederick Co., Woodsboro Maryland sometime before 1786, and was taxed in Rockingham Co., Virginia in 1787. He was taxed at Keezeltown (Captain Richard Ragan's Company East District, East Portion of Central District and Linville) with his son, Martin in 1792, and he was residing there on Dec. 7, 1791. He moved to Warren Co., Franklin Twp., Ohio sometime between Feb., 1797, and 1800, d. there, intestate, on Feb. 5, 1817 (at age 96 ?b. 1721?). His estate was administered by Nicholas and George Ehrhardt on Nov. 7, 1817. They were the parents of the following children: Martin$^{1\cdot4\cdot1g}$, b. c.1758; Nicholas$^{1\cdot4\cdot2g}$, b. c.1761, taxed in Frederick Co., Virginia in 1787, helped to administer his father's estate in 1817; Elisabeth$^{1\cdot4\cdot3g}$, b. c.1771, m. Alpert Eger in Rockingham Co., Virginia in 1792.

Martin Ehrhardt

Martin$^{1\cdot4\cdot1g}$ m. Eva. He was residing in Warren Co., Turtle Creek Twp. in 1806-19, and Darke Co., Ohio on Feb. 28, 1822. They had the following children: Susanna$^{1\cdot4\cdot1\cdot1g}$, b. c.1780, m. Edward Thompson in Rockingham Co., Virginia Aug. 15, 1801; Johan Jacob$^{1\cdot4\cdot1\cdot2g}$, bapt. at Frederick Co., Woodsboro, Rocky Hill (Grace) Lutheran Church on Aug. 2, 1786; Christina$^{1\cdot4\cdot1\cdot3g}$, b. May 1, 1792, bapt. at Glade Reformed Church at Frederick Co., Maryland/Virginia Aug. 5, 1792, sponsored by Andrew and Christina Hedge.

Christian Ehrhardt

Christian$^{1\cdot7g}$ m. Barbara. He was taxed in Rapho Twp. in 1770, and in Londonderry Twp., as a freeman in 1775. He took the Oath of Allegiance in Lancaster Co. on June 13, 1777. Christian d. in Rapho Twp. in Feb., 1809. They had the following children in Rapho Twp.: Christian$^{1\cdot7\cdot1g}$; Jacob$^{1\cdot7\cdot2g}$; John$^{1\cdot7\cdot3g}$; Mary$^{1\cdot7\cdot4g}$; Ann$^{1\cdot7\cdot5g}$.

****

Wilhelm Ehrhardt

Wilhelm$^{1g(b)}$ m. Anna Catarina Schreiner in Lancaster Co., Warwick Twp., Pennsylvania Dec. 1, 1746. They resided in Shrewsbury Twp. in July, 1766, and had the following children (several baptized at Christ's

Lutheran): Thomas$^{1.1g(b)}$, b. April 24, 1749; Johan Peter$^{1.2g(b)}$, b. May ?, 1751; Eva Elizabeth$^{1.3g(b)}$, b. Aug. 22, 1753; Johannes$^{1.4g(b)}$, b. c.1755.

Thomas Ehrhardt

Thomas$^{1.1g(b)}$ m. Rosina Michael, and had the following children in York Co., Shrewsbury Twp., Pennsylvania: Wilhelm$^{1.1.1g(b)}$, b. c.1768; Jacob$^{1.1.2g(b)}$, b. c.1770; Johannes$^{1.1.3g(b)}$, b. June 10, 1779, bapt. at Friedensaal on July 4, 1779, sponsored by Philip and Anna Barbara Shaffer; Rosina$^{1.1.4g(b)}$, b. in Shrewsbury Twp. on March 19, 1781, m. Daniel Diehl$^{1.1.1.4.11}$; Thomas$^{1.1.5g(b)}$, b. Feb. 13, 1787, bapt. at Friedensaal Feb. 18, 1787, sponsored by Jacob and Catharine Ulp; Eva$^{1.1.6g(b)}$, b. Aug. 13, 1788, bapt. at Friedensaal Oct. 11, 1788, sponsored by Wilhelm Ehrhard and wife.

Wilhelm Ehrhardt

Wilhelm$^{1.1.1g(b)}$ m. Susanna, and had the following children in Shrewsbury Twp.: Peter$^{1.1.1.1g(b)}$, b. Sept. 7, 1788, bapt. at Friedensaal on Oct. 11, 1788, sponsored by Peter Kleinfelter and wife; Jacob$^{1.1.1.2g(b)}$, b. May 6, 1794, bapt. at Friedensaal on May 29, 1794, sponsored by Jacob and Catherine Ehrhard.

Jacob Ehrhardt

Jacob$^{1.1.2g(b)}$ m. Catherine, and had a son in Shrewsbury Twp.: Jacob$^{1.1.2.1g(b)}$, b. 1792, bapt. at Friedensaal, sponsored by Michael and Susanna Spessert.

Johannes Ehrhardt

Johannes$^{1.1.3g(b)}$, m. Esther$^{1.1.1.1.4.51}$, dau. of Georg and Anna Maria (Liebenstein) Diehl. She was b. Aug. 23, 1781, bapt. at St. Paul's Nov. 8, 1781, sponsored by her uncle and aunt, Carl and Christina Diehl. She d. sometime after Nov. 24, 1826. John d. Sept. 20, 1825. They had a dau.: Maria$^{1.1.3.1g(b)}$, b. May 26, 1824.

Johannes Ehrhardt

Johannes$^{1.4g(b)}$ m. Margaretha$^{1.4.8b}$, dau. of Johan David$^{1.4b}$ and Anna Catharina (Simon) Schaffer, and had the following children in Shrewsbury/Hopewell Twp.: Catharina$^{1.4.1g(b)}$, b. June 2, 1795, bapt. at Saddler's (St. John's) Lutheran Church on Nov. 8, 1795, sponsored by Catharina Ehrhart; Margaretha$^{1.4.2g(b)}$, b. Dec. 20, 1797, bapt. at Saddler's, sponsored by Rosina Ehrhart (single); Eva$^{1.4.3g(b)}$, b. June 6, 1800, bapt. at Saddler's, sponsored by Jacob Ehrhart and wife.

****

Peter Grimm

Peter[1h] resided in Lancaster Co., Earl Twp., New Holland, Pennsylvania. He may have been the Peter Grimm that immigrated to America from Unkenbach Germany in the ship *Forest* on Oct. 11, 1752. Peter was a freeman in Earl Twp. in 1771/72. A Margreta Grimin took communion at Seltenreich on May 25, 1765. Peter was the father of the following children: Johan Heinrich[1.1h], b. c.1749; Johan Peter[1.2h], b. c.1751; Susanna Margaret[1.3h], b. c.1753, m. Johannes Friesner[1f]; Jacob[1.4f], b. c.1754; Eva[1.5f,] b. 1755, confirmed at Cocalico Reformed Church April 28, 1771; John[1.6f], b. c.1759.

Johan Heinrich Grimm

Johan Heinrich[1.1h] m. Anna Christina, dau. of Johan Leonhard and Maria Sophia Mueller, at Lancaster Co., Seltenreich Lutheran Church on Nov. 16, 1773, and Maria Sophia, dau. of Johann Leonhardt (1712-1785) and Anna Maria (Lang) Stein, on May 3, 1778. Anna Christina was b. Sept. 10, 1753, d. in Earl Twp. on Dec. 22, 1776. Maria Sophia was b. 1752. Johan Heinrich was a freeman in Earl Twp. in 1771, and a meson in 1770. In 1769, he was a freeman at George Schyker's in Earl Twp. Johan Heinrich had the following children in Earl Twp.:

Johan Leonhard[1.1.1h], b. Nov. 21, 1774, bapt. at Seltenreich Dec. 18, 1774, sponsored by his grandparents, Johan Leonhard and Maria Sophia Mueller.

Maria Christina[1.1.2h], b. Dec. 22, 1776, bapt. at Seltenreich on Dec. 30, 1776, sponsored by Leonard and Sophia Mueller.

Anna Maria[1.1.3h], b. Jan. 29, 1779, bapt. at Seltenreich on May 2, 1779, sponsored by Leonard and Anna Maria Stein.

Henry[1.1.4h], b. Nov. 13, 1784, bapt. at Seltenreich in 1785, sponsored by Peter and Sophia Grimm.

Peter[1.1.5h], b. Aug. 21, 1785, bapt. at Seltenreich on Dec. 15, 1785, sponsored by David and Margaret Diefendoerfer.

John[1.1.6h], b. April 6, 1788, and bapt. at Seltenreich on May 1, 1788.

Elizabeth[1.1.7h], b. Dec. 6, 1789, and bapt. at Seltenreich on Jan. 1, 1790.

Catherine[1.1.6h], b. July 16, 1792, bapt. at Seltenreich on Aug. 5, 1792, sponsored by her parents.

Maria Margaret[1.1.7h], b. Oct. 5, 1794, bapt. at Seltenreich on Nov. 9, sponsored by her parents.

Johan Peter Grimm

Johan Peter[1.2h] m. Anna Maria Sophia, dau. of Johan Leonhard and Maria Spohia Mueller, at Lancaster Co., Seltenreich Lutheran Church on Jan. 5, 1773. He resided in Rockingham Co., Timberville, (Captain Ezekiel Harrison's Company, East District) Virginia in 1792. Peter and

Sophia had the following children in Earl Twp.:

Adam[1.2.1h], b. c.1773, and m. Elizabeth, dau. of John Croy/Gray, in Rockingham Co. in 1792. He has not been confirmed as a son.

Johan Peter[1.2.2h], b. June 29, 1777, bapt. at Seltenreich on Aug. 10, 1777, sponsored by Michael and Eleonore Schnoeder.

Sophia[1.2.3h], b. July 15, 1779, bapt. at Seltenreich on Aug. 22, 1779, sponsored by Henry and Sophia Grimm. She m. John Leonard in Rockingham Co. on Jan. 29, 1798.

Catharina[1.2.4h], b. July 15, 1779, bapt. at Seltenreich on Aug. 22, 1779, sponsored by Henry and Sophia Grimm. She m. Jacob Groff in Rockingham Co. on March 25, 1799. He was b. 1774. Catharina and Jacob were confirmed at Rader's on Oct. 25, 1801.

John[1.2.5h], b. Nov. 10, 1780, bapt. at Seltenreich on Dec. 4, sponsored by Michael Schneder and wife, and confirmed at Rader's Lutheran Church on Oct. 25, 1801.

Peter[1.2.6h], b. Oct. 3, 1784, bapt. at Seltenreich on May 1, 1788, and confirmed at Rader's on Oct. 25, 1801. He m. Elizabeth Shaver in Rockingham Co. in 1805.

Salome[1.2.7h], b. Jan. 25, 1787, bapt. at Seltenreich on May 1, 1788, and confirmed at Rader's on Oct. 25, 1801.

Polly[1.2.8h], b. c.1786, and m. Abraham Heed in Rockingham Co. in 1808.

Jacob Grimm

Jacob[1.4h] m. Christine, and had the following dau. in Earl Twp.:
Anna Maria[1.4.1h], b. June 2, 1776, bapt. at Seltenreich on July 28, 1776, sponsored by Leonard and Anna Maria Stein.

Eva Grimm

Eva[1.5h] m. Johan Frederick Schuetz in Lancaster Co., Seltenreich Lutheran Church May 7, 1775. They bapt. the following children at the White Oaks Congregation in Lancaster Co.: Susanna[1.5.1h], b. Feb. 7, 1779; Catharina[1.5.2h], b. May 14, 1780; Eva[1.5.3h], b. April 25, 1783; Anna Maria[1.5.4h], b. Aug. 31, 1784.

John Grimm (Crim, Krim)

John[1.6f] resided in Rockingham Co., Timberville, (Captain Ezekiel Harrison's Company, East District) Virginia in 1792, as Jno. Crim. He m. Juliana. John and Juliana had a dau. Elizabeth[1.6.1f], b. c.1781, m. Daniel Hoof/Hooft in Rockingham Co. Nov. 28, 1802.

****

John Bieri

John[11] m. Catharina, and had a son, Nicholas[1.1g], b. c.1697.

Nicholas Bieri

Nicholas$^{1.11}$ m. Barbara, dau. of Michael Jeremiah George and Magdalena Miller, in York Co., East Manchester Twp., Pennsylvania on Dec. 1, 1728. Nicholas came to America on the ship *Friendship of Bristol* Oct. 16, 1727. Barbara was b. in the Palatinate in 1710, d. Dec. 2, 1791. She m. Rev. Jacob Kagy (1719-1788) on Nov. 17, 1769. Nicholas and Barbara had the following children in York Co., Springettsbury, Pennsylvania: John$^{1.1.11}$, b. Aug. 2, 1729; Catharina$^{1.1.21}$, b. c.1730; Susanna$^{1.1.31}$, b. c.1732; Margaret$^{1.1.41}$, b. c.1734; Abraham$^{1.1.51}$, b. c.1736; Nicholas$^{1.1.61}$, b. June 16, 1739; George$^{1.1.71}$, b. c.1741.

John Beery

John$^{1.1.11}$ m. Catherina, dau. of Hartman and Anna (Stirtz) Hunsaker, in York Co., Pennsylvania in 1748. Hartman was b. in Aargau, Switzerland in 1695/7, and came to America on the ship *Pennsylvania Merchant* on Sept. 10, 1733. After Hartman's widow m. Jacob Gochenour Feb. 1740, d. 1745. They had the following children: Daniel$^{1.1.1.11}$, b. 1755; Anna$^{1.1.1.21}$, b. Jan. 30, 1768, m. Ludwig Seitz.

Abraham Beery

Abraham$^{1.1.51}$ m. Elizabeth Gochenour, and had the following children: Abraham$^{1.1.5.11}$, b. 1762; Jacob$^{1.1.5.21}$, b. Sept. 11, 1769, and is probably the Jacob that m. Nancy Geil in Albemarle or Rockingham Co. (Edom), Virginia on Nov. 27, 1794; John$^{1.1.5.31}$, b. c.1773; Christian$^{1.1.5.41}$, b. c.1782.

Abraham Beery

Abraham$^{1.1.5.11}$ m. Magdalena Rife in Harrisburg on Sept. 28, 1786, and Barbara Good before 1802. He had the following children at Edom: Anna$^{1.1.5.1.11}$, b. 1802; David$^{1.1.5.1.21}$, b. Oct. 8, 1808.

John Beery

John$^{1.1.5.31}$ m. Barbara Kagy, and had the following children: Barbara$^{1.1.5.3.11}$, b. Shenandoah Co., New Market, Virginia March 12, 1795; Daniel$^{1.1.5.3.21}$, b. Rockingham Co., Edom, Virginia April 5, 1798; Samuel$^{1.1.5.3.31}$, b. New Market Nov. 3, 1799.

Christian Beery

Christian$^{1.1.5.41}$ m. Catharine Frank in Harrisburg Feb. 25, 1798, and had the following children: John$^{1.1.5.4.11}$, b. Rockingham Co., Edom, Virginia Nov. 24, 1801.

Nicholas Beery

Nicholas$^{1.1.61}$ m. Maria, dau. of Jacob Keller, c.1763, and Mrs. Mary Good (Gro) c.1789. He d. in Fairfield Co., Rush Creek Twp., Ohio on Feb. 16, 1811, and is buried in Miller cemetery. They moved to Ohio in 1805. Nicholas had the following children in Shrewsbury Twp.: Barbara$^{1.1.6.11}$, b. April 6, 1764, m. Jacob Blosser at York Feb. 12, 1788; John$^{1.1.6.21}$, b. Nov. 4, 1765; Jacob$^{1.1.6.31}$, b. 1766; Elizabeth$^{1.1.6.41}$, b. April 11, 1771; Abraham$^{1.1.6.51}$, b. July 20, 1773; Mary$^{1.1.6.61}$, b. Sept. 4, 1775, m. Henry Stemen (1775-1855); Isaac$^{1.1.6.71}$, b. June 10, 1777; Nicholas$^{1.1.6.81}$, b. 1780, d. young; Henry$^{1.1.6.91}$, b. April 30, 1781; George$^{1.1.6.101}$, b. April 4, 1783, m. Susanna Funk in Rockingham Co., Virginia in 1796; Susan$^{1.1.6.111}$, b. 1785; Martha$^{1.1.6.121}$, b. 1787; Joseph$^{1.1.6.131}$, b. Feb. 8, 1790, m. Frances Garber in Rockingham Co. Nov. 15, 1811; Christian$^{1.1.6.141}$, b. Aug. 1, 1792; Margaret$^{1.1.6.151}$, b. June 15, 1795; Francis$^{1.1.6.161}$, b. 1796.

John Beery

John$^{1.1.6.21}$ m. Margaret, dau. of Nicholas Shafer, in Rockingham Co., Virginia March 15, 1788, and had the following children in Harrisburg: Nicholas$^{1.1.6.2.11}$, b. March 8, 1789; Elizabeth$^{1.1.6.2.31}$, b. July 4, 1791; Henry$^{1.1.6.2.31}$, b. Oct. 2, 1793; David$^{1.1.6.2.41}$, b. July 21, 1797; Abraham Washington$^{1.1.6.2.51}$, b. Dec. 12, 1799; Katherine$^{1.1.6.2.61}$, b. April 15, 1802; Margaret$^{1.1.6.2.71}$, b. Sept. 26, 1804.

Abraham Beery

Abraham$^{1.1.6.51}$ m. Catherine Fast in Rockingham Co., Harrisonburg, Virginia on March 7, 1802. She was b. in Berks Co., Reading, Pennsylvania April 17, 1786, d. in Fairfield Co., Rush Creek Twp., Ohio Jan. 2, 1870. In 1803, they settled on the bluff, on the north side of the Raccoon and one mile east of Berne. Abraham d. in Rush Creek Twp. June 15, 1845. They are buried in Miller cemetery. They had the following children: Abraham$^{1.1.6.5.11}$, m. Elizabeth Weldy, and resided in Adams Co., Decatur, Indiana; Joel$^{1.1.6.5.21}$, m. Sarah Huddle, resided in Drake Co., Ohio; Elizabeth$^{1.1.6.5.31}$, m. Abraham Geil, resided in Fairfield Co., Rush Creek Twp; Sarah$^{1.1.6.5.41}$, b. July 2, 1807, m. Henry Swartz$^{1.5.4.7a}$; Catherine$^{1.1.6.5.51}$, b. Feb. 26, 1809, m. Joseph Swartz$^{1.5.4.1a}$; Mary$^{1.1.6.5.61}$, b. Aug. 25, 1812, m. George Swartz$^{1.5.4.6a}$.

Mary Beery

Mary$^{1.1.6.61}$ m. Reverend Henry Stemen, and had the following children: John$^{1.1.6.6.11}$, b. 1796, m. Catharine Mericle; Isaac$^{1.1.6.6.21}$, b. 1798, m. Mary Mericle, and had Lydia in 1827. Lydia m. Benjamin

Friesner and after his death, Adam Strickler in Fairfield Co. on Nov. 21, 1864.

****

Jacob Keller

Jacob[1] may have been the Jacob Keller in Dover Twp. in 1762 (possibly a son of Antony and Maria Barbara). He was taxed in Shrewsbury Twp. with 150 acres one horse, and three cattle in 1779, and 100 acres, one horse, and two cattle in 1780. His will was probated on July 27, 1791, in Shrewsbury Twp. His executers were Christian Keller and Andrew Meyer. Jacob had the following children:

Maria[1.1], b. c.1743, m. Nicholas Beery[1.1.61].

dau.[1.2], b. c.1749, m. Andreas Meyer.

Christian[1.3], b. 1752, and was taxed in Shrewsbury Twp. in 1780 with two horses, and three cattle. He may have m. Elizabeth Nissley in 1781, and had John in 1783, Christian in 1785, Anna in 1787, and Susanna in 1789.

Henry[1.4], b. May 13, 1755. He was not in Jacob's will, but some researchers have said that Henry and Maria were siblings.

John[1.5], b. c.1758. He was not on Jacob's will, but he was residing in Shrewsbury Twp. in 1780 with 100 acres, two horses and three cattle, and 140 acres, three horses and four cattle in Shrewsbury Twp. in 1779.

Samuel[1.6], b. c.1761. He was not mentioned in Jacob's will, but he had 150 acres in Shrewsbury Twp. in 1780, and 200 acres in Shrewsbury Twp. in 1779.

Henry Keller

Henry[1.4] m. Catharina, dau. of Johannes and Anna Catharina Seitz, in York Co., Pennsylvania on April 6, 1784. He was taxed as single in Shrewsbury Twp. in 1779, and 1780. They moved to Fairfield Co., Pleasant Twp., Ohio sometime between 1803 and 1810. Henry d. Feb. 13, 1838, and Catharina on Nov. 26, 1843. They had the following children in Shrewsbury Twp.:

John[1.4.1], b. July 17, 1785, d. in Seneca Co., Tiffin, Ohio Oct. 9, 1859, m. Elizabeth Mitzell (b. Aug. 11, 1784) 1804.

Jacob[1.4.2], b. Jan. 7, 1787, d. Oct. 21, 1870, m. Anna Miller in Fairfield Co., 1810.

Benjamin[1.4.3], b. May 28, 1789.

Elizabeth[1.4.4], b. June 15, 1791, d. in Fairfield Co. Feb. 20, 1859, m. Henry Seever in Fairfield Co. Feb. 5, 1810.

Henry[1.4.5], b. April 21, 1793, d. in August, 1870, m. Catherine Hoover in Fairfield Co. 1818.

Joseph[1.4.6], b. Oct. 27, 1795, d. in Seneca Co., Tiffen, Ohio Jan. 15, 1855, m. Catherine Bright c.1816, and Elizabeth Tussing

Nov. 14, 1830, and Nancy Good sometime after 1840.

Daniel$^{1.4.7j}$, b. Oct. 25, 1797.

Catherine$^{1.4.8j}$, b. April 2, 1800, d. in Perry Co., Somerset, Ohio, m. George Groves in Fairfield Co. Oct. 10, 1823.

Magdalena$^{1.4.9j}$, b. July 2, 1801, d. in Fairfield Co. Sept. 24, 1885, m. Isaac Montieth in Fairfield Co. April 6, 1823.

Mary$^{1.4.10j}$, b. May 12, 1803, m. Jacob Miller in Fairfield Co. on April 6, 1823.

Benjamin Keller

Benjamin$^{1.4.3j}$ m. Maria Keller in York Co., Pennsylvania Feb. 14, 1813, and Sarah Layman sometime after 1825. Benjamin d. in Miami Co., Pleasant Hill, Ohio Sept. 18, 1870. Benjamin and Maria had a dau. Leah$^{1.4.3.1j}$, b. York Co. on May 27, 1825.

****

Christian Stabler

Christian^{1k} arrived at Philadelphia in 1752. He m. Anna, and settled in York Co., Shrewsbury Twp., Pennsylvania in 1761. He d. Sept., 1784. They had the following children: Catharina$^{1.1k}$, b. c.1755; Christina$^{1.2k}$, b. Nov. 3, 1757, bapt. Jan. 8, 1758, m. Johan Carl, son of Carl Adam and Maria Elisabeth (Ehrhardt) Diehl; Johann$^{1.3k}$, b. c.1758; Maria Barbara$^{1.4k}$, b. c.1760; Johan Jacob$^{1.5k}$, b. Oct. 10, 1762; Christian$^{1.6k}$, b. July 21, 1764; Adam$^{1.7k}$, b. c.1765; Georg Jacob$^{1.8k}$, b. Dec. 26, 1768; Anna$^{1.9k}$, b. c.1770.

Catharina Stabler

Catharina$^{1.1k}$ m. Andreas Muller, and had the following children:

Barbara$^{1.1.1k}$, b. Jan. 23, 1774, bapt. at Friedensaal Feb. 27, 1774, sponsored by her aunt, Barbara Stabler.

Christina$^{1.1.2k}$, b. April, 1776, bapt. at Friedensaal May 19, 1776, sponsored by her aunt, Christina Stabler.

Christian$^{1.1.3k}$, b. Sept. 1780, bapt. at Friedensaal, sponsored by his grandparents, Christian and Anna Stabler.

Maria Magdalena$^{1.1.4k}$, b. Nov. 16, 1782, bapt. at Friedensaal Dec. 1, 1782, sponsored by Barbara, dau. of Christian Lang.

Michael$^{1.1.5k}$, b. March 5, 1785, bapt. at Friedensaal April 17, 1785, sponsored by his uncle, Christian Stabler.

Catharina$^{1.1.6k}$, b. Dec. 2, 1789, bapt. at Fissel's Feb. 25, 1790, sponsored by Georg and Catharina Nabelen.

Johann Stabler

Johann$^{1.3k}$ m. Margaret sometime before 1783, and had the following children: Christina$^{1.3.1k}$, bapt. at Friedensaal April 4, 1784, sponsored by her uncle and aunt, Carl Diehl and wife; Susanna$^{1.3.2k}$, b. Dec. 16,

1790, bapt. at St. Peter's (Yellow) Church Dec. 16, 1790, sponsored by
her uncle and aunt, Christian and Elisabeth Stabler.

Maria Barbara Stabler

Maria Barbara$^{1.4k}$ m. Johan Peter, son of Peter and Catharina
Gudling. He was bapt. at Strayer's on June 21, 1761, sponsored by
Peter and Elisabeth Benss. Peter and Barbara had the following
children:

Christian$^{1.4.1k}$, b. July 15, 1783, bapt. at Friedensaal Aug. 3, 1783,
sponsored by his uncle and aunt, John and Margaret Stabler.

Catharina$^{1.4.2k}$, b. April 30, 1785, bapt. at Friedensaal June 12,
1785, sponsored by the uncle and aunt, Andreas Muller and
wife.

Elizabeth$^{1.4.3k}$, b. March 10, 1787, bapt. at Friedensaal April 1,
1787, sponsored by Tobias and Catharina Muller.

Adam$^{1.4.4k}$, b. May 12, 1788, bapt. at Friedensaal June 9, 1788,
sponsored by his uncle and aunt, Adam Stabler and wife.

Barbara$^{1.4.5k}$, b. April 20, 1790, bapt. at Friedensaal May 23, 1790,
sponsored by her uncle and aunt, Adam and Christina Stabler.

Susanna$^{1.4.6k}$, bapt. at St. Peter's (Yellow) Church Jan. 15, 1792,
sponsored by Adam and Elisabeth Schaffer.

Eva$^{1.4.7k}$, b. June 22, 1800, bapt. at Friedensaal July 27, 1800,
sponsored by Johannes and Eva Seitz.

Johan Jacob Stabler

Johan Jacob$^{1.5k}$ m. Catharina, and had the following children:
Catharina$^{1.5.1k}$, b. Jan. 1, 1791, bapt. at St. Peter's (Yellow) Church
May 1, 1791, sponsored by her uncle and aunt, Andreas and Catharina
Muller; Susanna$^{1.5.2k}$, b. July 11, 1799, bapt. at Saddler's Nov. 17,
1799, sponsored by Susanna Zeitt.

Christian Stabler

Christian$^{1.6k}$ m. Elisabeth and Anna Maria$^{1.1.1.5.2d}$, dau. of Johannes
and Anna Catharina Seitz, in York Co. April 11, 1812. He d. in
Baltimore Co., Stablerville, Maryland on Dec. 6, 1846. Anna Maria d.
at Stablerville March 19, 1845. They are buried in Stablersville
cemetery. Christian and Elisabeth had a son Adam$^{1.6.1k}$, b. April 1,
1799, and bapt. at Fissel's.

Adam Stabler

Adam$^{1.8k}$ m. Christina Diehl. They had a dau. Eva$^{1.8.1k}$, b. March 15,
1785, bapt. at Friedensaal on April 17, 1785, sponsored by Eva, dau. of
Michael Kleinfelter. She m. Johannes Seitz.

Georg Jacob Stabler

Georg Jacob[1.8k] m. Catharina, dau. of Johannes Michael and Appolonia Kleinfelter. She was bapt. at St. Jacob's Dec. 12, 1768, d. Sept. 1807. George d. 1830. They had the following children in Shrewsbury Twp.:

Johann Georg[1.8.1k], b. March 6, 1789, bapt. at Fissel's May 21, 1789, sponsored by his uncle and aunt, Johannes and Anna Barbara Kunckel. He d. in 1847.

Christian[1.8.2k], b. May 3, 1790, and bapt. at Fissel's May 18, 1790.

Johann Michael[1.8.3k], b. Feb., 1791, bapt. at Fissel's Nov. 20, 1791, sponsored by Johan Michael and Catharina Kleinfelter.

Anna Elizabeth[1.8.4k], b. July 14, 1793, bapt. at Fissel's, sponsored by Salmon Flauer and wife.

Justina[1.8.5k], b. Oct. 4, 1795, bapt. at Fissel's, sponsored by Justina Kunckel (old mother).

Christina[1.8.6k], b. 1798.

Catharina[1.8.7k], b. Sept. 5, 1800, bapt. at Fissel's, sponsored by Justina Kunckel.

Joseph[1.8.8k], b. 1802.

****

Melchior Diehl

Melchior[11] m. Eva, d. in Unden-Cappeln on Sept. 1, 1677, and had a son, Hans Georg[1.11].

Hans Georg Diehl

Hans Georg[1.11] m. Anna Catharina, dau. of Peter Hertz of Schweinscheid, at Unden-Cappeln on Jan. 20, 1680, and had a son, Johan Adam[1.1.11], b. Sept. 12, 1690.

Johan Adam Diehl

Johan Adam[1.1.11] was confirmed at Herran-Sultzbach in 1704, d. in York Co., Pennsylvania April 1755. He m. Maria Catharina, dau. of Johan Daniel and Anna Catharina (Esch) Kreischer, of Homberg on Dec. 4, 1712. She was bapt. Oct. 28, 1696, d. before 1767.

Johann Daniel Kreisher

Johann Daniel, son of Georg Kreisher of Mertzweiler, Gerichtsschoffe and Kirchencensor, m. Anna Catharina, dau. of Abraham Esch of Deimberg, at Deimberg on Nov. 18, 1687. They immigrated to America on the ship *Samuel* on Aug. 27, 1739, and settled in York Co., Pennsylvania. Adam's will was written on March 31, 1755. They had the following children at Homberg, Germany: Johann Daniel[1.1.1.11], b. 1713; Maria Elisabeth[1.1.1.21], b. April 4, 1715, m. Johan Adam Simon[1.1.1.3c]; Carl Adam[1.1.1.31], b. 1717; Eva Margaretha[1.1.1.41], bapt. Aug. 27, 1718; Angelica Elizabeth[1.1.1.51], b. c.1721;

Nicholas$^{1.1.1.61}$, b. c.1724; Peter$^{1.1.1.71}$, b. c.1728; Johan
Georg$^{1.1.1.81}$, b. c.1732; Johan Adam$^{1.1.1.91}$, b. April, 1734.

Johann Daniel Diehl

Johann Daniel$^{1.1.1.11}$ m. Maria Elisabeth$^{1.1.1.4c}$, dau. of Johan Nickel
Simon in Lancaster Co., Warwick Twp., Pennsylvania Dec. 26, 1740.
He was b. near Homberg, Landkreis of Kusel, Pfaltz in 1713. He
immigrated to Pennsylvania on the ship *Samuel* Aug. 27, 1739. In
1751, Daniel received a land warrant in Codorus Twp. near Seven
Valleys, and built a mill within a year. He d. intestate in Dec., 1761,
and is buried at Friedensaal Lutheran Church. At the time of his
death he owned over 500 acres and four mills. He was naturalized on
April 10/11, 1761. Daniel and Maria bapt. the following children at
Christ's Lutheran Church of York: Johan Carl$^{1.1.1.1.11}$, b. Oct. 19,
1742, bapt. at Christ's Lutheran Church on Nov. 24, 1742; Anna
Maria$^{1.1.1.1.21}$, b. Feb. 11, 1744, bapt. at Christ's Lutheran on March
17, 1744; Johan Adam$^{1.1.1.1.31}$, b. Dec. 16, 1746, bapt. at Christ's
Lutheran on Feb. 24, 1747, d. in August, 1764; Georg$^{1.1.1.1.41}$, b. Feb.
24, 1750.

Johan Carl Diehl

Carl$^{1.1.1.1.11}$ d. in Adams Co., Cumberland Twp., Pennsylvania on
Aug. 20, 1820. He m. Christina Catharina, dau. of Georg and
Catharina (Rausher) Liebenstein, in Christ's Lutheran Church of York
Oct. 11, 1763. She was b. in Manchester Twp. on Aug. 5, 1746, d. in
Adams Co. May 5, 1809. He inherited his father's mill property, and
between 1768 and 1783, he built a brick addition to the original stone
home. In 1783, he had 2 houses, 1 outhouse, 250 acres, 2 negroes, 4
horses, 8 horned cattle, 10 sheep, 1 grist mill, 1 saw mill, 1 hemp mill,
and 2 stills. In addition to being a miller, he was a blacksmith. In
1773, he purchased *Groundhog Hill* in Shrewsbury Twp., which he
later sold part to Andrew Swartz. About 1787, he sold the mill
property to Jacob Sitler, moved to Baltimore, Maryland, and purchased
several town lots. In 1792, he sold the remainder of *Groundhog Hill*
to Jacob Bowman. About 1805, he moved to Adams Co., Pennsylvania,
and purchased over 775 acres in Columbiana Co., Ohio, with intentions
of moving there. His will was written on March 15, 1812, and probated
in 1851. They had the following children: Eve$^{1.1.1.1.11}$, b. c.1764, m.
Ephraim Robinson, d. in Baltimore, Maryland on Nov. 6, 1842;
son$^{1.1.1.1.21}$, b. c.1767; Daniel$^{1.1.1.1.31}$, b. 1776, d. before 1820;
Carl$^{1.1.1.1.41}$, b. 1780, d. April 17, 1808; Michael$^{1.1.1.1.51}$, b. Oct.
21, 1782, bapt. at St. Paul's on Nov. 24, 1782, sponsored by his uncle
and aunt, George and Eva Diehl, d. before 1820; George$^{1.1.1.1.61}$, b.
1784, m. Catherine Bomberger (b. c. 1780, d. Feb. 26, 1881), d. in
Baltimore, Maryland Sept. 20, 1820, served as Private under Captain

John Hanna in the War of 1812 from Aug. 19, 1814 to Nov. 18, 1814; Adam[1.1.1.1.1.71], b. c.1785, d. March 17, 1789; infant[1.1.1.1.1.81], b. Dec., 1786, d. July 13, 1788; Jacob[1.1.1.1.1.91], b. March, 1787.

Jacob Diehl

Jacob[1.1.1.1.1.91] m. Christina, dau. of Christian (son of Christian) and Hannah (Steitz) Diehl, in Baltimore, Maryland on June 24, 1807. She was b. 1785, d. in Adams Co., Germany Twp., Pennsylvania April 19, 1830. Jacob d. in Columbiana Co., Knox Twp., Ohio on June 24, 1862. He moved to Adams Co., Pennsylvania c.1809, and to Ohio c.1832. They had the following children:

    Daniel[1.1.1.1.9.11], b. May 13, 1808, d. in Ohio June 11, 1885.

    Jacob Henry[1.1.1.1.9.21], b. May 27, 1809, m. Sarah McCadden in Adams Co. on March 17, 1834, resided in Ohio in 1858.

    Charlotte[1.1.1.1.9.31], b. 1810, m. David Colestock, and was alive in 1850.

    Charles[1.1.1.1.9.41], b. Dec. 2, 1811, d. in Ohio March 28, 1865.

    David[1.1.1.1.9.51], b. 1814, m. Rebecca Weyganott, d. in Ohio June 11, 1885.

    Mariah[1.1.1.1.9.61], b. Jan. 26, 1817, m. Adam Hahn March 15, 1840, d. in Ohio March 26, 1874.

    William[1.1.1.1.9.71], b. April 25, 1819, m. Margaret Smalley Burchfield Oct. 18, 1849, d. in Ohio Oct. 3, 1900.

    Agnes[1.1.1.1.9.81], b. 1820, m. Peter Cressinger June 3, 1847 and Jesse Brooks April 1, 1852, d. in Columbiana Co., Ohio 1892.

    Matilda[1.1.1.1.9.91], b. April 10, 1827.

    Aaron[1.1.1.1.9.101], b. April 7, 1830, m. Sarah Boyce in Columbiana Co., Ohio Feb. 8, 1863, d. in Stark Co., Alliance, Ohio Dec. 23, 1908.

Anna Maria Diehl

Anna Maria[1.1.1.1.21] d. in York Co., York Twp., Jan. 10, 1800. She m. Frederick, son of Killian and Christina Fissel, and Captain John McDonald, probably son of John and Jane McDonald. Frederick was b. in Essenheim on the Maintz May 24, 1733, immigrated to America on the ship *Loyal Judith* Sept. 3, 1742, d. in Shrewsbury Twp. Jan. 1778. He purchased 170 acres and 116 perches in Shrewsbury Twp. in Nov 1765, and in 1771 gave the land for Fissel's (Jerusalem) Union Church. He was a millwright/miller, and operated the Diehl Mill while Daniel's estate was settled. Frederick was naturalized on April 3, 1763, and he served on the Committee for Defense during the Revolutionary War. When he died, he owned 250 acres and a mill tract consisting of 150 acres. John McDonald was b. 1749, d. in York Twp. March 19, 1813. During the Revolutionary War, he served as a Captain in Col. James Batt's Battalion. Anna Maria had the following children in

Shrewsbury Twp.: Elizabeth$^{1.1.1.1.2.11}$, b. c.1762. Henry$^{1.1.1.1.2.21}$, b. April 22, 1764; Eva$^{1.1.1.1.2.31}$, b. 1766; Margaret$^{1.1.1.1.2.41}$, b. Dec. 12, 1768, m. Daniel, son of Daniel Reider, moved to Wayne Co., Ohio in 1816; Frederick$^{1.1.1.1.2.51}$, b. 1769; Christina$^{1.1.1.1.2.61}$, b. 1772; Daniel$^{1.1.1.1.2.71}$, b. 1774, m. Elizabeth Frey, d. in Codorus Twp. Feb. 1824; Anna Maria$^{1.1.1.1.2.81}$, b. Feb. 22, 1777; Catherine$^{1.1.1.1.2.91}$, b. Dec. 28, 1782, d. April 28, 1788.

Elizabeth Fissel

Elizabeth$^{1.1.1.1.2.11}$ m. John, son of Johan Philip and Elizabeth (Flowers) Schneider, and had the following children in Shrewsbury Twp.: Johan George$^{1.1.1.1.2.1.11}$, b. Feb., 1781; Johan Philip$^{1.1.1.1.2.1.21}$, b. Feb. 14, 1783; Elizabeth$^{1.1.1.1.2.1.31}$, b. Sept. 16, 1785; Susan$^{1.1.1.1.2.1.41}$, b. Aug. 17, 1788, m. Anthony Kniesly, d. Nov. 11, 1869.

Henry Fissel

Henry$^{1.1.1.1.2.21}$ m. Barbara, dau. Michael Fissel, d. in Manheim Twp. in 1802. She d. in Paradise Twp. in April, 1823. They had nthe following children:

Anna Margaret$^{1.1.1.1.2.2.11}$, b. July 7, 1785, bapt. at Lischy's on Aug. 21, 1785, m. Adam Strasbaugh.

Catharina Barbara$^{1.1.1.1.2.2.21}$, b. Aug. 22, 1787, bapt. at Lischy's on Nov. 8, 1787, m. Michael Hoke.

John Michael$^{1.1.1.1.2.2.31}$, b. April 14, 1789, bapt. at Lischy's on May 17, 1789, sponsored by Michael and Margaret Fischel.

John$^{1.1.1.1.2.2.41}$, b. June 14, 1791, bapt. at Lischy's on Aug. 7, 1791, sponsored by Leonard and Margaret Reber.

John Henry$^{1.1.1.1.2.2.51}$, b. Aug. 2, 1793, bapt. at Lischy's on Sept. 1, 1793, sponsored by Michael Fischel.

Mary Magdalena$^{1.1.1.1.2.2.61}$, b. July 25, 1795, bapt. at Lischy's on Nov. 15, 1795, sponsored be Michael and Margaret Fischel.

John Jacob$^{1.1.1.1.2.2.71}$, b. Nov. 20, 1797, bapt. at Lischy's on Jan. 6, 1798, sponsored by his parents.

Elizabeth$^{1.1.1.1.2.2.81}$, b. March, 1800, and m. Abraham Spangler.

George$^{1.1.1.1.2.2.91}$, b. June 19, 1802.

Eva Fissel

Eva$^{1.1.1.1.2.31}$ m. Baltzer, son of John Faust of Lancaster Co., Pennsylvania, July 30, 1781. He founded the town of Shrewsbury, and had 150 acres, a grist mill and saw mill in Shrewsbury Twp. in 1780. He served in the Revolutionary War under Captain Henry Ferree in 1781. Baltzer and Eva had the following children (most of whom moved to Somerset Co., Pennsylvania):

Elizabeth$^{1.1.1.1.2.3.11}$, b. Dec. 27, 1783, m. George Berkebile.

John[1.1.1.1.2.3.21], b. Nov. 16, 1785, m. Dorothy Cable, d. May 12, 1861.

Baltzer[1.1.1.1.2.3.31], b. c.1787, m. Mary Kleinfelter.

Frederick[1.1.1.1.2.3.41], b. Oct. 1789, d. in 1856.

Catherine[1.1.1.1.2.3.51], b. c.1791, m. David Schaffer.

Eve[1.1.1.1.2.3.61], b. Dec. 25, 1795, m. ____ Fitzgerald, and John Oaks, d. Dec. 27, 1831.

Susanna[1.1.1.1.2.3.71], m. Samuel Oaks.

Daniel[1.1.1.1.2.3.81], b. March 7, 1798, bapt. at Saddler's, sponsored by Daniel Fischel and wife.

Lydia[1.1.1.1.2.3.91], b. Feb. 23, 1804.

Frederick Fissel

Frederick[1.1.1.1.2.51] m. Phillippina Morgethal on Oct. 18, 1810, d. in 1817. She d. in Paradise Twp. in Oct., 1837. They had the following children: Leah[1.1.1.1.2.5.11]; Samuel[1.1.1.1.2.5.21].

Georg Diehl

Georg[1.1.1.1.41], d. in Codorus Twp. on July 28, 1804. He m. Anna Eva, dau. of Georg and Catharina (Rausher) Liebenstein, c.1774. She was b. in Manchester Twp. on April 7, 1753, d. Oct. 10, 1835. Georg received his father's farm land. He was a tax assessor in 1781, and in 1783 had 300 acres. He was a Private in the Second Class of Captain George Geilelman's Company. When he died, he owned 484 acres. Georg and Anna Eva had the following children:

Daniel[1.1.1.1.4.11], b. March 27, 1775, bapt. at Friedensaal Aug. 18, 1776, sponsored by his uncle and aunt, Carl and Christina Diehl.

Catherine[1.1.1.1.4.21], b. June 30, 1776, bapt. at St. Paul's (Ziegler's) Church Aug. 10, 1776, sponsored by her uncle and aunt, Carl and Christina Diehl. She m. Jacob Ebert, d. Jan. 6, 1862.

Adam[1.1.1.1.4.31], b. Oct. 15, 1777, bapt. at St. Paul's Dec. 6, 1777, sponsored by his uncle and aunt Carl Diehl and wife.

George[1.1.1.1.4.41], b. July 12, 1779, bapt. at St. Paul's Aug. 4, 1779, sponsored by his uncle and aunt, Carl and Christina Diehl, d. in Germany Twp. Aug. 6, 1803.

Esther[1.1.1.1.4.51], b. Aug. 23, 1781, bapt. at St. Paul's Nov. 8, 1781, sponsored by her uncle and aunt, Carl and Christina Diehl. She m. John, son of Thomas and Rosina (Michael) Ehrhart, d. sometime after Nov. 24, 1826. John was b. June 10, 1779, d. Sept. 20, 1825. They had Maria on May 26, 1824.

Christina Eva[1.1.1.1.4.61], b. Nov. 20, 1782, bapt. at St. Paul's on Dec. 25, 1782, sponsored by Eva Diehl. She was unmarried in 1806.

Jacob$^{1.1.1.1.4.7^1}$, b. c.1785.

Anna Maria$^{1.1.1.1.4.8^1}$, b. Oct. 16, 1788.

John$^{1.1.1.1.4.9^1}$, b. c.1791, d. sometime after 1856.

Charles$^{1.1.1.1.4.10^1}$, b. c.1792.

David$^{1.1.1.1.4.11^1}$, b. July 14, 1794, bapt. at St. Paul's July 30, 1794, sponsored by his parents. He d. May 1812.

Daniel Diehl

Daniel$^{1.1.1.1.4.11}$ m. Rosina, dau. of Thomas and Rosina (Michael) Ehrhart. She was b. in Shrewsbury Twp. March 19, 1781, d. in Codorus Twp. Feb. 20, 1847. He d. in Codorus Twp. on March 5, 1842. He erected a tannery at Seven Valleys, and had 100 acres of land in 1805. They are buried in Ziegler's cemetery. They had the following children:

Lydia$^{1.1.1.1.4.1.11}$, b. Feb. 19, 1800, bapt. at St. Paul's April 13, 1800, sponsored by Eva Diehl, m. Michael Hartman, d. in York Oct. 7, 1886.

Peter$^{1.1.1.1.4.1.21}$, b. April 23, 1802, m. Anna Maria Smyser Nov. 13, 1823, d. in Adams Co., Pennsylvania April 13, 1887.

Juliana$^{1.1.1.1.4.1.31}$, b. Jan. 27, 1804, m. Jacob Albert Jan. 8, 1824, d. in Northampton Co., Pennsylvania April 26, 1855.

Daniel$^{1.1.1.1.4.1.4^1}$, b. Aug. 19, 1807, m. Anna Maria Kohler Nov. 23, 1830 and Katie Lichtenwalter in 1850, d. in Evansville, Illinois March 18, 1867.

Henry Adrain$^{1.1.1.1.4.1.51}$, b. June 1, 1809, m. Mary Ann Smyser, d. in Buchanan Co., Iowa Jan. 28, 1881.

Anna Mary$^{1.1.1.1.4.1.61}$, b. April 18, 1811, m. Philip Menges and Jacob Allison, resided in Littletown, Pennsylvania.

Andrew$^{1.1.1.1.4.1.71}$, b. July 20, 1812, m. Rebecca Bollinger, d. in York Feb. 20, 1892.

Sarah$^{1.1.1.1.4.1.81}$, b. c.1814, and m. George Schlider.

Elizabeth$^{1.1.1.1.4.1.91}$, b. Oct. 18, 1816, d. Aug. 14, 1843.

Cassia$^{1.1.1.1.4.1.101}$, b. 1818, m. Joseph Barker, d. in Adams Co., Pennsylvania Nov. 11, 1910.

Heneritta$^{1.1.1.1.4.1.111}$, b. c.1819, m. Adam Smith in 1844, d. in Hanover, Pennsylvania in 1857.

Alexander$^{1.1.1.1.4.1.121}$, b. July 24, 1822, m. Sarah Julius Sept. 14, 1843, d. in Codorus Twp. on Sept. 20, 1849.

Adam Diehl

Adam$^{1.1.1.1.4.31}$ m. Catherine, dau. of Peter and Barbara Krebs, d. in Frederick Co., Walkersville, Maryland Dec. 24, 1856. She was b. April 20, 1779, d. April 19, 1817. In 1805, he had 250 acres and a tanyard. About 1834, he moved to Walkersville, Maryland. He is buried at St. John's at Woodsboro, Maryland, and his wife is buried at Zeigler's

cemetery in York Co. They had the following children:
George[1.1.1.1.4.3.11], b. Sept. 24, 1803, d. in Walkersville Jan. 5, 1881;
Elizabeth[1.1.1.1.4.3.21], b. Aug. 14, 1805, m. Jonas Gladfelter and
Jacob Smyser, d. in York Co., Pennsylvania April 30, 1879;
Jesse[1.1.1.1.4.3.31], b. Oct. 28, 1807, m. Anna Maria Spangler, d. in
York Co. Dec. 4, 1843; John[1.1.1.1.4.3.41], b. Dec. 16, 1809, m. Lydia
Ramer, d. in Adams Co., Pennsylvania Aug. 6, 1890;
Ephraim[1.1.1.1.4.3.51], b. April 22, 1812, m. Susanna Long, d. in Ohio
Sept. 21, 1889; Leah[1.1.1.1.4.3.61], b. Sept. 22, 1814, m. John Lishy
Smyser, d. in Buchanan Co., Iowa Nov. 9, 1900; Adam[1.1.1.1.4.3.71], b.
Sept. 22, 1814, m. Sarah Kroh, d. in Frederick Co., Maryland Aug. 3,
1905.

Jacob Diehl

Jacob[1.1.1.1.4.71] m. Mary, d. in Adams Co., Tyrone Twp.,
Pennsylvania in June, 1823. He was a tanner, and had land in
Manheim Twp. About 1812, he moved to Adams Co., Tyrone Twp. He
had purchased land in Stark Co., Ohio, but d. before he could make the
move. Mary moved to Stark Co., Canton, Ohio after Jacob's death,
and only her son, William, remained behind. Jacob and Mary had the
following children: William[1.1.1.1.4.7.11], b. Jan. 4, 1809, m. Lydia
Gladfelter, d. in York Co., Codorus Twp., Pennsylvania Oct. 9, 1878;
Elizabeth[1.1.1.1.4.7.21], b. April 10, 1811, m. Daniel Smith, d. in Stark
Co., Ohio sometime after 1874; Isaac[1.1.1.1.4.7.31], b. Nov. 25, 1812, m.
Susanna Daily, resided in DeKalb Co., Indiana in 1885;
Sally[1.1.1.1.4.7.41], b. Oct. 18, 1814; Jacob[1.1.1.1.4.7.51], b. Nov. 28,
1816, m. Julia Kirk in Ohio on May 3, 1842; Daniel[1.1.1.1.4.7.61], b.
Feb. 5, 1819, m. Hannah Harter, resided in Summit Co., Ohio in 1874;
Samuel[1.1.1.1.4.7.61], b. May 5, 1822, m. Elizabeth Snyder in Ohio Oct.
8, 1840.

Anna Maria Diehl

Anna Maria[1.1.1.1.4.81] m. Andrew, son of Jacob and Susanna
(Schreiber) Sheely, d. in Adams Co., Littlestown, Pennsylvania Feb. 29,
1850. He was b. Dec. 28, 1774, d. Nov. 1, 1850. They had the
following children: Jacob[1.1.1.1.4.8.11], b. Dec. 11, 1808, m. Mary
Hartman in 1832, d. April 2, 1860; Mary J.[1.1.1.1.4.8.21], b. June 6,
1811, m. Jacob Hartman May 27, 1834, d. Jan. 17, 1884;
Hester[1.1.1.1.4.8.31], b. April 10, 1813, m. Jacob Sponseller, d. Dec. 11,
1857; J. George[1.1.1.1.4.8.41], b. July 14, 1818, m. Anna, d. Sept. 6,
1898.
Daniel[1.1.1.1.4.8.51], b. 1820, m. Hannah M. Lightner, d. Nov. 3, 1901.

Charles Diehl

Charles[1.1.1.1.4.101] m. Elizabeth Sheets in Columbiana Co., Ohio June

16, 1818, d. in Randolph Co., Indiana between 1840 and 1850. She was b. in Maryland to Christian and Margaret (Wetzel) Sheets in 1800. In 1830, they resided in Drake Co., Ohio, and in 1840, they resided in Randolph Co., Jackson Twp., Indiana. They had the following children: Margaret$^{1.1.1.1.4.10.11}$, b. 1819; John$^{1.1.1.1.4.10.21}$, b. 1820, m. Martha; Mary Ann$^{1.1.1.1.4.10.31}$, b. Nov. 15, 1821, m. Elerson Fields, d. in Onaga, Kansas April 22, 1912; Ephraim$^{1.1.1.1.4.10.41}$, b. Sept. 22, 1822, m. Margaret Baugh, d. April 10, 1864; Eliza$^{1.1.1.1.4.10.51}$, b. c.1826; Lottie$^{1.1.1.1.4.10.61}$, b. c.1828; Harriet Sarah$^{1.1.1.1.4.10.71}$, b. 1837; Amanda$^{1.1.1.1.4.10.81}$, b. 1840; Catherine$^{1.1.1.1.4.10.91}$, b. 1841; Martha J.$^{1.1.1.1.4.10.101}$.

Carl Adam Diehl

Carl Adam$^{1.1.1.31}$ m. Maria Elisabeth, dau. of Johan Peter and Anna Margarethe (Becker) Ehrhardt, in Codorus Twp. Nov. 24, 1742. She was bapt. at Staudernheim in the Palatinate Nov. 30, 1716, d. in Shrewsbury Twp. c.1795. On March 1, 1755 (issued April 10, 1749 and Oct. 18, 1753) he received a land warrant in Shrewsbury Twp. called *Diehls Folly*. He applied for naturalization on Sept. 24, 1755, and was naturalized Sept. 24, 1763. On Oct. 3, 1763, he purchased 118 acres and 40 perches called *Diehl's Chance*. On Dec. 22, 1764, he had surveyed, 394.5 acres called *Shrewsbury Town*, 344 acres 50 perches on a branch of Codorus Creek, and 249 acres on Deer Creek. On April 4, 1769, he purchased a grist and saw mill on Deer Creek, which he sold to his brother Peter in 1771. Carl also had a mill in Shrewsbury Twp. He d. in Shrewsbury Twp. April 18, 1800. Carl and Maria Elisabeth had the following children: Adam$^{1.1.1.3.11}$, b. Aug. 12, 1743, bapt. at Christ's Lutheran Church on Sept. 18, 1743; Eva Christina$^{1.1.1.3.21}$, b. 1744; Elizabeth$^{1.1.1.3.31}$, b. c.1746; Johan Carl$^{1.1.1.3.41}$, b. Oct. 14, 1750; Anna Catharina Elisabetha$^{1.1.1.3.51}$, b. Dec. 3, 1752, bapt. at Christ's Lutheran Dec. 25, 1752.

Adam Diehl

Adam$^{1.1.1.3.11}$ m. Anna Elizabeth Seyler, d. in York Co., Windsor Twp. Oct. 30, 1820. She d. in Chanceford Twp. March 7, 1831. Adam served under Captain Aquilla Wiley and John Ehrman in the Revolutionary War. In 1783, he was in Shrewsbury Twp., operating his father's mill on an 115-acre tract. On May 2, 1786, he purchased 71 acres 115 perches in Windsor Twp. By 1795, he had a mill and 200 acres. The mill was located on Muddy Creek. Adam is buried in Lebanon Lutheran cemetery. Adam and Anna Elizabeth had the following children:

Elizabeth$^{1.1.1.3.1.11}$, b. Feb. 28, 1772, and m. William McClorg. He d. in Ohio in May, 1831, while looking for land to settle on. Elizabeth resided in York Co. in 1831.

Anna Catherina$^{1.1.1.3.1.21}$, b. Oct. 15, 1774, bapt. at Friedensaal
   Oct. 30, 1774, sponsored by Dewaldt and Maria Catharina
   Scharer. She m. George Robb (d. in Aug., 1855), son of Peter
   Robb, and d. May 5, 1843.
Anna Christina$^{1.1.1.3.1.31}$, b. Aug. 13, 1777, bapt. at Friedensaal
   Aug. 31, 1777, m. Jacob Byer.
Eva Margaret$^{1.1.1.3.1.41}$, b. Dec. 9, 1780, bapt. at Friedensaal Jan.
   21, 1781, m. David, son of John Sherg, Jan. 14, 1813.
Johan David$^{1.1.1.3.1.51}$, b. June, 1782, d. April 18, 1783.
Anna Maria Susanna$^{1.1.1.3.1.61}$, b. Aug. 20, 1783, bapt. at
   Friedensaal Sept. 21, 1783, m. Henry, son of Andrew and Anna
   Margaret Barsinger, d. c.1818 in Windsor Twp. He was b. Oct.
   26, 1779, d. in Windsor Twp. April 26, 1849.

Eva Christina Diehl

Eva Christina$^{1.1.1.3.21}$ m. Frederick Schinleber and Martin, son of
Christopher and Philipena Kurtz. Frederick immigrated to America on
the ship *Richmond* Oct. 5, 1763, d. c.1777. He took over Charles
Diehl's mill on Deer Creek, and later Martin Kurtz took it over.
Martin was b. 1745, d. 1836. He was a teamster in the Revolutionary
War, and one of the founders of Saddler's Church. Eva Christina d. in
Shrewsbury Twp. Aug. 22, 1828. She had the following children:
   Charles$^{1.1.1.3.2.11}$, b. 1775, m. Jane, resided in Anderson Co.,
      Tennessee in 1850. She was b. 1780, and living in 1860.
   Frederick$^{1.1.1.3.2.21}$, b. 1777, and m. Christine.
   Joshua$^{1.1.1.3.2.31}$, b. c.1781, d. in Ohio.
   Johan Christopher$^{1.1.1.3.2.41}$, b. Oct. 28, 1783, bapt. at Friedensaal
      Nov. 16, 1783, m. Nancy Lowe, d. in Ohio.
   Michael$^{1.1.1.3.2.51}$, b. Sept. 10, 1786, bapt. at Friedensaal June 25,
      1786, m. Mary, d. in York Co. Nov. 11, 1870. She was b. 1800.
      They are buried in Stewartstown.
   Maria Elizabeth$^{1.1.1.3.2.61}$, b. Feb. 14, 1788, bapt. at Fissel's Aug.
      31, 1788, m. George Ebaugh, d. in Illinois. He was b. Sept. 19,
      1789, to John and Sarah (Flowers) Ebaugh. He served in the
      War of 1812, worked the mill on Deer Creek for a time, and
      then moved to Illinois.
   Christina$^{1.1.1.3.2.71}$, b. March 1, 1791, bapt. at Friedensaal Nov.
      20, 1791.
   Frederick$^{1.1.1.3.2.81}$, b. Sept. 5, 1797, bapt. at Saddler's Oct. 15,
      1797.

Elizabeth Diehl

Elizabeth$^{1.1.1.3.31}$ m. Jacob, son of Jacob and Catharina Scharer, d. in
Stark Co., Osnaburg Twp., Mapleton, Ohio in 1825. He was b. Jan. 9,
1744, d. in Stark Co. Jan. 29, 1823. Jacob worked a mill he received

from his father in Shrewsbury Twp., until c.1805, when he moved to Ohio. Jacob was a Private in Captain George Long's Sixth Battalion, during the Revolutionary War. They had the following children:

Johan Jacob$^{1.1.1.3.3.11}$, b. Jan. 27, 1775, bapt. at Friedensaal Feb. 19, 1775, m. Catherine, d. in Stark Co., Ohio in 1832. She was b. 1778, d. in 1824.

Johann Adam$^{1.1.1.3.3.21}$, b. Sept. 15, 1778, bapt. at Friedensaal Sept. 27, 1778, sponsored by Adam and Elisabeth Diehl. He m. Barbara Hart, d. Nov. 26, 1836. She was b. in Baltimore Co., Maryland June 8, 1778, d. in Ohio Aug. 21, 1866.

Maria Elizabeth$^{1.1.1.3.3.31}$, b. August, 1783, bapt. at Friedensaal Aug. 31, 1783, sponsored by Dewald and Catharina Scharer.

Catherine$^{1.1.1.3.3.41}$, b. Sept. 20, 1785, bapt. at Friedensaal Oct. 16, 1785, d. before 1793.

John$^{1.1.1.3.3.51}$, b. Jan. 8, 1787, bapt. at Friedensaal March 13, 1787, m. Elizabeth Singhouse and Elizabeth Kiefer, d. in Indiana Sept. 30, 1871. Elizabeth Singhouse was b. May, 1783, d. in Mapleton, Ohio March 1, 1815. Elizabeth Kiefer b. Feb. 28, 1799, d. Oct. 20, 1864.

Carl$^{1.1.1.3.3.61}$, b. June 23, 1789, bapt. at Friedensaal July 5, 1789.

Henry$^{1.1.1.3.3.71}$, b. Nov. 16, 1791, m. Dorothy Grim, d. in Kansas Jan. 29, 1878. She was b. Beaver Co., Pennsylvania Sept. 29, 1795, d. in Ohio Feb. 3, 1845.

Anna Catherine$^{1.1.1.3.3.81}$, b. Oct. 9, 1795, bapt. at Friedensaal Nov. 8, 1795, sponsored by Catharine Scharer. She m. George Augustine in 1817, d. in La Salle Co., Illinois.

Johan Carl Diehl

Johan Carl$^{1.1.1.3.11}$ m. Christina$^{1.2k}$, dau. of Christian and Anna Stabler, c.1777. He d. in Shrewsbury Twp. Aug. 1, 1817, and she d. there in 1811. In 1785, he received 356.11 acres from his father, and took over the family farm. He was overseer for Shrewsbury Twp. in 1780, and tax collector in 1783. Carl served in the York Co., Militia in the Revolutionary War under Captain Henry Ferree as a Private, 6th Class, and later in Captain John Ehrmans Company. They had the following children:

Johann$^{1.1.1.3.4.11}$, b. June 20, 1778, bapt. at Friedensaal Aug. 2, 1778.

Carl$^{1.1.1.3.4.21}$, b. June 11, 1779, bapt. at Friedensaal Aug. 8, 1779, sponsored by his grandfather, Carl Diehl.

Catharina$^{1.1.1.3.4.31}$, b. Dec. 6, 1780, bapt. at Friedensaal Dec. 24, 1780, sponsored by her aunt, Maria Barbara Stabler. She m. John Koller, d. May 20, 1863.

Maria Elisabetha$^{1.1.1.3.4.41}$, b. Nov. 13, 1782, bapt. at Friedensaal Nov. 30, 1782, sponsored by Jacob and Elisabeth Scharer.

Susana[1.1.1.3.4.51], b. Feb. 2, 1785, bapt. at Friedensaal April 17,
   1785, sponsored by Adam and Anna Fritz.
Johan Adam[1.1.1.3.4.61], b. Feb. 26, 1787, bapt. at Friedensaal
   March 18, 1787, sponsored by his uncle and aunt, Adam and
   Christina Stabler.
Christina[1.1.1.3.4.71], b. May 8, 1789, bapt. at Friedensaal May 31,
   1789, sponsored by her uncle and aunt, Andreas and Catharina
   Muller. She m. Adam Seitz, and was alive in 1870.
John[1.1.1.3.4.81], b. Sept. 3, 1791, bapt. at Friedensaal Oct. 10,
   1791, sponsored by his uncle and aunt, Christian and Elisabeth
   Stabler. He d. c.1818.
Magdalena[1.1.1.3.4.91], b. Dec. 5, 1793, bapt. at Friedensaal Jan. 18,
   1794, sponsored by Adam Seitz and wife.
Barbara[1.1.1.3.4.101], b. March 27, 1796, bapt. at Friedensaal in
   April, 1796, sponsored by Barbara Miller. She d. before 1817.

Carl Diehl

Carl[1.1.1.3.4.21] m. Catherine, dau. of Jacob and Catherine (Miller)
Koller, d. March 10, 1839. She d. June 24, 1865. They are buried in
Lebanon Lutheran cemetery in North Hopewell Twp. He was a miller,
and bought the family mill from his uncle, Adam, in 1823. They had
the following children in Windsor Twp.:
Christina[1.1.1.3.4.2.11], b. March 6, 1803, m. Jacob Flinchbaugh, d.
   March 1, 1841.
Jacob[1.1.1.3.4.2.21], b. April 27, 1805, m. Anna Mary Kohler, d.
   April 28, 1883.
Catherine E.[1.1.1.3.4.2.31], b. April 1, 1807, m. Frederick Grove, d.
   May 5, 1882.
Charles[1.1.1.3.4.2.41], b. Feb. 12, 1809, d. April 18, 1820.
Adam[1.1.1.3.4.2.51], b. and d. in 1813.
Julia Ann[1.1.1.3.4.2.61], b. March 22, 1825, m. Jacob Herbst, d.
   March 20, 1907.

Maria Elisabetha Diehl

Maria Elisabetha[1.1.1.3.4.41] m. Johann Georg, son of Peter and
Elisabetha (Schaffer) Kleinfelter. He was b. Sept. 26, 1779, bapt. at
Friedensaal Oct. 3, 1779, sponsored by his grandparents, Georg and
Barbara Kleinfelter. She d. Aug. 17, 1820. They had the following
children:
Elizabeth[1.1.1.1.1.2.11], b. April 16, 1803, sponsored by her
   grandmother, Elizabeth Kleinfelter.
Carl[1.1.1.1.1.2.21], b. Oct. 16, 1804, bapt. Nov. 18,1804, sponsored
   by Carl Diehl and wife. He d. in 1885.
Magdalena[1.1.1.1.1.2.31], b. Dec. 19, 1808, bapt. Jan. 14, 1809,
   sponsored by Catherine Shoffer. She d. Feb. 9, 1830.

Catherine$^{1.1.1.1.1.2.41}$, b. c.1812, m. Jesse Shaffer.
Henry$^{1.1.1.1.1.2.51}$, b. Aug. 24, 1813, bapt. Sept. 26, 1813,
   sponsored by Henry Reiman. He d. Aug. 18, 1820.
Adabina$^{1.1.1.1.1.2.61}$, b. c.1815, d. before
   1820.Samuel$^{1.1.1.1.1.2.71}$, b. April, 1818, d. Aug. 1,
   1820.Juliana$^{1.1.1.1.1.2.81}$, b. July 23, 1820, d. April 7, 1821.

Susanna Diehl

Susanna$^{1.1.3.4.51}$ m. Michael, son of Johan Heinrich and Elisabetha
Christina (Kleinfelter) Kunckel, c.1804. He was b. Feb. 12, 1784, bapt.
at Friedensaal May 2, 1784, sponsored by Michael and Justina Kunckel.
Susanna d. Dec. 1, 1814, and Michael m. Anna Catherine Sentz c.1815.
Anna Catherine was b. 1791, d. in 1870. Michael moved to Richland
Co., Ohio in 1828, d. there in 1846. Michael and Susanna had the
following children:
   Catherine$^{1.1.3.4.5.11}$, b. c.1805, d. in York Co. Feb. 1, 1897, m.
      Henry Markel.
   Susanna$^{1.1.3.4.5.21}$, b. c.1807, m. Lawrence Kerschner, and
      moved to Ohio.
   Joseph$^{1.1.3.4.5.31}$, b. March 9, 1809, d. in York Co., Pennsylvania
      Nov. 1, 1850. He m. Catherine Shaffer Feb. 2, 1832.
   Charles$^{1.1.3.4.5.41}$, b. c.1812, and moved to Richland Co., Ohio.
   Henry$^{1.1.3.4.5.51}$, b. 1814, d. in 1894.

Johan Adam Diehl

Johan Adam$^{1.1.3.4.61}$ m. Catherine, dau. of Johan Adam and
Elizabeth (Kleinfelter) Schaffer. She was b. in Shrewsbury Twp. Aug.
18, 1788, d. there May 13, 1871. Adam d. in Shrewsbury Twp. Sept.
11, 1849. They had the following children:
   Magdalena$^{1.1.3.4.6.11}$, b. Feb. 20, 1810, d. Feb. 25, 1891, and m.
      William Ehrhardt.
   Elizabeth$^{1.1.3.4.6.21}$, b. Nov. 25, 1812, d. May 25, 1888, and m.
      John Myers March 18, 1834.
   Catherine$^{1.1.3.4.6.31}$, b. Oct. 11, 1814, d. May 16, 1886, and m.
      John Dise in 1836.
   Levi$^{1.1.3.4.6.41}$, b. Sept. 30, 1816, d. March 22, 1885, and m.
      Juliana, dau. of Peter and Rosina (Ruhl) Kleinfelter.
   Charles$^{1.1.3.4.6.51}$, b. Oct. 28, 1818, d. Jan. 6, 1893, and m.
      Elizabeth Attig.
   Adam$^{1.1.3.4.6.61}$, b. Feb. 25, 1821, d. June 28, 1912, and m.
      Nancy Ann Tyson Nov. 26, 1846.
   Isaac$^{1.1.3.4.6.71}$, b. Nov. 8, 1822, d. March 7, 1899, and m.
      Rosina, dau. of Peter and Rosina (Ruhl) Kleinfelter.
   Julia$^{1.1.3.4.6.81}$, b. May 9, 1825, d. Sept. 2, 1908, and m. Henry
      Ehrhart.

Christina$^{1.1.1.3.4.6.91}$, b. June 1, 1829, d. Nov. 2, 1846.

Magdalena Diehl

Magdalena$^{1.1.1.3.4.91}$ m. John/Jacob, son of John and Christina (Gebel) Kramer, d. in Shrewsbury Twp. June 10, 1855. He was b. Dec. 9, 1787, d. in Shrewsbury Twp. March 31, 1868. They are buried in the Evangelical Lutheran cemetery of Shrewsbury. They had the following children:

Charles$^{1.1.1.3.4.9.11}$, b. March 1, 1813.

Anna Maria$^{1.1.1.3.4.9.21}$, b. Dec. 15, 1815, m. Peter Frederick March 15, 1832 and Samuel Kleinfelter, d. March 4, 1899.

Maria$^{1.1.1.3.4.9.31}$, b. May 5, 1818, m. John Nealey Hendrix, d. May 2, 1895.

Sarah Christina$^{1.1.1.3.4.9.41}$, b. June 6, 1822, and m. Henry Everding in April, 1850.

John$^{1.1.1.3.4.9.51}$, m. Elizabeth Hunt.

Lucinda$^{1.1.1.3.4.9.61}$, m. _____ Mason and Julius Kling, and resided in Williamsport, Pennsylvania.

J. Frank$^{1.1.1.3.4.9.71}$, m. Basal Breford, and resided in Annapolis, Maryland.

Anna Catharina Elisabetha Diehl

Anna Catharine$^{1.1.1.3.51}$ m. Dewalt/Theobald, son of Jacob and Catherine Scharer. They resided on the border between Shrewsbury and Hopewell Twp., and had the following children:

Johan Jacob$^{1.1.1.3.5.11}$, b. April, 1776, bapt. at Friedensaal May 19, 1776, sponsored by Jacob and Elisabeth Scharer. He m. Elizabeth, dau. of John Schrock, d. in York Twp. April 15, 1857. She was b. Dec. 25, 1777, d. June 14, 1851.

Adam$^{1.1.1.3.5.21}$, b. June 5, 1779, bapt. at Friedensaal July 4, 1779, sponsored by Adam and Elisabeth Diehl. He m. Dorothea, dau. of Jacob Olp, Nov. 29, 1810, d. in Springfield Twp. Dec. 26, 1863. She was b. April 11, 1788, d. June 23, 1865.

Eve Elisabeth$^{1.1.1.3.5.31}$, b. Feb. 19, 1784, bapt. at Friedensaal April 4, 1784, sponsored by Johan Martin and Christina Kurtz. She d. Feb. 29, 1864.

Catherine$^{1.1.1.3.5.41}$, b. June 15, 1787, and m. George Shirey. He d. in 1831.

Eva Margaretha Diehl

Eva Margaretha$^{1.1.1.41}$ m. Johan Michael, son of Hans Michael Ebert of Unter-Anfrach and York Co., Manchester Twp. He immigrated to America on the ship *Britania* Sept. 21, 1731, d. in May/June, 1785. Michael was Co. Assessor from 1767 to 1770 and tax collector in Manchester Twp. in 1775. He was Supervisor of the Highways in

1757. At the time of his death, Michael owned 780 acres in Manchester Twp. along the Codorus Creek. They had the following children in Manchester Twp.:

Johan Michael[1.1.1.4.11], b. Dec. 28, 1742, and bapt. at Christ's Lutheran Church of York Feb. 9, 1743. He m. Elizabeth, dau. of Jacob and Anna Margaret Rudisill, Aug. 8, 1764, d. c.April, 1790. She d. in May, 1791. Michael served in the Revolutionary War.

Helena[1.1.1.4.21], b. Dec. 5, 1744, bapt. at Christ's Lutheran June 10, 1745, d. before 1757.

Johan Jacob[1.1.1.4.31], b. Oct. 2, 1746, bapt. at Christ's Lutheran Oct. 4, 1746, d. before March, 1786.

Maria Elizabeth[1.1.1.4.41], b. Dec. 16, 1748, and bapt. at Christ's Lutheran Feb. 2, 1749. She m. Zachariah, son of Zachariah and Margaret Shugart. He was an innkeeper in York, served in the Committee of Correspondence Nov. 3, 1775, and was a 1st Lt. in Captain Michael Smyser's, Col. Michael Swope's Company, Flying Camp. They moved to Alexandria, Virginia between 1787 and 1790, and then moved to southwestern Virginia.

Johan Martin[1.1.1.4.51], b. Jan. 9, 1751, and bapt. at Christ's Lutheran Feb. 24, 1751. He m. Anna Maria, dau. of Mathias and Anna Catharina (Koppenhoffer) Smyser, d. in West Manchester Twp. in May, 1814. She was b. Nov. 10, 1756, d. March 29, 1833. Martin served in the Revolutionary War.

Maria Margaret[1.1.1.4.61], b. June 21, 1753, and bapt. at Christ's Lutheran July 22, 1753. She m. Martin, son of Peter and Elisabetha (Kramer) Gaertner, d. in Hellam Twp. April 14, 1824. He was b. June 21, 1744, d. march 30, 1818.

Philip Adam[1.1.1.4.71], b. July 2, 1755, and bapt. at Christ's Lutheran Sept. 2, 1755. He m. Susanna, dau. of Mathias and Anna Catharina (Koppenhoffer) Smyser, d. in St. Louis, Missouri Dec. 6, 1803. She was b. March 31, 1760, d. April 2, 1840. Philip served in the Revolutionary War, and was a merchant in St. Louis.

Helena[1.1.1.4.81], b. May 20, 1757.

Daniel[1.1.1.4.91], b. June 25, 1759, bapt. at Christ's Lutheran July 29, 1759, d. before March, 1786.

Johannes[1.1.1.4.101], b. June 26, 1761, and bapt. at Christ's Lutheran June 28, 1761. He m. Elizabeth, probably a dau. of Col. Michael and Anna Maria (Hoke) Smyser, and Anna Weyle Aug. 22, 1805, d. in Huron Co., Norwalk, Ohio July 14, 1835. Elizabeth was b. c.1766, d. in Dauphin Co., Harrisburg, Pennsylvania Feb. 19, 1803. Anna was b. Feb. 13, 1780, d. April 11, 1806. Johannes moved to Ohio in 1820.

Adam$^{1.1.1.4.111}$, b. Sept. 15, 1763, and bapt. at Christ's Lutheran Oct. 10, 1763. He m. Clarissa, dau. of Peter and Dorothy (Smyser) Hoke, d. in York Co., Pennsylvania c.Sept., 1808. She was b. 1767, d. April 13, 1838.

Angelica Elisabetha Diehl

Angelica Elisabetha$^{1.1.1.51}$ m. Johan Valentine, son of Johannes Verdriess, c.August, 1742. He was b. in Fussengonheim in the Palatinate, and was residing in Frederick Co., Maryland in 1779. Angelica was alive in 1772. Valentine received a land grant in Frederick Co., Monocacy, Maryland in 1743, and settled on Little Hunting Creek. He was naturalized in Maryland in Oct., 1743. They had the following children:

Maria Catrina$^{1.1.1.5.11}$, b. May 6, 1743, and baptized at Monocacy Lutheran Church.

Johannes$^{1.1.1.5.21}$, b. March 11, 1744, bapt. at Monocacy, and was residing in Greenbriar Co., Virginia in 1790. He m. Maria Catharina, dau. of Jacob Zither, in Frederick Maryland in 1772.

Maria Magdalena$^{1.1.1.5.31}$, b. Jan., 1747, bapt. at Monocacy, and appears as a sponsor to a baptism of a child of Peter Diehl in Lancaster Co., Pennsylvania in 1767.

Valentine$^{1.1.1.5.41}$, b. c.1750.

Nicholas Diehl

Nicholas$^{1.1.1.61}$ m. Maria Catherina, dau. of Johan Nicholas and Anna Barbara (Burkhart) Hantz, d. in York Twp. in May, 1790. She was b. in Sponheim, Germany Feb. 3, 1734, d. in York in Oct., 1817. Nicholas worked for his father in the milling business, and received 230 acres and instructions to continue operating the mill with his brother Peter, when his father d. On Oct. 8, 1767, he received a warrant in York Twp., adjoining the land he received from his father in all consisting of 260 acres and 27 perches which he named *Diehlsburg*. He was overseer of the poor in 1757, tax assessor for York Twp. in 1769, and was Vestryman at Christ's Lutheran Church of York. In 1783, he had 245 acres, one horse and 2 horned cattle. Nicholas and Maria Catharina had a son Peter$^{1.1.1.6.11}$, b. Feb. 23, 1760, bapt. at Christ's Lutheran Church of York March 2, 1760, d. young.

Peter Diehl

Peter$^{1.1.1.71}$ m. Anna Maria Margaretha, dau. of Johan Nicholas and Anna Barbara (Burkhart) Hantz. She was b. in Sponheim Sept. 5, 1737, d. before Jan., 1801. Peter d. in York Twp. in Dec., 1812. When his father d., Peter received 130 acres and the mill property. On June 18, 1765, Peter had 160 acres and 94 perches surveyed. Peter and his brother, Nicholas, ran their father's farm and mill until 1762, when

Peter sold the mill property to Casper Weaver who sold it the same day to Mathias Sitler. On Sept. 14, 1762, Peter purchased 96.5 acres in Lancaster Co., Donegal Twp., and remained there until Feb. 5, 1771, when he purchased a mill property and 248 acres in Shrewsbury Twp. from his brother, Carl. He also purchased 72 acres and 90 perches in Hopewell Twp. Peter and Maria Margaretha had the following children:

Johan Peter[1.1.1.7.11], b. Aug. 8, 1761, m. Susanna, dau. of George Krantz, and Catherine, dau. of Casper Diller June 18, 1809. Susanna was b. Aug. 14, 1769, d. Aug. 9, 1806. Peter served in the Revolutionary War as a Private in the Fifth Class, Captain Frey's Company from 1777-1780. He served in Captain Peter Ford's Company from 1782 to 1783. He worked with his father in the mill business and 1801, he purchased a tract on the Little Conewago at the Ox Head Inn. He d. in Adams Co. Aug. 1, 1839.

Nicholas[1.1.1.7.21], b. Feb. 4, 1765, bapt. at the First Reformed Congregation of Lancaster Feb. 28, 1765, sponsored by Nicholas and Maria Catharina Diehl. He m. Elizabeth, dau. of George and Anna Maria (Holtsinger) Bentz, d. in York Twp. Oct. 11, 1847. She was b. 1767, d. Jan. 14, 1818. He was a Private in Captain Godfrey's Company in the Revolutionary War from 1777 to 1780. He was a farmer in York Twp., and later purchased lots in Freytown with his brother, Jacob. He was Director of the Poor for York Twp. from 1831 to 1834.

Johan Adam[1.1.1.7.31], b. Feb. 26, 1767, bapt. at Maytown Lutheran Church April 17, 1767, sponsored by Andreas Arntz and Catharina and Mage. Verdruss, d. young.

Jacob[1.1.1.7.41], b. March 25, 1769, bapt. at Maytown Lutheran Church March 30, 1769, sponsored by Jacob and Elizabeth Kinter. He m. Anna Maria, dau. of Jacob Pflieger, April 13, 1797, d. in York Twp. June 3, 1854. He was Director of the Poor in York Twp. from 1826 to 1829. He purchased lots in Freystown with his brother Nicholas. He inherited the mill property and Adjoining land from his father.

Elizabeth[1.1.1.7.51], b. Nov. 26, 1771, m. Henry, son of Philip Jacob and Maria Catherina (Ziegler) King, d. in York Co. in Dec., 1812.

George[1.1.1.7.61], b. Feb. 3, 1774, bapt. at Christ's Lutheran Church of York May 8, 1774, d. young.

Catherine[1.1.1.7.71], b. June 26, 1776, bapt. at Christ's Lutheran Church of York Sept. 1, 1776, m. John Brillinger, d. Jan. 24, 1846. He was b. Feb. 5, 1772, d. April 5, 1820. They had 50 acres in Spring Garden Twp., a mill property consisting of 160 acres in Manchester Twp., 400 acres in Windsor Twp., 50 acres

in Hellam Twp., and 2 lots in New Holland. He was one of the
original directors of the York National Bank.

Daniel[1.1.1.7.81], b. June 11, 1779, bapt. at Christ's Lutheran
Church of York Aug. 8, 1779, m. Barbara, dau. of Jacob and
Barbara (Kohr) Stoehr, d. March 10, 1824. She was b. Feb. 1,
1786, d. Feb. 2, 1871. He inherited 44 acres and 77 perches
from his father, which he sold to purchase land in Newberry
Twp. (200 acres) and Conewago/Newberry Twp. (115 acres and
a mill).

Johan Georg Diehl

Georg[1.1.1.81] m. Christina, dau. of Heinrich and Susanna (Miller)
Spengler, May 30, 1758, and Maria Magdalena Kohler. Christina d. in
York Co. c.1782/83. While in York Co., he resided in Dover Twp., and
his children were bapt. at Strayer's. He was naturalized April 1, 1765.
He served in the Revolutionary War as a Private in Captain Godfrey
Frey's Company, Third Battalion. He moved to Botetourt Co., Virginia
in the fall of 1787. He had the following children:

Susanna[1.1.1.8.11], b. c.1759, m. Charles, son of Philip Casper and
Margaret Spengler, d. in Botetourt Co. c.1803/4. He was b.
1746, d. Sept. 16, 1833. Charles was a Private in Captain
Philip Albright's Company, and later an Ensign in the Fourth
Company, First Battalion during the Revolutionary War. On
April 9, 1790 he purchased 150 acres the North Side of the
James River in Botetourt Co. He was a blacksmith.

Johan Adam[1.1.1.8.21], b. Jan. 28, 1763, d. c.1783.

Eva Margaretha[1.1.1.8.31], b. June 28, 1765, bapt. Aug. 18, 1765,
sponsored by Michael and Eva Margaretha Ebert, d. c.1783.

Nicholas[1.1.1.8.41], b. c.1768, d. c.1810.

Johan Georg[1.1.1.8.51], b. Nov. 17, 1770, bapt. May 13, 1770,
sponsored by George, Susanna and Henrich Spengler, d.
c.1783.

Magdalena[1.1.1.8.61], b. Feb. 23, 1774, bapt. at Christ's Lutheran
Church of York April 3, 1774, and m. John Hinderleiter, d. in
Botetourt Co., Virginia. He was b. in Berks Co., Pennsylvania,
d. in Botetourt Co. in 1844. He had land on Catawba Creek.

Peter[1.1.1.8.71], b. Oct. 12, 1776, bapt. at Christ's Lutheran Church
of York Dec. 25, 1776, and m. Catherine, d. in Botetourt Co. in
Feb., 1827. She d. c.Sept., 1843. He inherited land on
Looney's Mill Creek (purchased by his father in 1791) from his
father.

Johan Adam Diehl

Adam[1.1.1.91] m. Maria Magdalena, dau. of Paul and Anna Eva
(Schwab) Burkhart, June 17, 1760. She was b. Oct. 13, 1740. Adam

was residing in York Co. in 1796. He worked in his father's mill with his brother's Peter, and Nicholas after his father's death. He was naturalized Aug. 23, 1764. He was an elder of Strayer's Church in 1767, and Supervisor of the Highways in 1775. He served in the York Co. Militia under Captain Adam Schaffer's Company, and Captain Christian Coffman's Company from 1777-79. He resided in Dover Twp., and purchased 80 acres Feb. 19, 1773. He probably went to live with one of his children, and it is uncertain which Twp. he d. in. Adam and Maria Magdalena had the following children:

Anna Maria[1.1.1.9.11], b. June 9, 1763, bapt. at Strayer's July 24, 1763, sponsored by Michael Eberth and Anna Maria Eckert. She was living in Dec. 25, 1778.

Christina[1.1.1.9.21], b. Sept. 28, 1765, bapt. at Strayer's Oct. 19, 1765, sponsored by Johan Georg and Christina Diehl.

Johan Nicholas[1.1.1.9.31], b. 1766, m. Mary (1776- after 1850), and resided in York Co., Spring Garden Twp. in 1850. He had land in Manchester Twp. for a time.

Johan Adam[1.1.1.9.41], b. June 18, 1769, bapt. at Strayer's Aug. 6, 1769, sponsored by Vendel Gross and Anna Margareth Burckert.

Johan Peter[1.1.1.9.51], b. Jan. 19, 1772, bapt. at Strayer's April 5, 1772, sponsored by Peter and Barbara Weinbrenner, d. Jan. 22, 1775.

Maria Catharina[1.1.1.9.61], b. Aug. 25, 1774, bapt. Sept. 24, 1774, sponsored by Vendel and Margaretha Gross.

Peter[1.1.1.9.71], b. Nov. 3, 1776, bapt. at Strayer's Dec. 1, 1776, sponsored by Peter Diehl.

****

Johannes Hildebrand

Johannes[1m] was b. in Switzerland in 1715 to Hans Jacob, d. in York Co., Shrewsbury Twp., Pennsylvania April 2, 1782. He m. Anna Barbara, dau. of Hans Peter and Salomea (Berg) Glatfelter. Anna Barbara was b. in Switzerland in 1729, d. Aug. 18, 1794.

Hans Peter was b. 1700 to Felix (March 7, 1669-August 23, 1724(42)) and Barbara (Glorius) Glatfelter, d. in York Co., Pennsylvania in 1743. Felix was the son of Felix Glatfelter (Oct. 21, 1632-Jan. 1, 1709) and Barbara (d. July 22, 1694).

Johannes and Anna Barbara had the following children in York Co., Shrewsbury Twp., Pennsylvania:

Felix[1.1m], b. Nov. 14, 1749, bapt. by Reverend Jacob Lischy May 13, 1750, sponsored by Felix and Elisabeth Glatfelder.

Dorothea[1.2m], bapt. by Reverend Jacob Lischy June 21, 1751, sponsored by Heinrich and Dorethea Walther. She m. Jacob Swartz[1.3a].

Catharina[1.3m], bapt. by Reverend Jacob Lischy Dec. 22, 1751,
sponsored by Johan Michel and Catharina Knotel.

Johan Jacob[1.4m], bapt. by Reverend Jacob Lischy Nov. 12, 1752,
sponsored by Jacob and Elisabeth Rein.

Casper[1.5m], bapt. by Reverend Jacob Lischy April 13, 1755,
sponsored by Casper and Anna Maria Glatfelter.

Heinrich[1.6m], bapt. by Reverend Jacob Lischy May 8, 1757,
sponsored by Heinrich and Dorothea Walther.

Anna Maria[1.7m], bapt. by Reverend Jacob Lischy Sept. 14, 1760,
sponsored by Casper and Anna Maria Glatfelter.

Sarah[1.8m], b. c.1762.

Anna Barbara[1.9m], b. Sept. 29, 1766, bapt. at Friedensaal Oct. 19,
1766, sponsored by Conrad and Dorothea Swartz.

Maria Margaretha[1.10m], b. c.1769, bapt. at Friedensaal between
Dec., 1768 and July, 1769, sponsored by Michael and Margaret
Geisselman.

Felix Hildebrand

Felix[1.1m] m. Maria Elisabeth[1.1.1.5.1c], dau. of Johann Philipp and
Anna Gertrude (Schneider) Simon, c.1772. He d. in Shrewsbury Twp.
March 26, 1820. She d. in Shrewsbury Twp. Oct. 31, 1820, buried in
Strine cemetery, beside her husband. They had the following children
in Shrewsbury Twp.:

Anna Elisabeth[1.1.1.5.1.1c], b. Nov. 20, 1774, bapt. at Friedensaal
Dec. 25, 1774, sponsored by her grandparents, Johannes and
Anna Barbara Hildebrand.

Eva[1.1.1.5.1.2c], b. Oct. 28, 1778, bapt. at Friedensaal Nov. 8, 1778,
sponsored by Thomas and Rosina Ehrhardt.

Anna Dorothea[1.1.1.5.1.3c], b. Oct. 30, 1780, bapt. at Friedensaal
Nov. 26, 1780, sponsored by her uncle and aunt, Jacob and
Dorothea Swartz.

Johann Jacob[1.1.1.5.1.4c], b. Aug. 8, 1782, bapt. at Friedensaal Aug.
26, 1782, sponsored by Philip and Barbara Schaffer.

Johan Henrich[1.1.1.5.1.5c], b. April 8, 1787, bapt. at St. Peter's
(Yellow) Church May 19, 1787, sponsored by Conrad and
Dorothea Swartz.

Anna Maria[1.1.1.5.1.6c], b. March 12, 1789, bapt. at St. Peter's
(Yellow) Church May 9, 1789, sponsored by Johann and Anna
Maria Sheurer.

Johan Jacob Hildebrand

Johan Jacob[1.4m] m. Maria Elisabeth, and had the following children in
Shrewsbury Twp.:

Elisabeth[1.4.1m], b. Oct., 1777, bapt. at Friedensaal Nov. 23, 1777,
sponsored by Felix and Elisabeth Hildebrand.

Maria Eva$^{1.4.2m}$, b. Oct. 23, 1779, bapt. at Friedensaal Dec. 9, 1779, sponsored by Michael and Dorothea Zech.

Anna Elisabeth$^{1.4.3m}$, b. Nov. 12, 1782, bapt. at Friedensaal, sponsored by Jacob and Dorothea Swartz.

Johannes$^{1.4.4m}$, b. Jan. 8, 1789, bapt. at St. Peter's (Yellow) Church Feb. 14, 1789, sponsored by Johannes and Susanna Hildebrand.

Mary Magdalene$^{1.4.5m}$, b. May 6, 1794, bapt. at St. Peter's, sponsored by Magtalena Raberin.

Casper Hildebrand

Casper$^{1.5m}$ m. Barbara Cramer at the First Reformed Church of York June 3, 1783. They had the following children in Shrewsbury Twp.:

Eva$^{1.5.1m}$, b. June 21, 1784, bapt. at St. Peter's (Yellow) Church Sept. 6, 1784, sponsored by Anna Maria Hildebrandin.

Johannes$^{1.5.2m}$, b. Oct. 5, 1786, bapt. at St. Peter's (Yellow) Church Nov. 19, 1786, sponsored by Jacob and Dorothea Swartz.

Daniel$^{1.5.3m}$, b. Oct. 31, 1788, bapt. at St. Peter's (Yellow) Church Dec. 11, 1788, sponsored by Henrich and Margaret Glatfelter.

Petrus$^{1.5.4m}$, b. Oct. 1, 1790, bapt. at St. Peter's (Yellow) Church, sponsored by Johan and Barbara Schmit.

Johan Heinrich$^{1.5.5m}$, b. April 7, 1793, bapt. at St. Peter's (Yellow) Church, sponsored by Henrich and Magtalena Hildebrand.

Fredrich$^{1.5.6m}$, b. Jan. 21, 1796, and bapt. at St. Peter's (Yellow) Church.

Casper$^{1.5.7m}$, b. April 14, 1798, bapt. at St. Peter's (Yellow) Church, sponsored by Felix Hildebrand and wife.

Heinrich Hildebrand

Heinrich$^{1.6m}$ m. Magdalene Kraut at the First Reformed Church of York Nov. 14, 1787. They had the following children in Shrewsbury Twp.:

Johannes$^{1.6.1m}$, b. April 30, 1788, bapt. at St. Peter's (Yellow) Church May 7, 1788, sponsored by Jacob and Dorothea Swartz.

Catharina$^{1.6.2m}$, b. Oct. 11, 1789, bapt. at St. Peter's (Yellow) Church Jan. 12, 1790, sponsored by Michael and Anna Maria Glatfelter.

Michael$^{1.6.3m}$, b. July 27, 1791, bapt. at St. Peter's (Yellow) Church Sept. 20, 1791, sponsored by Johannes and Susanna Hildebrand.

Susanna$^{1.6.4m}$, b. April 10, 1793, bapt. at St. Peter's (Yellow) Church, sponsored by Johannes and Susanna Hildebrand.

Michael$^{1.6.5m}$, b. March 9, 1795, bapt. at St. Peter's (Yellow) Church April 12, 1795, sponsored by Michael and Elizabeth Graut.

Jacob$^{1.6.6m}$, b. Aug. 29, 1796, bapt. at St. Peter's (Yellow) Church,

sponsored by Casper Hildebrand and wife.
Margaretha Magtalena$^{1.6.7m}$, b. May 21, 1799, bapt. at St. Peter's (Yellow) Church, sponsored by Magtalena Bender.

Anna Maria Hildebrand

Anna Maria$^{1.7m}$ m. John Cheyry/Scheure/Scheiry in the First Reformed Church of York March 29, 1785, and had the following children in Shrewsbury Twp.:
  Maria Eva$^{1.7.1m}$, b. Aug. 10, 1788, bapt. at St. Peter's (Yellow) Church Aug. 30, 1788, sponsored by Felix and Elisabeth Hildebrand.
  Dorothea$^{1.7.2m}$, b. Nov. 25, 1789, bapt. at St. Peter's (Yellow) Church June 12, 1790, sponsored by Jacob and Dorothea Swartz.
  Wilhelm$^{1.7.3m}$, b. Sept. 23, 1791, bapt. at St. Peter's (Yellow) Church, sponsored by Peter and Elisabeth Kleinfelter.
  Christina$^{1.7.4m}$, b. July 24, 1793, bapt. at St.Peter's (Yellow) Church, sponsored by Elisabeth Hildebrand.
  Ana Maria$^{1.7.5m}$, b. July 24, 1795, bapt. at St. Peter's (Yellow) Church, sponsored by Casper and Barbara Hildebrand.

Sarah Hildebrand

Sarah$^{1.8m}$ m. John Hartman at the First Reformed Church of York Jan. 21, 1783, and had the following children in Shrewsbury Twp.: Catherine$^{1.8.1m}$, b. July 22, 1787, bapt. at Friedensaal on the 7th Sunday after Trinity, sponsored by John and Anna Maria Sheiry.
Johan Hennrich$^{1.8.2m}$, b. Aug. 15, 1791, bapt. at St. Peter's (Yellow) Church, sponsored by Hennerich and Magtalena Hildebrand.

Anna Barbara Hildebrand

Anna Barbara$^{1.9m}$ m. Ludwig Hartman at the First Reformed Church of York in August/Sept., 1787, and had the following dau. in Shrewsbury Twp.: Barbara$^{1.9.1m}$, b. Feb. 12, 1792, bapt. at St. Peter's (Yellow) Church, sponsored by Jacob and Filbina Dippel.
****

Johannes Abraham Baehli

Johannes Abraham^{1h} m. Anna Maria. He was residing in Berks Co., Albany Twp., Pennsylvania in 1754. His religion is unknown prior to his immigration to America, since most of his children underwent adult Lutheran baptisms in Berks Co. He was probably of Swiss descent, since that name is prevalent there. Johannes and Anna Maria disappear from the records of Berks Co. after the baptism of their son Abraham in 1763. Johannes and Anna Maria were the parents of the following children: Annastass$^{1.1h}$, b. c.1728, and bapt. by Reverend

Daniel Schumacher on Jan. 28, 1755; Frantz$^{1.2h}$, b. 1730; Daniel$^{1.3h}$, b. c.1732; Jacob$^{1.4h}$, b. Sept. 1, 1734; Peter$^{1.5h}$, b. c.1738; Johan Nickel$^{1.6h}$, b. c.1740; Johann Abraham$^{1.7h}$, b. 1742; Carl Ludwig$^{1.8h}$, b. c.1744.

Frantz Baehli

Frantz$^{1.2h}$ was bapt. by Reverend Daniel Schumacher on May 25, 1755, m. Christina about 1752. Frantz d. Albany Twp. in March, 1805. Frantz and Christina had the following children in Albany Twp.:

Johan Andreas$^{1.2.1h}$, b. 1753, bapt. by Reverend Daniel Schumacher on May 25, 1755, sponsored by Andreas and Maria Margaretha Hagenbuch.

Johan Martin$^{1.2.2h}$, b. 1754, bapt. by Reverend Daniel Schumacher on May 25, 1755, sponsored by Andreas and Maria Margaretha Hagenbuch.

Maria Magdalena$^{1.2.3h}$, b. May 12, 1756, bapt. by Reverend Daniel Schumacher on June 24, 1756, sponsored by Reverend Daniel Schumacher and Magdalena Stebelton.

Johan Daniel$^{1.2.4h}$, b. April 17, 1758, bapt. at Allemangel Lutheran Church on April 17, 1760, and sponsored by his uncle and aunt, Daniel and Rosina Baehli. He m. Elisabeth, who was b. 1763.

Johannes$^{1.2.5h}$, bapt. March 12, 1764 at Zion Lutheran Church.

Christina Barbara$^{1.2.6h}$, b. May 23, 1766, bapt. at Allemangel Lutheran Church on Sept. 21, 1766, sponsored by Tobias and Barbara Stebelton.

Daniel Baehli

Daniel$^{1.3h}$ m. Anna Rosina (Hoell). He resided in Berks Co., Windsor Twp., Pennsylvania in the 1750s and early 1760s. About 1765, Daniel and his brother, Jacob moved to York Co., Shrewsbury Twp., Pennsylvania. In the period, 1779-1783, Daniel possessed 100 acres, two horses and a few cattle. Anna Rosina's maiden name was probably Hoell because Daniel and Rosina appeared as sponsors on numerous baptisms of the Hoell family at Zion's Moselem Church in Richmond Twp. Daniel d. in Shrewsbury Twp. Jan. 1811, and Anna Rosina in May 1815. Daniel's will was written on June 5, 1798, and probated by Rosina Baehli and Henry Ruhl on Jan. 21, 1811. Rosina's will was written on March 28, 1815, and probated on May 2, 1815 by Henry Ruhl and George Frederick. The beneficiaries of Rosina's estate were Jacob Baehli, Henry Baker, Lydia Baker, Rosina Baker, and Henry Ruhl.

Jacob Baehli

Jacob$^{1.4h}$ was bapt. by Reverend Daniel Schumacher on Oct. 29, 1755, sponsored by Anthony and Elisabeth Pettersheimer. He was on the

tax lists of Albany Twp. in 1754, 1758, and 1759. In 1758, he is listed as poor. He m. Anna Maria, had one dau., and m. Eva Elisabetha, dau. of Hans Peter and Eva Elisabetha (Kunckel) Kleinfelter, in Berks Co., Pennsylvania c.1759/60. Eva was b. in Florsbach, Hessen, Germany in 1732, m. Johan Gottleib Volck about 1754. Gottleib d. in Berks Co., Ruscombe Manner Twp. in 1759. Gottleib and Eva Elisabetha had a dau. in Ruscombe Manner Twp., Elisabetha[1.1.3.11], b. July 22, 1755, bapt. at Mertz Church in Rockland Twp. on Aug. 31, 1755, and sponsored by Michael and Elizabeth Homan. She was mentioned in her stepfather, Jacob Baehli's, will in 1812, as Elizabeth Folk.
Jacob moved to York Co., Shrewsbury Twp., Pennsylvania with his brother Daniel in 1765. Jacob was a weaver and yeoman. In 1779, he had 70 acres, two horses, and one head of cattle; in 1780 and 1781, 100 acres, two horses, and three cattle; in 1782, he had 50 acres, two horses, and three cattle; and in 1783, 100 acres with four inhabitants in the household. During the Revolutionary War, Jacob served as a Private in the York Co. Militia, Captain John Ehrman's Company in 1776 and 1778. Eva Elisabetha d. in Shrewsbury Twp. on June 24, 1809, and Jacob on Aug. 1, 1812. They are buried in Fissel's cemetery. Jacob was the father of the following children: Anna Catharina[1.4.1h], b. Feb. 12, 1758; Jacob[1.4.2h], b. c.1760; George[1.4.3h], b. Dec. 13, 1762; Margaretha Barbara[1.4.4h], b. July 23, 1764; Anna Barbara[1.4.5h], b. April 17, 1766; Anna Rosina[1.4.6h], b. March 27, 1769; Susanna[1.4.7h], b. c.1771; Johannes[1.4.8h], b. c.1773.

Anna Catharina Baehli
Anna Catharina[1.4.1h] was bapt. by Reverend Daniel Schumacher on April 2, 1758, and sponsored by Conrad Bielmann and Catherina Grimmen. It has not been confirmed, but she probably married Michael, son of Adam and Catharina Roser. Michael was a Private in the Sixth Company, Seventh Battalion in 1778-80, and the Eighth Company, Fifth Battalion as a Corporal 1782-83 during the Revolutionary War. He had a land draft called Roseborough, consisting of 27 and 3/4 acres in Shrewsbury Twp., on the Maryland line on Oct. 29, 1786. In 1783, he resided in Codorus Twp. He was later resided in Baltimore Co., Maryland. Michael and Catharina had the following children:

Catharina[1.4.1.1h], b. April 4, 1782, bapt. at Fissel's on May 18, 1782, and sponsored by her grandparents, Adam and Anna Catherina Roser.
Elisabetha[1.4.1.2h], b. March 8, 1785, bapt. at Fissel's on May 1, 1785, and sponsored by Jacob and Susanna Baehli.
Eva[1.4.1.3h], b. Dec. 10, 1791, bapt. at Fissel's, and sponsored by Georg Baehli and wife.

Anna Rosina[1.4.1.4h], b. Jan. 20, 1793, bapt. at Fissel's, and sponsored by Daniel and Rosina Baehli.

Jacob Baehli

Jacob[1.4.2h] m. Susanna about 1784. Jacob resided in Codorus Twp. with 10 acres, a horse and one or two cattle during the period, 1779-1783. Jacob moved to Lycoming Co., Elmsport, Pennsylvania between 1812 and 1817, where Susanna d. sometime before 1817, and Jacob d. 1829. after Susanna's death, Jacob m. Elizabeth Conrad, widow of Michael Fisher. Michael d. 1799. Elizabeth was b. 1760. Jacob and Susanna were the parents of the following children, b. in Codorus Twp.:

Anna Eva[1.4.2.1h], b. Sept. 7, 1784, bapt. at Fissel's on Sept. 14, 1784, and sponsored by her uncle and aunt, Henry and Margaretha Ruhl. She m. George Markel at Christ Lutheran Church of York on Feb. 22, 1803 (this may have been her cousin, Eva).

Jacob[1.4.2.2h], b. April, 1787.

Elisabeta[1.4.2.3h], b. May 7, 1788, bapt. at Fissel's on May 23, 1788, and sponsored by Wentel and Elisabetha Heuss.

Anna Barbara[1.4.2.4h], b. Jan. 3, 1790, bapt. at Fissel's in 1790, sponsored by her uncle and aunt, Bernhard Hamsher and wife.

Catherina[1.4.2.5h], b. c.1792, m. Johannes (b. 25 Aug. 1792), son of Michael and Elizabeth (Conrad) Fisher.

Johannes[1.4.2.6h], b. Aug. 7, 1794, bapt. at Fissel's, and sponsored by his great uncle and aunt, Daniel and Rosina Baehli.

Susanna[1.4.2.7h], b. May 22, 1796, bapt. at Fissel's, sponsored by Jacob and Susanna Kerchner.

Lulisabini[1.4.2.8h], b. Aug. 31, 1798, bapt. at Fissel's, and sponsored by Hannes and Lulisabini Groh.

Jacob Baehli

Jacob[1.4.2.2h] m. Christina, dau. of Michael and Elizabeth (Conrad) Fisher, of Carroll Co., Bachman's Valley, Maryland, d. on Sept. 28, 1846. She was born on March 30, 1794, d. on June 30, 1876. They had the following children: David[1.4.2.2.1h]; Sarah[1.4.2.2.2h]; Jacob[1.4.2.2.3h]; Christina[1.4.2.2.4h], m. William Trump; John[1.4.2.2.5h], m. Elizabeth; Susanna[1.4.2.2.6h], m. Charles Myhart; Eleanora[1.4.2.2.7h], m. Benjamin Smith; Elizabeth[1.4.2.2.8h], m. Moses Allen; Henry[1.4.2.2.9h]; George[1.4.2.2.10h], m. Ellen Trump; Leah[1.4.2.2.11h]; Rebecca[1.4.2.2.12h], m. Adam Benner.

George Baehli

George[1.4.3h] m. Margaretha dau. of Peter and Anna Margaretha (Rudolph) Gerberich, and an unknown woman sometime after 1802.

During the period, 1779-1781, George had 100 acres, two horses, and some cattle in Shrewsbury Twp. George was a Private in the Revolutionary War. He was drafted into the York Co., Militia in July, 1776, and served in Captain Long's Company and Col. Swope's Battalion for three months. He marched from York to Lancaster, and then to Philadelphia, Trenton, and Brunswick. He then marched to Amboy, and Newark, and was discharged Oct. 1776. He was drafted again in the fall of 1782, and served in Captain Furry's Company under Major Austin. He was assigned to guard (at Camp Security, York) British prisoners taken with Cornwallis for three months. He applied for pension in Jan., 1834. George d. Codorus Twp. on Nov. 24 (23), 1843. George resided with Henry Baehli in later years. George and Margaretha had the following children, in Shrewsbury Twp.:
Peter[1.4.3.1h], b. c.1782; Elisabeth[1.4.3.2h], b. c.1783, m. Jacob Kerchner; John[1.4.3.3h], b. c.1785; Jacob[1.4.3.4h], b. c.1787; Eve[1.4.3.5h], b. c.1789; Margaret[1.4.3.6h], b. c.1790; possibly Henry[1.4.3.7h], b. 1808 (this speculation is based on the fact that George was residing with him before his death).

Peter Baehli
Peter[1.4.3.1h] m. Christina, and had the following children: Catharina[1.4.3.1.1h], bapt. at St. Jacob's Lutheran Church in York Co. on April 30, 1803; Petrus[1.4.3.1.2h], bapt. at St. Jacob's on Aug. 8, 1819.

Henry Baehli
Henry[1.4.3.7h] m. Mary, dau. of Christian and Susanna (Lau) Rohrbaugh, d. Shrewsbury Twp. on Jan. 20, 1892. She was born on Dec. 1, 1816, d. Shrewsbury Twp. April 26, 1857. They had the following children: Jesse R.[1.4.3.7.1h], b. Jan. 5, 1836, m. Sarah Brenneman; Jacob R.[1.4.3.7.2h], b. May 15, 1839, m. Sarah Markel, d. Codorus Twp. on Oct. 10, 1911; Samuel R.[1.4.3.7.3h], b. March 23, 1841, m. Christina (Dec. 28, 1848 - April 10, 1913), dau. of George B., and Nancy (Brenneman) Merckel, Aug. 4, 1864, d. York Co. Aug. 13, 1910, buried in Zion Church cemetery; Mary Ann R.[1.4.3.7.4h], b. 1843, d. Nov. 7, 1920, buried in Fissel's cemetery; John R.[1.4.3.7.5h], b. July 4, 1847, d. March 3, 1878, buried in Fissel's cemetery; Sarah[1.4.3.7.6h], b. 1849; Henry R.[1.4.3.7.7h], b. March 12, 1853, d. Nov. 13, 1926, buried in Fissel's cemetery; Levi R.[1.4.3.7.8h], b. March 12, 1856, m. Ellen C., d. on July 12, 1918, buried at St. Jacob's.

Margaretha Barbara Baehli
Margaretha Barbara[1.4.4h] m. Heinrich, son of Frederick and Maria Elisabetha (Bahn) Ruhl. He was bapt. at Christ Lutheran Church of York Feb., 13, 1763, and sponsored by his grandparents, Henry and

Eva Bahn. Heinrich m. Margaretha Barbara, dau. of Jacob and Eva Elisabetha (Kleinfelter) Baehli, at the First Reformed Lutheran Church of York Sept. 24, 1782. Margaretha was born July 23, 1764, bapt. Albany Twp., Berks Co., Pennsylvania, at the Allemangel Lutheran Church on Sept. 2, 1764, and sponsored by Andreas Kunckell and Margaretha Barbara Probst. Henry owned 100 acres in Shrewsbury Twp. in 1783. He received Pleasant Ridge from his father in 1802, which he in turn deeded to his son, Johannes[1.4.4.2h], on Jan. 26, 1811, along with the tract of 2Q,299 supra, which was patented to Henry on June 25, 1810. In 1828, he and his sister-in-law, Rosina (Baehli) Ruhl's, family moved to Ohio. Henry settled in Sandusky Twp., Richland Co., where he d. between Jan. 5, and March 9, 1830. Margaret d. sometime after Jan., 1830. They were the parents of the following children, who were b. Shrewsbury Twp.:

> Johan Jacob[1.4.4.1h], b. Aug. 21, 1783, bapt. at Fissel's on Sept. 14, 1783, and sponsored by his grandparents Jacob and Elisabeth Baehli. Johan Jacob d. sometime before 1797.
>
> Johannes[1.4.4.2h], b. Nov. 18, 1785.
>
> Elisabetha[1.4.4.3h], b. Jan. 9, 1788, m. Johannes Gerberich.
>
> Henrich[1.4.4.4h], b. Aug. 10, 1792, bapt. at Fissel's about 1792, and sponsored by his uncle and aunt, Johannes Baehli and wife. He d. Shrewsbury Twp. on Dec. 28, 1815, buried in Lischy's Reformed Church cemetery.
>
> Michael[1.4.4.5h], b. 1795.
>
> Jacob[1.4.4.6h], b. Jan. 7, 1797.
>
> Eva[1.4.4.7h], b. July 17, 1800.
>
> Susanna[1.4.4.8h], b. c.1802.
>
> Mary[1.4.4.9h], b. May 4, 1804, m. Georg Ruhl[1.4.6.8h].
>
> Lydia[1.4.4.10h], b. c.1806. She was unmarried in 1830, and received "one-third of land on middle one-third half section cut off North end by an east-west line, two cows, bureau, bed, two iron pots" from her father's will. She may have been the Lydia Ruhl, b. 1810, residing in Shrewsbury Twp., York Co., Pennsylvania with Ese Geisey and Jacob and Christian Smith in 1850.

Johannes Ruhl

Johannes[1.4.4.2h] was bapt. at Fissel's on Dec. 18, 1785, and sponsored by his father's uncle and aunt, Johannes and Helena Ruhl. Johannes m. Catherina on Dec. 23, 1809. She was born on Dec. 3, 1791, d. Shrewsbury Twp. on June 18, 1882. Johannes was a blacksmith, and received Pleasant Ridge, and tract of 2Q, 299 supra from his father in 1811. Johannes sold part of the land of 2V, 420 supra to John Grove on July 26, 1817, and Johannes bought the tract of 3C,266 supra from John and Elizabeth Grove on April 1, 1825. John bought 8 acres and 51 perches in Shrewsbury Twp. from Daniel and Isabella Kauffelt on

June 7, 1834. Johannes d. Shrewsbury Twp. on Feb. 19, 1858, and is
buried beside his wife in the Lutheran cemetery. Johannes and
Catherina had the following children in Shrewsbury Twp.:

Samuel$^{1\cdot4\cdot4\cdot2\cdot1h}$, b. 1817. He has not been confirmed as a son of
Johannes, but seems to fit nowhere else. Samuel, a farmer,
m. Margaret, who was b. Pennsylvania in 1817. They resided
in Shrewsbury Twp. in 1850.

Noah G.$^{1\cdot4\cdot4\cdot2\cdot2h}$, b. Feb. 19, 1823, m. Anna M., who was b.
Pennsylvania in 1824. He was a Major during the Civil War,
and served from 1861-65. He d. at York on July 19, 1890,
buried in the Lutheran Church cemetery in Shrewsbury Twp.

Possibly Mary Catherine$^{1\cdot4\cdot4\cdot2\cdot3h}$, b. Feb. 8, 1827, d. April 5, 1828,
buried in the Lutheran cemetery in Shrewsbury Twp. close to
John and his wife.

Jeremiah$^{1\cdot4\cdot4\cdot2\cdot4h}$, b. 1831, d. on Dec. 27, 1849. He is buried in
the Lutheran cemetery in Shrewsbury Twp.

Joseph$^{1\cdot4\cdot4\cdot2\cdot5h}$, b. 1832, m. Lucy Ann.

Margaret$^{1\cdot4\cdot4\cdot2\cdot6h}$, b. 1834.

Michael Ruhl

Michael$^{1\cdot4\cdot4\cdot5h}$ m. Rebecca Richey in Shrewsbury Twp., York Co.,
Pennsylvania on April 18, 1822. He received "one-third of middle
one-third half section" of his father's land from his father's will.
Rebecca d. sometime before 1850, and Michael resided in Crawford Co.,
Jackson Twp., Ohio in 1850. Michael and Rebecca had a dau.
Catherine$^{1\cdot4\cdot4\cdot5\cdot1h}$, b. 1834.

Jacob Ruhl

Jacob$^{1\cdot4\cdot4\cdot6h}$ received the "privilege of living on, clearing, and
improving" his father's land after his mother's death. Jacob d.
Crawford Co., Galion, Ohio Aug. 8, 1842. Jacob and his wife, Catherine
Fate, are believed to be the parents of a son
Jacob$^{1\cdot4\cdot4\cdot6\cdot1h}$, b. c.1817, m. Maria Burden in Crawford Co., Ohio on
April 9, 1838.

Eva Ruhl

Eva$^{1\cdot4\cdot4\cdot7h}$ was bapt. at Fissel's c.1800, and sponsored by her uncle
and aunt, Johann and Margareta Baehli. She m. Jacob Nunemaker
c.1822. He was b. York Co., Codorus Twp., Pennsylvania in 1800 to
Jacob and Anna Maria Nunemaker. He was bapt. at Steltz Union
(Bethlehem) Church in Jan., 1800, and sponsored by Solomon
Nunemaker and wife. Eva d. sometime before Jan. 5, 1830 in York
Co., Shrewsbury Twp. In her father's will, each of her sons was given
fifty dollars upon attaining their twenty-first birthday. Jacob was
residing in Shrewsbury Twp. in 1850 with his second wife. Jacob and

Eva had the following children in Shrewsbury Twp.: ohn$^{1.4.4.7.1h}$, b. c.1823; Isaac$^{1.4.4.7.2h}$, b. 1825, resided with his father in 1850.

Susanna Ruhl

Susanna$^{1.4.4.8h}$ m. Johan Adam, son of Adam and Maria Barbara Hoffman. He was b. Codorus Twp. April 11, 1781. They resided in Codorus Twp. until 1838, when they moved to Richland Co. (now Morrow), Perry Twp., Ohio. Adam d. May 22, 1848, buried in North Woodbury Lutheran cemetery. Adam and Susanna had the following children in Codorus Twp.:

  Michael$^{1.4.4.8.1h}$, b. Nov. 11, 1819, m. Sarah A. Bortner in Richland Co., Ohio Nov. 26, 1840. She was b. in Pennsylvania in 1822. They were residing in Morrow Co., North Bloomfield Twp. in 1850.

  Jacob$^{1.4.4.8.2h}$, b. Dec. 9, 1820, d. Perry Twp. on Sept. 12, 1846. He m. Elizabeth Hassler in Richland Co., Ohio Jan. 29, 1843.

  Samuel$^{1.4.4.8.3h}$, b. Nov. 20, 1822, m. Lucinda H. Derius in Richland Co., Ohio April 27, 1845. She was b. Pennsylvania Nov. 2, 1820, d. Perry Twp. Dec. 30, 1890. Samuel d. Perry Twp. Feb. 22, 1890, buried beside Lucinda in North Woodbury Lutheran cemetery.

  Adam$^{1.4.4.8.4h}$, b. 1825.

  George$^{1.4.4.8.5h}$, was under the age of 21 in May, 1848; his uncle, Georg Ruhl, was appointed as his guardian.

  Jesse$^{1.4.4.8.6h}$, was under the age of 21 in May, 1848; Henry R. Hosler was appointed his guardian.

Anna Barbara Baehli

Anna Barbara$^{1.4.5h}$ was bapt. at St. Jacob's May 10, 1766, sponsored by Ludwig Hahnawaldt and Anna Barbara Gerberich. She m. Barnet Hamschear in Trinity Reformed Church of York, Pennsylvania Dec. 24, 1780. Barnet d. in Shrewsbury Twp. in 1792. Barnet and Barbara had the following children in Shrewsbury Twp.: Barnet$^{1.4.5.1h}$, b. 1783; Margaretha$^{1.4.5.2h}$, b. 1786; Eva$^{1.4.5.3h}$, b. 1787; Heinrich$^{1.4.5.4h}$, b. 1790; Johannes$^{1.4.5.5h}$, b. May 15, 1791, bapt. at Fissel's June 5, 1791, sponsored by his uncle, Hannes Baehli (single).

Johan Georg Ruhl

Anna Rosina$^{1.4.6h}$ m. Johan Georg, son of Johannes and Helena (Schenck) Ruhl. He was bapt. at St. Jacob's July 30, 1765, sponsored by his uncle and aunt, Georg Ruhl and Rosina Schenck. He m. Anna Rosina, dau. of Jacob and Eva Elisabetha (Kleinfelter) Baehli, in York Co., Pennsylvania in 1786. Anna Rosina was b. Shrewsbury Twp. March 27, 1769, bapt. at St. Jacob's on May 28, 1769, sponsored by her uncle and aunt, Daniel and Anna Rosina Baehli. Georg purchased 140

acres, 27 perches in Codorus Twp. on March 12, 1787 from Jacob and
Maria Catherina Noll. On March 24, 1795, Georg and Rosina deeded
to Philip Ruhl, three tracts in Codorus Twp.- (a) 60 acres 127 perches
surveyed to Martin Anthony in 1767, called Hard Scoffle; (b) 79 acres
60 perches surveyed to Martin Anthony in 1768, called Hog's Manor;
(c) 50 acres warranted to Georg Ruhl on April 5, 1788. In Feb. 1794,
Georg signed an agreement for the founding of a union congregation at
New Freedom in Codorus Twp., called Steltz Union (Bethlehem)
Church. During the War of 1812, Georg served as a Private in the
York Co. Militia. Georg and Rosina lived in the borderland region
between Codorus Twp., and Baltimore Co., Mine Run Hundred,
Maryland, and appeared on census and tax record records of both
areas, but their sons indicated that they were b. Baltimore Co.,
Maryland. Georg and Rosina moved to Mine Run Hundred in
Maryland in 1795, and Georg d. there March 15, 1815. His will was
probated in Baltimore Co., Maryland; he is buried in Steltz cemetery in
York Co., Pennsylvania beside his parents. In his will, he mentions his
land in Ohio, where Rosina, and her sons, Johannes[1.4.6.4h] and
Georg[1.4.6.8h], moved in 1828. The journey was made by team with
the family of Rosina's brother-in-law, Henry Ruhl[1.2.2]. During the trip
they cut a portion of the road to Mansfield, Ohio, and after their
arrival lived in a covered wagon until they cleared a site to build a
cabin. Rosina d. on Dec. 8, 1855, and is buried in North Woodbury
Lutheran Church cemetery. Georg and Rosina were the parents of the
following children:

Elisabetha[1.4.6.1h], b. Feb. 2, 1787, bapt. at Fissel's on Feb. 26,
1787, sponsored by her parents.
Eve[1.4.6.2h], b. c.1790, m. Jacob, son of Jacob and Anna Maria
(Heibele) Dick, before 1815. Jacob was b. Shrewsbury Twp.
Oct. 10, 1784, bapt. at Fissel's Nov. 14, 1784, sponsored by his
parents.
Caterina[1.4.6.3h], b. c.1793.
Johannes[1.4.6.4h], b. Dec. 14, 1796.
Maria[1.4.6.5h], b. 1799, bapt. at Steltz Union Dec. 27, 1799,
sponsored by Johannes Huber.
Johan Jacob[1.4.6.6h], b. 1802.
Susanna[1.4.6.7h], b. c.1804.
Georg[1.4.6.8h], b. July 6, 1806.

Johannes Ruhl
Johannes[1.4.6.4h] was bapt. at Steltz Union in Dec., 1796, and
sponsored by his uncle and aunt, Johannes and Margaretha Gerberich.
He m. Susannah Blossner in York Co., c.1820. She was b. York Co.
Jan. 30, 1802, d. Morrow Co., Perry Twp., Ohio April 7, 1895.
Johannes was a farmer in Perry Twp., where he d. March 12, 1874.

They are buried in Shauck cemetery. They were the parents of the following children (the first two were b. Baltimore Co., Maryland):

John[1.4.6.4.1h], b. March 27, 1821, m. Mary E. Pugh in Morrow Co., Ohio Dec. 12, 1850. She was b. in Virginia June 9, 1826, d. Perry Twp. Sept. 19, 1912. John d. Perry Twp. May 23, 1903, buried beside his wife in North Woodbury Lutheran cemetery.

Isaac[1.4.6.4.2h], b. June 16, 1823, m. Maria, dau. of John and Martha Price, in Morrow Co., Ohio Dec. 8, 1855. She was b. Ohio in 1835. Isaac and Maria resided in Morrow Co., North Bloomfield Twp. in 1880, where they moved sometime after 1860.

Amos[1.4.6.4.3h], b. June 2, 1832, m. Caroline Bruchner in Morrow Co., Ohio April 5, 1855. She was b. Ohio on Aug. 15, 1832, d. Perry Twp. Nov. 6, 1919. In 1853, Amos became a clerk in the store of Morgan Levering at Woodbury, while he studied medicine, for two years. Soon after his marriage, he moved to Nebraska, where he practiced medicine for two years, before returning to North Woodbury. After returning to Ohio, he entered the mercantile business with Allen Levering. After six years, Levering sold out his interest to Amos' brother-in-law, Norman Merwine. This partnership lasted briefly, and Norman sold out to Robert Levering. In 1876, Robert retired and left Amos as sole proprietor. Amos continued to practice medicine, was the Treasurer of Perry Twp. for twelve years, as well as the Post Master. He d. Perry Twp. Feb. 16, 1897, buried in North Woodbury Lutheran Cemetery beside his wife.

Lovina[1.4.6.4.4h], b. 1841, m. Norman Merwine in Morrow Co., Ohio on Feb. 11, 1858. He was b. 1832.

Johan Jacob Ruhl

Jacob[1.4.6.6h] was bapt. at Steltz Union on Oct. 22, 1802, and sponsored by his grandfather, Jacob Baehli. Initially, he remained in Baltimore Co., Maryland, after his mother and brothers headed west. Jacob resided in Mine Run Hundred, District 6 in 1850, and moved to Morrow Co., Perry Twp., Ohio in the 1860s. His son, Adam[1.4.6.6.1h], moved to Perry Twp. in the 1850s. Jacob was a farmer and a wagon maker. He m. Elizabeth sometime prior to 1831. She was b. Pennsylvania in 1805, d. Richland Co., Troy Twp., Ohio in 1882. In 1880, Elizabeth was residing in Troy Twp. with Ellen Ruhl, a 32-year old tailoress, who was b. in Maryland and her parents b. Pennsylvania. Ellen's relationship to this family has not been established. Jacob d. Morrow Co., Perry Twp., in 1875, and is buried beside his wife in Shauck cemetery. They had the following children in Baltimore Co., Maryland:

Adam H.[1.4.6.6.1h], b. 1831, m. Louisa c.1857, and Cordilla A.

Feigley in Morrow Co., Ohio on July 18, 1872. Louisa was b. Pennsylvania on Jan. 17, 1837, d. Perry Twp. on Sept. 23, 1870, buried in North Woodbury Lutheran cemetery. Adam probably d. between 1872 and 1880.

Probably, Jacob[1.4.6.6.2h], b. 1834. He has not been proven to be Jacob's son, but he was a laborer in the home of Jacob Bollinger, close to Jacob's home, in 1850.

Washington[1.4.6.6.3h], b. 1839.

Martha[1.4.6.6.4h], b. 1847, m. Ezra S. McDonel in Richland Co., Ohio Feb. 6, 1868.

Probably, John[1.4.6.6.5h], b. 1852. He has not been confirmed to be Jacob's son, but in 1880, he names his father's birth place as Maryland, and his mother's as Pennsylvania. In 1880, he was a blacksmith residing in Richland Co., Mansfield, Ohio.

Georg Ruhl

Georg[1.4.6.8h] was bapt. at Steltz Union on Aug. 8, 1806, and sponsored by Jacob Nunnemacher and wife. He m. his first cousin, Mary[1.4.4.9h], dau. of Henry and Margaret (Baehli) Ruhl, in York Co., Pennsylvania on Nov. 16, 1826. Mary received one hundred dollars from her father's will. Georg and Mary moved with their families to North Woodbury, Ohio in 1828, and erected a cabin with a puncheon floor. Their farm consisted of 160 acres on NE 1/2 of Section 19 Range 19 W Twp. 19 N. They lived in the cabin for some time before finally clearing the land, and building the home, which he later sold to his brother's son-in-law, Norman Merwine, when he left Ohio. Georg sold eight lots from his farm for the village of Woodbury, and donated one to the United Brethren Church. He farmed in Perry Twp. until 1863, when he engaged in trade at different places, first at West Point, Ohio, then at Galion, Ohio. About 1865, he moved his family to Marshall Co., Indiana, and settled first at Bourbon and then on a small farm in Green Twp., just southwest of Argos, Indiana. In Indiana he worked as a farmer and carpenter. He was Justice of the Peace for many years as well as the Assessor and Trustee of Green Twp. He was a member, and elder of the Evangelical Lutheran Church. Mary d. Green Twp. on May 9, 1870, and Georg m. Mary Ann Newhouse in Marshall Co., Dec. 11, 1872. Mary Ann d. Dec. 22, 1921. In 1867, George converted from the Lutheran faith to the Methodist Episcopal Church. Georg d. on June 2 (3), 1890, and is buried beside his first wife, in Gilead cemetery. Georg and Mary were the parents of the following children (the first was b. York Co., Pennsylvania):

Catherine A.[1.4.6.8.1h], b. Oct. 13, 1827, m. Adam Grove, d. Kosciusko Co., Milford, Indiana Feb. 28, 1899. Adam was b. 1808, d. 1899. They were buried in the Milford Twp. cemetery.

Eliza J.[1.4.6.8.2h], b. March 29, 1829, m. Eliah, son of Samuel and

Catherine (Crack) Dennis, in Richland Co., Ohio on Sept. 17, 1846. He was b. in Ohio Sept. 17, 1824, d. Morrow Co., Perry Twp., Ohio March 22, 1883. At age nineteen, Eliah learned the trade of wagon making from his brother in North Woodbury. After 18 months, he quit, took charge of George Ruhl's farm, and farmed it for two years. Next, he went to the homestead, where he farmed for ten years, then moved to North Woodbury, where he worked in a steam saw-mill for a year. After the mill, he bought interest in the Fish farm, and lived on that for two years before buying 80 acres of the Gabriel McWilliams' farm, which he promptly sold to buy 60 acres of the Gantz farm. After ten years, he sold the Gantz farm, and bought the 83-acre homestead of his wife's cousin, Samuel Hoffman, in the spring of 1875. Eliza d. Oct. 14, 1895, buried beside her husband in Shauck cemetery.

Josiah[1.4.6.8.3h], b. Nov. 26, 1830, m. Rebecca Keefer in Morrow Co., Ohio on Nov. 1, 1855. She was b. Pennsylvania in 1831, d. Marshall Co. June 20, 1911. In 1866/67, Josiah moved his family to Marshall Co., Bourbon, Indiana, d. before 1911. Josiah served in the Civil War, buried in Marshall Co., Indiana.

Henry R.[1.4.6.8.4h], b. Sept. 3, 1832, m. Matilda, dau. of Georg Keller and Perneleper (Lightfoot) Gantz, in Morrow Co., Ohio Oct. 14, 1856. Henry moved his family to Marshall Co., Indiana in 1865, and settled on a farm in Green Twp. Between 1874 and 1879, Henry and Matilda moved their family to Reno Co., Kansas, settling near Huntsville. Henry d. in Kansas in 1890, and Matilda d. Marshall Co., Argos, Indiana while on a visit to her brother Nov. 23, 1904.

Margaret[1.4.6.8.5h], b. Nov. 22, 1834, m. John Lightfoot, son of Georg Keller and Perneleper (Lightfoot) Gantz, in Morrow Co., Ohio on Sept. 11, 1856. In 1865/66, John sold 60 acres of the farm to his brother-in-law, Eliah Dennis, and moved to Marshall Co., Bourbon, Indiana, where one dau. was born. In 1868, John and Margaret moved to Walnut Twp., two miles southwest of Argos, Indiana. The farm eventually consisted of 22 acres. John was a farmer and a carpenter in the summer months, and during the remainder of the year, was employed at the David and Asher Boyce saw mill. He held the office of Assessor for numerous years. After moving to Indiana, he converted to Methodism, and became church choir leader, and a bass singer in the choir. When he was 76, John suffered a stroke of apoplexy which affected his sight until he was totally blind at age 78. In 1919, old age forced John and Margaret to leave their farm. On Oct. 25, 1919, Margaret d. in St. Joseph Co., South Bend, Indiana at the home of her dau. Hannah.

John moved in with his son Frank, (in 1920 he was living with his dau., Eva McAfee) where he d. on July 16, 1924 at age 90. Both are buried in Gilead cemetery, about six miles southwest of Argos, Indiana.

Levi$^{1.4.6.8.6h}$, b. May 30, 1838, m. Priscilla A., dau. of Israel and Elizabeth Huntsman, in Morrow Co., Ohio on July 3, 1864. She was born at North Woodbury on Oct. 19, 1844, d. Marshall Co., Bremen, Indiana on April 10, 1911. Levi moved to Marshall Co., Green Twp., Indiana in 1866, and later moved to German Twp., and farmed near Bremen, until his death from dropsy July 8, 1908.

Jacob$^{1.4.6.8.7h}$, b. Nov. 24, 1842, m. Catherine, dau. of Henry Hassler and Catherine (Patterson) Ruhl, in Morrow Co., Ohio April 21, 1866. Catherine was b. Perry Twp., Richland Co., Ohio Sept. 10, 1838, d. Morrow Co., Perry Twp. Jan. 15, 1911. In 1911, Jacob was considered to be an influential and honored agriculturist of Perry Twp., Morrow Co., Ohio. At that time he had a 160 acre farm in Perry Twp., and an 80- acre tract in Congress Twp.

George W.$^{1.4.6.8.8h}$, b. Feb. 1, 1849, m. Laura Leonard in Marshall Co., Indiana Sept. 19, 1871, and Sarah F. Castetter in Elkhart Co., Indiana May 13, 1877. Laura d. Marshall Co., Indiana April 10, 1876. Sarah was b. Ohio, d. sometime after 1900. In 1880, George resided in New Paris, Indiana, and worked in a carriage shop. He was a business man in Elkhart Co., Goshen, Indiana in 1911.

Susanna Baehli

Susanna$^{1.4.7h}$ probably m. Jacob Kerchner c.1787. After Susanna's death, Jacob m. Elisabetha$^{1.4.3.2h}$, dau. of Georg and Margaretha (Gerberich) Baehli, at Christ Lutheran Church of York on June 14, 1803. Jacob d. York Co., Pennsylvania prior to May 13, 1828, when the probate was begun on his estate. Jacob had the following children in Shrewsbury Twp.: Johannes$^{1.4.7.1h}$, b. Oct., 1791, bapt. at Fissel's Nov. 1791;; Eva$^{1.4.7.2h}$, b. July 9, 1794, bapt. at Fissel's July 30, 1794; Jacob$^{1.4.7.3h}$, b. 1797; Rosina$^{1.4.7.4h}$, b. 1800, m. James Thompson; Elizabeth$^{1.4.7.5h}$, b. c.1802, m. Henry Hetrick; George$^{1.4.3.2.1h}$, b. c.1804; Margaret$^{1.4.3.2.2h}$, b. c.1806, m. George Trouett; Catharine$^{1.4.3.2.3h}$, b. c.1807; Susanna$^{1.4.3.2.4h}$, b. c.1809; John B.$^{1.4.3.2.5h}$, b. April 21, 1812; Henry$^{1.4.3.2.6h}$, b. c.1814; Lydia$^{1.4.3.2.7h}$, b. c.1816; Charles$^{1.4.3.2.8h}$, b. c.1818.

Eva Kerchner

Eva$^{1.4.7.2h}$ m. Ludwig Krebs, and had the following children: Amos$^{1.4.7.2.1h}$, bapt. at St. Jacob's (Stone) Lutheran Church in York

Co. on Dec. 5, 1824; Catharina Eva$^{1.4.7.2.2h}$, bapt. at St. Jacob's on Nov. 30, 1828.

Jacob Kerchner

Jacob$^{1.4.7.3h}$ m. Anna Mary, dau. of Peter Lau, and Catharine Rohrbach, before 1850. Anna Mary was b. 1794, d. before 1835. Jacob d. 1872. Jacob and Anna Mary had the following children in Shrewsbury Twp.: John$^{1.4.7.3.1h}$, b. 1820; Jacob$^{1.4.7.3.2h}$, b. 1823; Daniel$^{1.4.7.3.3h}$, b. 1823; Adam$^{1.4.7.3.4h}$, b. 1829.

John B. Kerchner

John B.$^{1.4.3.2.5h}$ m. Elizabeth (Sept. 20, 1819-March 6, 1894), dau. of Adam and Anna Behler, d. on May 8, 1880. They had the following children in Codorus Twp.: Julyann$^{1.4.3.2.5.1h}$, b. 1836; Isabel$^{1.4.3.2.5.2h}$, b. Jan. 13, 1839; Jacob$^{1.4.3.2.5.3h}$, b. 1842; Adam$^{1.4.3.2.5.4h}$, b. 1843; Matilda$^{1.4.3.2.5.5h}$, b. 1846.

Isabel Kerchner

Isabel$^{1.4.3.2.5.2h}$ m. Lewis Kline, son of Charles and Leah (Klinedinst) Glatfelter, d. on May 1, 1900. He was born on Oct. 19, 1843, d. on March 13, 1916. They had the following children: Franklin$^{1.4.3.2.5.2.1h}$, b. c.1862; Emma J.$^{1.4.3.2.5.2.2h}$, b. 1864, d. 1923; Lucy Ann$^{1.4.3.2.5.2.3h}$, b. Jan. 6, 1867, m. Levi M. Baehli, d. Dec. 4, 1942; Alice A. Elizabeth$^{1.4.3.2.5.2.4h}$, b. 1868, d. 1870; Maranda$^{1.4.3.2.5.2.5h}$, b. 1870, d. 1870; Paul$^{1.4.3.2.5.2.6h}$, b. 1880, d. 1881; Rose$^{1.4.3.2.5.2.7h}$, b. c.1882.

Henry Kerchner

Henry$^{1.4.3.2.6h}$ is probably the Henry Kerchner who m. Christina Lenden in York Co., Hanover, St. Matthews Lutheran Church Jan. 7, 1847. Henry and Christina had the following children: Levi$^{1.4.3.2.6.1h}$; Amos$^{1.4.3.2.6.2h}$; Sarah Amar Feny$^{1.4.3.2.6.3h}$; Henry Noah$^{1.4.3.2.6.4h}$; Mary Alice$^{1.4.3.2.6.5h}$. All the above children were bapt. at St. Jacob's. Lutheran Church between 1848 and 1860 in the order given.

Charles Kerchner

Charles$^{1.4.3.2.8h}$ m. Mary Ann, and had a son Jacob$^{1.4.3.2.8.1h}$, bapt. at St. Jacob's Lutheran Church in York Co. April 16, 1848.

Johannes Baehli

Johannes$^{1.4.8h}$ d. Codorus Twp. in Aug., 1841. His will was written on Feb. 4, 1841, and probated on Aug. 21, 1841 by John Ruhl and Jacob Kerschner. Johannes m. Margaretta and had a dau., Mary$^{1.4.8.1h}$, m. ____ Moyer.

Peter Baehli

Peter[1.5h] m. Margaretha and had the following children in Berks Co., Albany Twp.: Anna Rosina[1.5.1h], bapt. Aug. 1, 1762, by Reverend Daniel Schumacher; Johan Abraham[1.5.2h], bapt. Dec. 30, 1764, by Reverend Daniel Schumacher.

Johan Nickel Baehli

Johan Nickel[1.6h] m. Catharina, and had a dau. in Berks Co., Greenwich Twp., Pennsylvania: Catharina[1.6.1h], b. March 15, 1763.

Johann Abraham Baehli

Johann Abraham[1.7h] was bapt. April 28, 1763 at Rosenthal Lutheran Church, and sponsored by his brother, Jacob Baehli. Abraham m. Catharina, who d. c.1770, and then m. Margaretha in 1770. Abraham moved to Frederick Co., Middletown, Maryland with his brother, Carl Ludwig, c.1770. Abraham had the following children (the first three, b. Albany Twp.):

Johan Peter[1.7.1h], bapt. at Allemangel Lutheran Church on June 3, 1764, and sponsored by Peter and Anna Elisabeth Scheibeli.

Johan Abraham[1.7.2h], b. Sept. 21, 1766, bapt. at Allemangel Lutheran Church on Oct. 12, 1766, and sponsored by Peter and Anna Elisabeth Scheibeli.

Maria Margaretha[1.7.3h], b. March 26, 1769, and bapt. at Allemangel Lutheran Church on April 9, 1769.

Wilhelm[1.7.4h], b. June 1, 1771, and bapt. at Middletown on Sept. 25, 1771.

Carl Ludwig Baehli

Carl Ludwig[1.8h] m. Anna Elisabeth. They moved to Frederick Co., Middletown, Maryland with Carl's brother, Abraham, in 1770. Carl Ludwig and Anna Elisabeth had the following children: Jacob[1.8.1h], bapt. Jan. 30, 1766 at Berks Co., Reading, Pennsylvania; Daniel[1.8.2h], b. April 18, 1773, bapt. at the Evangelical Reformed Church of Frederick, Maryland on May 30, 1773, and sponsored by Daniel and Catherine Hauwet; Susanna[1.8.3h], b. Feb. 25, 1779.

****

Johan Christopffel Leonhard

Johan Christopffel[1n] m. Anna Eva[1.4o], dau. of Hanss Peter and Anna Christina (Peters) Kessler, in Horn Hunsrueck, Rheinland, Preussen on Nov. 10, 1693. They had the following children in Horn Hunsrueck: Annam Margreta[1.1n], bapt. Aug. 28, 1695; Johannes Georg[1.2n], bapt. Nov. 15, 1705; Johannes Peter[1.3n], bapt. May 27, 1708, and presumed to be the Johann Peter, b. May 4, 1708, that immigrated to America; Johann Christopffel[1.4n], b. March 22, 1710/11.

Johann Peter Leonhardt

Johann Peter$^{1.3n}$ m. Maria Margaretha, and resided in Zweibrucken, before immigrating to America (according to tradition). They arrived at Philadelphia on the ship Two Brothers on Sept. 15, 1748, and settled in Berks Co., Greenwich Twp., Pennsylvania. Peter was a cooper, and moved to York Co., Dover Twp., Pennsylvania. He was residing there on April 13, 1763. Maria Magdalena was born on Sept. 28, 1715, d. on July 1, 1777. Peter d. on April 4, 1774. They are buried in Strayer's Lutheran cemetery. They had the following children: Philip$^{1.3.1n}$, b. 1734; Johan Jacob$^{1.3.2n}$, b. Nov. 18, 1736; Johann Georg$^{1.3.3n}$, b. 1738; Jon Christoph$^{1.3.4n}$, b. 1740; Heinrich$^{1.3.5n}$, b. 1742, m. Catherine, d. Somerset Co., Pennsylvania on March 21, 1837, moved to Bedford (now Somerset) Co. in 1785; Wilhelm$^{1.3.6n}$, b. 1745; Johan Peter$^{1.3.7n}$, b. Jan. 30, 1749/50; Frederick$^{1.3.8n}$, b. March 7, 1751/52, m. Catherine Kramer, d. York Co., Dover Twp., Pennsylvania in 1837; Gottfried$^{1.3.9n}$, b. March 17, 1754.

Philip Lenhart

Philip$^{1.3.1n}$ m. Anna. Philip d. Berks Co., Greenwich Twp., Pennsylvania in 1803. They had the following children in Greenwich Twp.: Johannes$^{1.3.1.1n}$, b. c.1753, took the Oath of Allegiance in 1778, and received land in Windsor Twp. from Phillip in 1794; Phillip$^{1.3.1.2n}$, b. 1755, served in the Revolutionary War, and received a pension in 1833; Johan Jacob$^{1.3.1.3n}$, bapt. April 24, 1757; Johan Peter$^{1.3.1.4n}$, bapt. Oct. 8, 1758; Johan Georg$^{1.3.1.5n}$, b. Aug. 16, 1770, bapt. Sept. 11, 1770, and sponsored by Johan Georg and Rebekah.

Johan Jacob Lenhart

Johan Jacob$^{1.3.2n}$ m. Anna Maria (Feb., 1738-Dec., 1791), dau. of Johannes Kuhl/Keel, in Berks Co., Pennsylvania on Jan. 21, 1760, and Barbara sometime after 1791. Jacob d. Greenwich Twp. on Aug. 3, 1793, and is buried in Jerusalem Church cemetery. Barbara d. 1793. Jacob had the following children in Greenwich Twp.: Jacob$^{1.3.2.1n}$, b. c.1762; Catharina$^{1.3.2.2n}$, m. Frederick Moyer; Christina$^{1.3.2.3n}$, m. Jacob Homberger; Johannes$^{1.3.2.4n}$, b. 1770, m. Catherine, d. 1839; Heinrich$^{1.3.2.5n}$, b. Aug. 13, 1773; Sebastian$^{1.3.2.6n}$, b. c.1775, m. Catherine Eliza Miller, d. 1856.

Heinrich Lenhart

Heinrich$^{1.3.2.5n}$ m. Christina. She was born on Aug. 30, 1773, d. Berks Co. on Jan. 18, 1825. Heinrich founded Lenhartsville, d. there on May 21, 1837. They had the following children: Jacob$^{1.3.2.5.1n}$, b. Oct. 6, 1792; Johannes$^{1.3.2.5.2n}$; Rebecca$^{1.3.2.5.3n}$, m. Jacob Reicheleiderfer; Samuel$^{1.3.2.5.4n}$, b. Feb. 28, 1798, m. Lydia Hamen (April 1, 1802-Feb. 1, 1872), d. Lenhartsville on Aug. 1, 1869;

Isaac$^{1.3.2.5.5n}$; Daniel$^{1.3.2.5.6n}$; Benjamin$^{1.3.2.5.7n}$, b. Oct. 13, 1802; Henry$^{1.3.2.5.8n}$, b. July 21, 1804; Frederick$^{1.3.2.5.9n}$; Lydia$^{1.3.2.5.10n}$, m. Jonathan Losher; Reuben$^{1.3.2.5.12n}$.

Jacob Lenhart
Jacob$^{1.3.2.5.1n}$ m. Esther Hahl, d. Berks Co., Albany Twp. on July 9, 1825, and had a dau., Lydia$^{1.3.2.5.1.1n}$, b. 1818, d. 1825.

Johannes Lenhart
Johannes$^{1.3.2.5.2n}$ m. Hannah Heinly (Sept. 13, 1792-May 6, 1878), d. Berks Co., Greenwich Twp. on Feb. 22, 1839, and had the following children: Jacob$^{1.3.2.5.2.1n}$; a dau.$^{1.3.2.5.2.2n}$, m. John Fister; a dau.$^{1.3.2.5.2.3n}$, m. John Reber.

Isaac Lenhart
Isaac$^{1.3.2.5.5n}$ m. Elizabeth Leiby (b.1801), and had a dau., Catherine$^{1.3.2.5.5.1n}$, b. Nov. 15, 1830.

Benjamin Lenhart
Benjamin$^{1.3.2.5.7n}$ m. Esther Hahl, widow of Jacob Lenhart, d. Albany Twp. on Jan. 8, 1858. She was born on Nov. 6, 1801, d. on Feb. 6, 1840. They had the following children: James$^{1.3.2.5.7.1n}$; a dau.$^{1.3.2.5.7.2n}$, m. Daniel Grim; a dau.$^{1.3.2.5.7.3n}$, m. John B. Hammerly.

Henry Lenhart
Henry$^{1.3.2.5.8n}$ m. Salome Leiby, d. Greenwich Twp. on Aug. 9, 1840, and had the following children: Augustus$^{1.3.2.5.8.1n}$; Alfred$^{1.3.2.5.8.2n}$.

Johann Georg Lenhart
Johann Georg$^{1.3.3n}$ m. Anna Catharina in York Co., Pennsylvania c.1767. They moved from Dover Twp. to Newberry Twp. between 1777 and 1779, and to Monaghan Twp. between 1779 and 1783. Georg served as a Private in the Revolutionary War. Between 1783 and 1784, he moved to Somerset Co., Pennsylvania, and settled in Milford Twp., and in 1784, he purchased 390 acres on Coxes and Middle Creek. Georg d. there in 1797. Georg and Anna Catharina had the following children:

Johan Peter$^{1.3.3.1n}$, bapt. at Strayer's March 31, 1768, sponsored by Johan Peter and Maria Margaretha Lenhart.

Anna Elisabetha$^{1.3.3.2n}$, bapt. at Strayer's on March 10, 1770, sponsored by Johan Adam and Anna Elisabetha Kramer.

Anna Maria$^{1.3.3.3n}$, b. c.1772, m. Abraham Whipkey in Somerset Co. on Dec. 25, 1792, d. Milford Twp. in 1832. Abraham d.

Milford Twp. in June 1820.

Catharina$^{1.3.3.4n}$, bapt. in the First Reformed Church of York on
June 5, 1774, and sponsored by Frederick and Catharine
Lenhart. She m. John Whipkey in Somerset Co. on Oct. 22,
1793.

Susanna$^{1.3.3.5n}$, b. 1776.

Maria Barbara$^{1.3.3.6n}$, b. Nov. 5, 1777, and bapt. at Strayer's on
June 7, 1778, and sponsored by Michael and Margetha Gross.

Hannah$^{1.3.3.7n}$, b. 1780.

Eva$^{1.3.3.8n}$, b. 1782.

Rebecca$^{1.3.3.9n}$, b. Nov. 1, 1785, bapt. at Samuel's Church, m.
Adam Harrah.

Johan Georg$^{1.3.3.10n}$, b. Jan. 3, 1789, and bapt. at Samuel's
Church.

Joseph$^{1.3.3.11n}$, b. Oct. 15, 1792.

Johan Peter Lenhart

Johan Peter$^{1.3.3.1n}$ m. Elizabeth, dau. of Yost Miller, in Bedford Co.,
Berlin, Pennsylvania on Aug. 13, 1793. They resided in Ohio in 1825,
and had the following children: Peter$^{1.3.3.1.1n}$, m. Catherine Yorty and
Nancy; Eve$^{1.3.3.1.2n}$, m. Jonathan Friedline; Samuel$^{1.3.3.1.3n}$, was
blind and unmarried; George$^{1.3.3.1.4n}$; Mary$^{1.3.3.1.5n}$, m. Phillip
Zimmerman; Elizabeth$^{1.3.3.1.6n}$; Sarah$^{1.3.3.1.7n}$, m. ____ Grady.

Anna Elisabetha Lenhart

Anna Elisabetha$^{1.3.3.2n}$ m. Andreas, son of Andreas and Catharina
Barbara (Bourgey) Boudemont, in Bedford (now Somerset) Co., Berlin,
Pennsylvania on May 4, 1790. Andreas d. Somerset Co., Middle Creek
Twp., Pennsylvania on Feb. 21, 1834. Anna Elisabetha d. in Somerset
Co., Spring Creek Twp., Pennsylvania on Aug. 12, 1832. They had the
following children: John$^{1.3.3.2.1n}$, b. Feb. 9, 1791; Mary$^{1.3.3.2.2n}$, b.
1793; Gabriel$^{1.3.3.2.3n}$, b. Jan. 24, 1794; Catherine$^{1.3.3.2.4n}$, b. 1797;
Eva$^{1.3.3.2.5n}$, b. March 15, 1799; Salome$^{1.3.3.2.6n}$, b. March 6, 1800,
m. George Pile; Peter$^{1.3.3.2.7n}$, b. March 2, 1802; Rosina$^{1.3.3.2.8n}$, b.
Dec. 18, 1804; Joseph$^{1.3.3.2.9n}$, b. Jan. 25, 1807, d. Westmoreland Co.,
Cook Twp., Pennsylvania March 3, 1880, m. Elizabeth (Aug. 22, 1811 -
Oct. 9, 1893), dau. of John and Catharine (Binfert) Bruner on Feb. 14,
1829; Elizabeth$^{1.3.3.2.10n}$, b. March 10, 1810; Hannah$^{1.3.3.2.11n}$, b.
July 14, 1812; Luiza$^{1.3.3.2.12n}$, b. 1815; Margaret$^{1.3.3.2.13n}$, b. Jan.
13, 1817.

John Putman

John$^{1.3.3.2.1n}$ m. Charlotte, dau. of Philip King, and Sarah Hall.
Charlotte was b. 1794, d. 1851. John d. Stark Co., Wilmont, Ohio on
May 3, 1872. John and Charlotte had the following children:

Mary$^{1.3.3.2.1.1n}$, b. 1815.

Andrew W. Justus$^{1.3.3.2.1.2n}$, b. Jan. 30, 1816.

Elizabeth$^{1.3.3.2.1.3n}$, b. c.1818, m. Abraham Spidle, and resided in Wilmot.

Phoebe$^{1.3.3.2.1.4n}$, b. Dec. 5, 1820, m. William Robinson, son of Samuel and Elisabetha Barbara (Robinson) Schlater, in Stark Co., Ohio on Oct. 28, 1841. She d. Mercer Co., Dublin Twp., Ohio on Feb. 18, 1891, and William d. there on April 17, 1884. William came to Mercer Co., Ohio with his brother, Peter, and his father, Samuel, in 1837. After Samuel's death, William returned to Stark Co., Ohio, briefly, but returned to Mercer Co. in 1841. He purchased 161 acres in section six of Dublin Twp. with his brother, Peter, from his brother-in-law, Peter Dull. William was b. Fayette Co., Salt Lick Twp., Pennsylvania on June 3, 1820.

Timothy C.$^{1.3.3.2.1.5n}$, b. Jan. 29, 1828.

Anna$^{1.3.3.2.1.6n}$, d. at age 11.

Mary Putman

Mary$^{1.3.3.2.1.1n}$ m. Jeremiah Agler. He was b. 1801, d. 1869. Mary d. 1902. They had the following children: Timothy$^{1.3.3.2.1.1.1n}$, b. 1834, d. 1924, m. Elizabeth Brewer (1838-1893); Harmen$^{1.3.3.2.1.1.2n}$, b. 1836; Wert$^{1.3.3.2.1.1.3a}$, b. 1838, d. 1924, m. Anna Krick (1842-1921); Morris$^{1.3.3.2.1.1.4n}$, b. 1841, m. Mollie Sinder; Andrew$^{1.3.3.2.1.1.5n}$, b. 1843, d. 1905, m. Sarah Elizabeth$^{1.3.3.2.7.13n}$ (1860-1940), dau. of Peter$^{1.3.3.2.7n}$ and Sarah E. (Neiferd) Putman; Sarah$^{1.3.3.2.1.1.6n}$, b. 1846, d. 1857; Charlotte$^{1.3.3.2.1.1.7n}$, b. 1851, m. Daniel Whitmore; John$^{1.3.3.2.1.3.3.2n}$, b. 1855.

Andrew W. Justus Putman

Andrew$^{1.3.3.2.1.2n}$ m. Judith, dau. of Samuel and Elizabeth Barbara (Robinson) Schlater, in Stark/Tuscarawas Co., Ohio on Sept. 28, 1837. Andrew d. Stark Co., Sugar Creek Twp., Ohio on Feb. 6, 1891, and Judith d. there on Feb. 16, 1898. She was b. Fayette Co., Salt Lick Twp., Pennsylvania on July 23, 1818. They had the following children: Clarissa$^{1.3.3.2.1.2.1n}$, b. 1838, d. 1865, m. William Wert McClintock (1832-1911); Harman$^{1.3.3.2.1.2.2n}$, b. March 12, 1843, d. Dec. 6, 1903, Sugar Creek Twp., Ohio, m. Mildred Samilda (1853-1903); Selecta$^{1.3.3.2.1.2.3n}$, b. 1844, d. 1926, m. Daniel Hoffman (1838-1895); Winfield Clark$^{1.3.3.2.1.2.4n}$, b. 1852, m. Catherine P. Gardner (b. 1853).

Elizabeth Putman

Elizabeth$^{1.3.3.2.1.3n}$ m. Abraham Spidle, and had the following children: Mary$^{1.3.3.2.1.3.1n}$, m. ____ Cole; John$^{1.3.3.2.1.3.2n}$,

Clark$^{1.3.3.2.1.3.3n}$; Lester$^{1.3.3.2.1.3.4n}$; Ida$^{1.3.3.2.1.3.5n}$;
Phoebe$^{1.3.3.2.1.3.6n}$, m. ____ Stoner; Charlotte$^{1.3.3.2.1.3.7n}$, m. ____
Clewell; Alice$^{1.3.3.2.1.3.8n}$, m. ____ Crossland; Charles
E.$^{1.3.3.2.1.3.9n}$.

Timothy C. Putman

Timothy C.$^{1.3.3.2.1.5n}$ m. Elizabeth, dau. of Hezekiah and Arvilla
(Curtis) Griffith on Oct. 3, 1850. She was b. 1833, d. 1903. Timothy d.
1898. He served in the Civil War in Co. K, 163rd O.N.G., and after the
war was the Captain of Company F., of the State Militia. He had 515
acres in Sugar Creek Twp. They had the following children:
Alice$^{1.3.3.2.1.5.1n}$, m. Carrell B. Allman and ____ Bartruff; John C.
F.$^{1.3.3.2.1.5.2n}$, b. 1856, d. 1903, m. Clara Beidler; Anne$^{1.3.3.2.1.5.3n}$.

Mary Putman

Mary$^{1.3.3.2.2n}$ m. John Shaffer. He was b. 1793, d. 1848. Mary d.
Stark Co., Massilon, Ohio in 1848. They had the following children:
Sarah E.$^{1.3.3.2.2.1n}$, b. 1817, d. 1871, m. Ephraim Trout;
George$^{1.3.3.2.2.2n}$, b. 1818, d. 1906, m. Margaret Carl/Gabriel and
Anna (Margaret was b. 1820); Gabriel$^{1.3.3.2.2.3n}$, b. 1820, m. Anna
Warner; child$^{1.3.3.2.2.4n}$, b. 1820, d. 1840; John Putman$^{1.3.3.2.2.5n}$, b.
1826, d. 1904, m. Maria Smith (1829-1877) c.1850, and Hilda Terrell
McCoy c.1880; Elizabeth$^{1.3.3.2.2.6n}$, b. 1827, d. 1910, m. Henry Clay
Younkin; William Samuel$^{1.3.3.2.2.7n}$, b. 1829, d. 1904, m. Jane Shaw;
Catherine$^{1.3.3.2.2.8n}$, b. 1832, m. William C. Stewart;
Josiah$^{1.3.3.2.2.9n}$, b. 1834, m. Margaret Dick.

Gabriel Putman

Gabriel$^{1.3.3.2.3n}$ m. Susanna Weimer, Rebecca White, and Sarah Hite.
Susan was b. 1797, d. 1865. Gabriel d. Stark Co., Wilmont, Ohio on
Nov. 27, 1882. Gabriel and Susanna had the following children:
   Christina$^{1.3.3.2.3.1n}$, b. 1822, m. Josiah Shunk, and ___ Kaylor.
   Mary$^{1.3.3.2.3.2n}$, b. 1823, d. 1841.
   Harriet$^{1.3.3.2.3.3n}$, b. c.1825, m. Alexander Shenk.
   Sallie$^{1.3.3.2.3.4n}$, b. c.1826, m. ____ Ash.
   Joseph Weimer$^{1.3.3.2.3.5n}$, b. Oct. 16, 1828, m. Hannah, dau. of
      Henry and Susan (Wallace) Stambaugh, in Aug., 1851. She
      was b. Sugar Creek Twp. in Jan., 1834. Joseph had a custom
      mill in New Hope Twp., and was a member of the milling
      company, Putman and Bro., in Wilmot.
   Hiram$^{1.3.3.2.3.4n}$, b. 1831, m. Mary Hobbs. She was b. 1836.

Catherine Putman

Catherine$^{1.3.3.2.4n}$ m. William Logan. He was b. 1781, d. 1883. She
d. Somerset Co., Pennsylvania on Sept. 23, 1837. They had the

following children: Andrew$^{1.3.3.2.4.1n}$; John$^{1.3.3.2.4.2n}$, b. 1820, m. Catherine Wyandt; Malinda$^{1.3.3.2.4.3n}$, b. 1845, d. 1930. She m. Benjamin Guise (1832-1913); Eva$^{1.3.3.2.4.4n}$; Canarissa$^{1.3.3.2.4.5n}$; William$^{1.3.3.2.4.6n}$, b. 1824, d. 1913.

Eva Putman

Eva$^{1.3.3.2.5n}$ m. George Barron. He was b. 1795, d. 1861. Eva d. Somerset Co., Middle Creek Twp., Pennsylvania on Jan. 15, 1868. They had the following children: Sarah$^{1.3.3.2.5.1n}$, b. 1819, d. 1903; Harriet$^{1.3.3.2.5.2n}$, b. c.1821, m. Daniel Dickey; Elizabeth$^{1.3.3.2.5.3n}$, b. 1825, d. 1888, m. Jeremiah Weimer (1826-1883); Rebecca$^{1.3.3.2.5.4n}$, b. 1827, m. Daniel W. Dull; Moses$^{1.3.3.2.5.5n}$, b. 1829, d. 1905, m. Martha Critchfield (1833-1892); John$^{1.3.3.2.5.6n}$, b. 1833, d. 1895; Simon$^{1.3.3.2.5.7n}$, b. 1836, d. 1913, m. Matilda Schlag (1840-1918); Mary$^{1.3.3.2.5.8n}$, b. 1836, m. Jacob Lenhart (b. 1835); Amanda$^{1.3.3.2.5.9n}$, b. 1840, m. John Schlag; Aaron$^{1.3.3.2.5.10n}$, b. c.1842, m. Catherine Walker.

Peter Putman

Peter$^{1.3.3.2.7n}$ m. Margaret/Mary Ann Adams c.1826 and Sarah E. Neiferd in Van Wert Co., Liberty Twp., Ohio on May 26, 1853. Margaret/Mary Ann d. 1844. Sarah was b. 1823. Peter d. Van Wert Co., Liberty Twp., Ohio on Jan. 13, 1885. He had the following children: Alexander$^{1.3.3.2.7.1n}$, b. 1827, m. Mary Temple and Sarah A. Shaffer; Isaac$^{1.3.3.2.7.2n}$, b. 1829, m. Sophia Mihm; Rosanna$^{1.3.3.2.7.3n}$, b. 1832, m. Josiah Ickes; John$^{1.3.3.2.7.4n}$, b. 1833, m. Martha Jane King; Mary$^{1.3.3.2.7.5n}$, b. 1839, m. Mac Brewer; Maria$^{1.3.3.2.7.6n}$, b. 1841, m. Marion B. Shaffer; Catherine$^{1.3.3.2.7.7n}$, b. 1844, m. Crayton Brewer; Winfield Scott$^{1.3.3.2.7.8n}$, b. 1854; Zachariah Taylor$^{1.3.3.2.7.9n}$, b. 1855; Jasper Newton$^{1.3.3.2.7.10n}$, b. 1857, m. Emma Frances Fortney; Peter Farmer$^{1.3.3.2.7.11n}$, b. 1858, d. 1900, m. Anna E. McClure (b. 1870); Tanner$^{1.3.3.2.7.12n}$, b. 1859; Sarah Elizabeth$^{1.3.3.2.7.13n}$, b. 1860, m. Andrew Agler$^{1.3.3.2.1.1.5n}$; Mary Ann$^{1.3.3.2.7.14n}$, b. 1862; Francis Marion$^{1.3.3.2.7.15n}$, b. 1863; Elder Willis$^{1.3.3.2.7.16n}$, b. 1864, m. Lena Gaier; Arminta$^{1.3.3.2.7.17n}$, b. 1866, m. Frank King (b. 1865); William Clark$^{1.3.3.2.7.18n}$, b. 1867; Clara B.$^{1.3.3.2.7.19n}$, b. 1872; Andrew$^{1.3.3.2.7.20n}$, b. c.1874.

Rosina Putman

Rosina$^{1.3.3.2.9n}$ m. John P. Cover. He was b. 1803, d. 1884. Rosina d. Somerset Co., Brother's Valley Twp., Pennsylvania on June 2, 1879. They had the following children: Phoebe$^{1.3.3.2.9.1n}$, b. 1826; Agnes$^{1.3.3.2.9.2n}$, b. 1828; Silas$^{1.3.3.2.9.3n}$, b. 1830; Amelia$^{1.3.3.2.9.4n}$, b. 1832; David J.$^{1.3.3.2.9.5n}$, b. 1834; Rosey Anne$^{1.3.3.2.9.6n}$, b. 1843; Peter J.$^{1.3.3.2.9.7n}$, b. 1845.

Elizabeth Putman

Elizabeth$^{1.3.3.2.10n}$ m. Joseph, son of Peter and Maria (Schneider) Boudemont, in Somerset Co., Pennsylvania on Oct., 1829. Elizabeth d. Stark Co., Sugar Creek Twp., Ohio on Oct. 6, 1893. Joseph was born on March 6, 1808, d. Sugar Creek Twp. on Nov. 23, 1892. In 1833, Joseph purchased 365 acres in Stark Co., Sugar Creek Twp., Ohio, and moved there. In the Spring of 1876, he moved to Wilmot. They had the following children: John$^{1.3.3.2.10.1n}$; Gabriel$^{1.3.3.2.10.2n}$; Harriet$^{1.3.3.2.10.3n}$, m. Benjamin Bumgardiner, d. 1862; Sevilla$^{1.3.3.2.10.4n}$, m. Henry Kreiling; Mary$^{1.3.3.2.10.5n}$, resided in Columbiana Co., Ohio; Catherine$^{1.3.3.2.10.6n}$, m. Frederick Nowman; William J.$^{1.3.3.2.10.7n}$, m. Caroline (b. Tuscarwas Co., Ohio, Dec 20, 1849), dau. of D. and Elizabeth (Ricksicker) Olmstead, on May 23, 1871.

Hannah Putman

Hannah$^{1.3.3.2.11n}$ m. Henry, son of John and Catherine (Binfert) Bruner. Henry was b. 1809, d. Baskerville, Pennsylvania in 1851. Hannah d. there on Oct. 26, 1894. They had the following children: Savila$^{1.3.3.2.11.1n}$, b. 1831, d. 1909; John Andrew$^{1.3.3.2.11.2n}$, b. 1832; Hiram$^{1.3.3.2.11.3n}$, b. 1834, d. 1883; Margaret$^{1.3.3.2.11.4n}$, b. 1835, d. 1854; George Washington$^{1.3.3.2.11.5n}$, b. 1837, d. 1936; Myria$^{1.3.3.2.11.6n}$, b. 1839, d. 1929; Harriet$^{1.3.3.2.11.7n}$, b. 1840; Louisa$^{1.1.4.1.3.3.2n}$, born and d. 1842; Elizabeth$^{1.3.3.2.11.9n}$, b. 1843, d. 1917; Josophene$^{1.3.3.2.11.10n}$, b. 1845, d. 1904; Israel$^{1.3.3.2.11.11n}$, b. 1847, d. 1939; Noah$^{1.3.3.2.11.12n}$, b. 1849, d. 1929.

Susanna Lenhart

Susanna$^{1.3.3.5n}$ m. John, son of John (b. Germany in 1740) and Susanna (1741-1812) Weimer. He was b. Somerset Co., Milford Twp., Pennsylvania on May 11, 1764, d. Westmoreland Co., Ligonier Twp., Pennsylvania in 1812. Susanna d. Stark Co., Sugar Creek Twp., Ohio on Oct. 1, 1829. She is buried in Weimer cemetery. They had the following children in Milford Twp.:

John Henry$^{1.3.3.5.1n}$, b. July 11, 1789, bapt. Sept. 20, 1789, m. Margaret Arenal Potts.

John$^{1.3.3.5.2n}$, bapt. at Sanner Lutheran Church on Feb. 15, 1793.

Elizabeth$^{1.3.3.5.3n}$, b. c.1794, d. before 1813.

Anna Catherine$^{1.3.3.5.4n}$, b. July 17, 1796, m. David Weimer in Westmoreland Co., Donegal Twp., Pennsylvania on Jan. 18, 1814.

Peter$^{1.3.3.5.5n}$, b. 1797.

Mary$^{1.3.3.5.6n}$, b. c.1799.

Gabriel$^{1.3.3.5.7n}$, b. May 13, 1801.

Gabriel Weimer

Gabriel[1.3.3.5.7n] m. Anna Overholser on Dec. 22, 1821, and Elizabeth, dau. of Philip and Susanna (Weimer) Dumbauld, in Stark Co., Ohio on March 28, 1840. Anna was b. Somerset Co., Pennsylvania on April 8, 1802, d. Stark Co., Sugar Creek Twp., Ohio on Jan. 15, 1839. Elizabeth was born on March 29, 1811. Gabriel had the following children in Stark Co., Ohio: Elias W.[1.3.3.5.7.1n], b. Sept. 15, 1824, m. Margaret (b.1829), d. Stark Co. on Sept. 6, 1898; Sarah A.[1.3.3.5.7.2], b. c.1826; Susan[1.3.3.5.7.3n], b. c.1828; Louisa[1.3.3.5.7.4n], b. c.1830; Josiah[1.3.3.5.7.5n], b. Feb. 26, 1831, d. April 7, 1842; Orlando B.[1.3.3.5.7.6n], b. Jan. 22, 1835, m. Amanda Ward in Millersburg, Ohio in 1863, d. Stark Co. on Jan. 22, 1901; Franklin[1.3.3.5.7.7n], b. Feb. 12, 1841, m. Oct 14, 1873, Catherine Crise (b. Somerset Co., Pennsylvania, 1851) Oct. 14, 1873; Oliver[1.3.3.5.7.8n], b. Feb. 12, 1843; Rose A.[1.3.3.5.7.9n], b. March 24, 1845, m. W. M. Stanford; Uriah[1.3.3.5.7.10n], b. May 26, 1847, d. April 8, 1889, m. Aug. 18, 1867, Magdalena Elizabeth Burris (b. Ohio, 1850); Mary C.[1.3.3.5.7.11n], b. Jan. 30, 1850; Solomon[1.3.3.5.7.12n], b. June 26, 1852, m. Katherine Diedler.

Maria Barbara Lenhart

Maria Barbara[1.3.3.6n] m. Samuel, son of John and Susannah (Whipkey) Berkey, in Somerset Co., Pennsylvania on June 13, 1797, and had the following children in Somerset Co.: Samuel[1.3.3.6.1n], b. 1798; a son[1.3.3.6.2n], b. 1800.

Hannah Lenhart

Hannah[1.3.3.7n] m. John, son of John and Elisabeth (Boudemont) Dull, in Somerset Co., Pennsylvania c.1799. She was b. York Co., Newbury Twp., Pennsylvania in 1780. He was b. Washington Co., Root's Hill, near Eakles Mills, Maryland in Oct., 1778. About 1814, John and Hannah moved to Fayette Co., Salt Lick Twp., Pennsylvania, near Champion, and in 1832, moved to Stark Co., Sugar Creek Twp., Ohio, near Wilmont. In Stark Co., John entered 320 acres of land. John d. from Asiatic Cholera on Sept. 20, 1834, and Hannah d. from the same disease on Sept. 27, 1834. They are buried in Weimer Church cemetery. A stone was erected several years after their death, by their son, Elias, but the bronze plaque, which held the inscription was melted down for the war effort. John and Hannah had the following children: Peter[1.3.3.7.1n], b. June 4, 1800; Anna Maria[1.3.3.7.2n], b. March 1, 1802; Joseph[1.3.3.7.3n], b. Feb. 9, 1804; Philipena "Phebe"[1.3.3.7.4n], b. March 7, 1806; John[1.3.3.7.5n], b. Jan. 15, 1808; infant[1.3.3.7.6n], b. c.1810; infant[1.3.3.7.7n], b. c.1812; Elizabeth[1.3.3.7.8n], b. June 4, 1813; Lenhart[1.3.3.7.9n], b. Aug. 11, 1815; Jacob[1.3.3.7.10n], b. May 1, 1817; Johannah[1.3.3.7.11n], b. May 11,

1819; Elias$^{1.3.3.7.12n}$, b. Feb. 3, 1822; Catherine$^{1.3.3.7.13n}$, b. Dec. 27, 1824.

Peter Dull

Peter$^{1.3.3.7.1n}$ m. Catherine, dau. of Samuel and Elisabetha Barbara (Robinson) Schlater, in Fayette Co., Pennsylvania in 1824. Peter moved to Stark Co., Ohio with his father in 1832, and in 1840, moved to Mercer Co., Dublin Twp., Ohio, settling just North East of Shanes Crossing. He purchased 161 acres in section six in 1840, and sold it to his brothers-in-law, W. R. and P. Schlater in 1841 to purchase 183 acres in section ten. In 1842, 1853, and 1855, He purchased land in section three. From 1867 to 1882, Peter deeded all of his land in section three to Josiah, Thomas, William Dull, and Nancy Jane Hooks. In 1882, Peter sold the home farm (consisting of 100 acres) in section ten to Nancy Jane Hooks, and the remaining 83 acres to William Dull. From 1882 till his death, Peter resided with his dau., Nancy Jane Hooks. Peter farmed northeast of Shane's Crossing until his death on April 7, 1888. Catherine was b. Fayette Co., Salt Lick Twp., Pennsylvania on Sept. 30, 1804, d. on Oct. 8, 1882, and is buried beside Peter in Ridge cemetery in Van Wert Co., Ohio. They had the following children:

Jeremiah$^{1.3.3.7.1.1n}$, b. 1825, m. Cynthia Ann, dau. of William and Catharine (Harp) Frysinger, in Van Wert Co., Ohio on Dec. 8, 1853, and Sarah Ann (Shaffer) Putman in Mercer Co. April 10, 1862. Cynthia was b. 1831, d. Dublin Twp. in 1859, buried in the Old Frysinger cemetery. Jeremiah enlisted on Sept. 7, 1864, killed in Chatham Co., Savannah, Georgia Jan. 30, 1865, buried in Laurel Grove cemetery, Georgia.

Mary$^{1.3.3.7.1.2n}$, b. May 13, 1827, m. Hugh Dobson in Mercer Co. Sept. 7, 1848. She d. Dublin Twp. Jan. 4, 1850, buried in Ridge cemetery.

Josiah$^{1.3.3.7.1.3n}$, b. March 5, 1829, m. Mary Ann, dau. of Abraham and Martha Miller, in Mercer Co. on Nov. 10, 1854, and Mary Jane, dau. of William and Lydia (Baltzell) Dilbone, c.1889/90. Mary Ann was b. Ohio in 1836, d. of typhoid in Dublin Twp. Oct. 31, 1889. Mary Jane was the widow of Jefferson Everett. She was born Miami Co., Ohio Aug. 1837, and was living in 1900. Josiah d. Dublin Twp. Aug. 13, 1909. They are buried in Mount Olive cemetery.

Lucinda$^{1.3.3.7.1.4n}$, b. Feb. 8, 1833, m. Seth Temple in Van Wert Co., Ohio on Dec. 2, 1852. He was b. 1824, d. Van Wert Co., Liberty Twp., Ohio Aug. 15, 1863. Lucinda d. Liberty Twp. on Sept. 20, 1861, and is buried beside her husband in Ridge cemetery.

Samuel$^{1.3.3.7.1.5n}$, b. March 17, 1834, and brought a load of horses for his father, by way of rail to Viroqua, Wisconsin in 1851. He sold all but two teams, which he traded for land in Vernon Co., Bad Ax, Wisconsin. He m. Mary O'Leary in Vernon Co., Bad Ax, Wisconsin in Sept. 1856. Samuel sold the land in Bad Ax, and purchased land on North Clayton, where he raised his family. Later he turned the farm over to his son, John, and moved to Readstown, Wisconsin. After a short stay, they returned to North Clayton. He d. Vernon Co., North Clayton, Wisconsin on April 21, 1918.

Hannah$^{1.3.3.7.1.6n}$, b. March 10, 1836, d. Mercer/Van Wert Co., Ohio Sept. 21, 1899, m. Lafayette Frazier (1818-1899) in Mercer Co. April 5, 1849.

Catherine$^{1.3.3.7.1.7n}$, b. March 10, 1836, d. in Mercer Co., Dublin Twp. in 1907, m. Alfred Frysinger in Mercer Co. Sept. 5, 1857. He was b. Ohio in 1834.

John$^{1.3.3.7.3.3.2n}$, b. Feb. 8, 1837, m. Susan, dau. of George and Katherine A. (Stophlet) Roebuck, in Mercer Co. Jan. 1, 1860, and Louisa, dau. of William and Lydia (Baltzell) Dilbone, in Mercer Co. Dec. 23, 1866. Susan d. Dublin Twp. Aug. 9, 1863, buried in Roebuck cemetery. Louisa d. Dublin Twp. in 1913. John d. Dublin Twp. Nov. 27, 1897. John and Louisa are buried in Mt. Olive cemetery. John had a 40-acre farm on the Louis Godfrey Reserve in Dublin Twp.

William S.$^{1.3.3.7.1.9n}$, b. March 15, 1840, m. Martha Shindeldecker in Mercer Co. on Aug. 18, 1861. She was b. Oct. 22, 1838, d. Mercer Co., Dublin Twp., Ohio on March 24, 1925. He d. Van Wert Co., Ohio City, Ohio Feb. 22, 1913, buried in Woodlawn cemetery.

Franklin$^{1.3.3.7.1.10n}$, b. 1843, m. Jane Miller in Mercer Co. on March 12, 1863. In the 1880s, they resided in Hamilton Co., Cincinnati, Ohio and Clermont Co., Goshen, Ohio.

Nancy Jane$^{1.3.3.7.1.11n}$, b. May 12, 1848, m. Abraham Hooks in Mercer Co. on Feb. 29, 1872. He was b. Dublin Twp. on Dec. 28, 1851, d. Allen Co., Lima, Ohio on Feb. 8, 1913. She d. in Lima on Jan. 8, 1901.

Phoebe$^{1.3.3.7.1.12n}$, b. March 15, 1849, d. on Jan. 27, 1853, buried in Ridge cemetery.

Anna Maria Dull

Anna Maria$^{1.3.3.7.2}$ m. Heinrich, son of Samuel and Elisabetha Barbara (Robinson) Schlater, in Fayette Co., Pennsylvania in 1821. Henry was b. Fayette Co., Salt Creek Twp., Pennsylvania in 1800, d. Tuscarwas Co., Wayne Twp., Ohio in 1847. Anna Maria d. Davies Co., Indiana in 1882. In 1850, Anna Maria resided in Tuscarwas Co., Ohio. They had the following children: Catherine$^{1.3.3.7.2.1n}$, b. 1827, m.

Crawford Arford in Tuscarwas Co., Ohio on March 3, 1850; Phebe Ann[1.3.3.7.2.2b], b. 1835, m. James M. Smith in Mercer Co., Ohio on Aug. 16, 1855.

Joseph Dull

Joseph[1.3.3.7.3n] m. Elizabeth Isabell, dau. of Frederick and Christina (Wolfe) Dumbauld, in Fayette Co., Pennsylvania March 29, 1827. She was b. Fayette Co., Pennsylvania Oct. 30, 1807, d. Licking Co., Ohio March 21, 1881. Joseph d. Licking Co., Liberty Twp., Ohio Oct. 17, 1891. They had the following children:

Phebe[1.3.3.7.3.1n], b. Fayette Co., Salt Lick Twp., Pennsylvania Jan. 7, 1829, m. Elisha T. P. Brooks.

Christina[1.3.3.7.3.2n], b. Fayette Co., Salt Lick Twp., Pennsylvania June 3, 1831, m. Joseph Perkins Brooks. He was b. Licking Co., Ohio May 29, 1831, and resided in Erie Co., Sandusky, Ohio in 1917.

Johannah[1.3.3.7.3.3n], b. Stark Co., Sugar Creek Twp., Ohio Aug. 1, 1833, m. Jackson Stephens in Licking Co., Ohio July 17, 1853. Joannah d. March 22, 1898.

Uriah[1.3.3.7.1.3.4n], b. Stark Co., Sugar Creek Twp., Ohio Nov. 15, 1835, m. Oelands/Lindy Ramsey. Uriah d. Aug. 31, 1909.

Nancy[1.3.3.7.1.3.5n], b. Ohio June 17, 1838, m. Jared Anderson.

John[1.3.3.7.1.3.6n], b. Ohio March 23, 1841, m. Mary Tippett.

Elias[1.3.3.7.1.3.7n], b. Ohio Oct. 10, 1843, m. Caroline Wright. She was b. 1851.

Charlotte[1.3.3.7.1.3.8n], b. Ohio June 15, 1848, m. Allen Stanbach/ Stanbaugh June 23, 1875. She d. Stark Co., Sugar Creek Twp., Ohio.

Lucenia Jane[1.3.3.7.1.3.9n], b. Ohio June 15, 1848, d. Ohio on Aug. 18, 1856.

Phillipena Dull

Phillipena "Phebe"[1.3.3.7.4n] m. John, son of Heinrich and Martha (Morrison) Schlater, in Fayette Co., Pennsylvania c.1824. They moved to Stark Co., Ohio before 1831, and Van Wert Co., Ohio c.1836. John was b. Fayette Co., Salt Lick Twp., Pennsylvania Feb. 13, 1800, d. Van Wert Co., Liberty Twp., Ohio Sept. 22, 1845. Phebe d. there Aug. 11, 1887. They had the following children:

Joseph[1.3.3.7.4.1n], b. 1825, m. Maria. They resided in Van Wert Co., Liberty Twp., Ohio in 1850. He was Mayor of Van Wert from 1862 to 1866, and managed the America House Tavern.

Mary A.[1.3.3.7.4.2n], b. 1826.

Nancy[1.3.3.7.4.3n], b. c.1828, m. O. W. Rose in Van Wert Co., Ohio Jan. 8, 1849.

Sarah[1.3.3.7.4.4n], b. Nov. 26, 1829, m. Abraham Balyeat in Van

Wert Co., Ohio May 13, 1852. He was b. 1823, d. 1881. Sarah
d. Van Wert Co., Pleasant Twp., Ohio Jan. 19, 1894.

Polly$^{1.3.3.7.4.5n}$, b. Dec. 16, 18(30), d. Stark Co., Sugar Creek
    Twp., Ohio March 17, 18(33). She is buried in Weimer
    cemetery.

Catherine$^{1.3.3.7.4.6n}$, b. 1830, m. R. Conn.

Hannah$^{1.3.3.7.4.7n}$, b. 1833, m. Z. A. Smith. They resided in
    Kansas.

Judith$^{1.3.3.7.4.8n}$, b. 1835, m. Robert Bruce Encill. They resided in
    Kosciusco Co., Warsaw, Indiana.

Benjamin F.$^{1.3.3.7.4.9n}$, b. July 5, 1837, m. Delilah Fortney in Van
    Wert Co., Ohio April 21, 1861. She was b. 1843, d. 1883.

Elizabeth$^{1.3.3.7.4.10n}$, b. Feb. 7, 1840, m. George F. Edson in Van
    Wert Co., Ohio March 29, 1857.

Jane$^{1.3.3.7.4.11n}$, b. 1841, m. William Henry McGough.

Samuel$^{1.3.3.7.4.12n}$, b. 1844.

John$^{1.3.3.7.4.13n}$, b. 1846.

John Dull

John$^{1.3.3.7.1.5n}$ m. Mary Jane Harbaugh in 1829. She was b.
Pennsylvania Feb. 17, 1813, d. Van Wert Co., Wilshire Twp., Ohio Nov.
20, 1882. John d. Wilshire Twp. Aug. 28, 1849. They had the following
children:

Lydia$^{1.3.3.7.1.5.1n}$, b. Fayette Co., Salt Lick Twp., Pennsylvania in
    1830, d. 1915. She m. Samuel Krick.

Franklin Benjamin$^{1.3.3.7.1.5.2n}$, b. Stark Co., Sugar Creek Twp.,
    Ohio in 1832, m. Rebecca Jane Walters in Van Wert Co. Dec.
    21, 1854. She was born Jan. 31, 1837, d. Wilshire Twp. Sept.
    30, 1894. Franklin d. Wilshire Twp. in 1910.

Sarah$^{1.3.3.7.1.5.3n}$, b. Stark Co., Sugar Creek Twp., Ohio in 1834,
    m. John Smith.

Joseph$^{1.3.3.7.1.5.4n}$, b. Stark Co., Sugar Creek Twp., Ohio in 1836.

George A.$^{1.3.3.7.1.5.5n}$, b. Van Wert Co., Wilshire Twp., Ohio Sept.
    27, 1841, d. Sept. 3, 1849.

John$^{1.3.3.7.1.5.6n}$, b. Wilshire Twp. c.1843.

Louisa Jane$^{1.3.3.7.1.5.7n}$, b. Wilshire Twp. in 1845, d. 1923. She
    m. Conrad Ault.

Mary J.$^{1.3.3.7.1.5.8n}$, b. Wilshire Twp. Aug. 23, 1849, d. March 23,
    1851.

Elizabeth Dull

Elizabeth$^{1.3.3.7.8n}$ m. Simon, son of Henry and Elizabeth (Warner)
Wyandt, in Stark Co., Ohio Nov. 5, 1834. They moved to Van Wert
Co., Harrison Twp., Ohio in 1839, and brought Elizabeth's sister
Catherine. Simon was born May 25, 1812, d. Harrison Twp. Jan. 4,

1859, and Elizabeth d. Van Wert Co., Convoy, Ohio Oct. 9, 1900. They had the following children: Henry$^{1.3.3.7.8.1n}$, b. 1835; John$^{1.3.3.7.8.2n}$, b. Jan. 30, 1837, m. Harriet Gunsett (b. 1839) in Van Wert Co., Ohio Dec. 5, 1861; Hannah$^{1.3.3.7.8.3n}$, b. Dec. 19, 1838, m. Josiah Gunsett (b. 1836) in Van Wert Co., Ohio March 3, 1860. He was b. 1836; David S.$^{1.3.3.7.8.4n}$, b. c.1840, d. c.1849; Jacob$^{1.3.3.7.8.5n}$, b. Aug. 3, 1842, m. Sarah E. North (b. Cumberland Co., Pennsylvania, May 11, 1846) in Van Wert Co., Ohio March 26, 1867; Catherine$^{1.3.3.7.8.6n}$, b. 1844, d. 1860; Franklin$^{1.3.3.7.8.7n}$, b. c.1846, d. c.1849; George W.$^{1.3.3.7.8.8n}$, b. 1847.

Lenhart Dull

Lenhart$^{1.3.3.7.1.9n}$ m. Susannah Ream in Van Wert Co., Feb. 17, 1842. She was born May 10, 1824, d. Tuscarwas Co., New Philadelphia, Ohio Nov. 10, 1924. After Lenhart's death, Susannah m. his brother, Elias (between 1900 and 1906). Lenhart d. Van Wert Co., Wilshire Twp., Ohio May 8, 1892. They had the following children in Wilshire Twp.: Celesta$^{1.3.3.7.1.9.1n}$, b. Dec. 2, 1844, d. 1937, m. Edward W. Robinson; James Monroe$^{1.3.3.7.1.9.2n}$, b. Jan. 23, 1846, d. Van Wert Co. June 6, 1916, m. Martha Ann Lintermoot (1851-1916) in Van Wert Co. May 17, 1868; Thomas Jefferson$^{1.3.3.7.1.9.3n}$, b. April 7, 1848, m. Mary Ursula Exline (1848-1918); George Washington$^{1.3.3.7.1.9.4n}$, b. June 2, 1850, d. 1892, m. Evaline Pickering in Mercer Co. March 7, 1875; Franklin Pierce$^{1.3.3.7.1.9.5n}$, b. Jan. 31, 1855, m. Hattie E. Martin (b. 1862) in Van Wert Co. Jan. 6, 1881; James Buchanan$^{1.3.3.7.1.9.6n}$, b. July 11, 1857, d. Mercer Co., Black Creek Twp., in 1945) m. Serena Lintermoot (b. Ohio, Nov 1863); Lafayette Jackson$^{1.3.3.7.1.9.7n}$, b. April 15, 1861, d. 1945, m. Cora McKillip in Mercer Co. Aug. 8, 1883, and Thursa Randels; Joseph Elmore$^{1.3.3.7.1.9.8n}$, b. Aug. 8, 1863, m. Augusta Krumboltz and Frances Krumboltz; Isabella$^{1.3.3.7.1.9.9n}$, b. Aug. 20, 1865, m. Victor Miller; Arabella$^{1.3.3.7.1.9.10n}$, b. Sept. 5, 1866, m. Frank Cushwa/Cushman; Mary C.$^{1.3.3.7.1.9.11n}$, b. March 5, 1871, m. Frank Estell.

Jacob Dull

Jacob$^{1.3.3.7.1.10n}$ m. Harriet Ream in Van Wert Co. Nov. 18, 1846. She was b. Ohio July 1, 1828, d. Van Wert Co., Wilshire Twp., Ohio April 12, 1914. Jacob d. Wilshire Twp. Aug. 15, 1904. They had the following children in Wilshire Twp.: Sylvester$^{1.3.3.7.1.10.1n}$, b. June, 1846, m. Rebecca Exline; Amos$^{1.3.3.7.1.10.2n}$, b. March, 1851, m. Emily E. Stewart (b. 1845) in Van Wert Co. March 8, 1873; Mariah Isabell$^{1.3.3.7.1.10.3n}$, b. 1855; Samuel$^{1.3.3.7.1.10.4n}$, b. Jan., 1858, m. Martha J. (b. 1856); Franklin Monroe$^{1.3.3.7.1.10.5n}$, b. April 3, 1860, d. Dec. 15, 1860; Margaret S.$^{1.3.3.7.1.10.6n}$, b. 1861;

Uriah$^{1.3.3.7.1.10.7n}$, b. 1875; Jacob A.$^{1.3.3.7.1.10.8n}$, b. 1878.

Johannah Dull

Johannah$^{1.3.3.7.1.11n}$ m. William Agler in Van Wert Co. March 21, 1847. He was b. Stark Co., Sugar Creek Twp., Ohio in 1824, d. Van Wert Co. in 1904. Johannah d. Van Wert Co. in 1894. They had the following children in Van Wert Co.: Mahala$^{1.3.3.7.1.11.1n}$, b. 1848, d. 1851; Emily Clara$^{1.3.3.7.1.11.2n}$, b. Jan. 6, 1850, d. in Lewiston, Michigan, Jan. 5, 1933, m. John William Lewellen (1844-1929) in Van Wert Co. Jan. 2, 1870; Valentine$^{1.3.3.7.1.11.3n}$, b. 1852, d. 1898, m. Mary Elizabeth Knight (b. 1857, d. 1898); Joseph R.$^{1.3.3.7.1.11.4n}$, b. 1854; Naomi$^{1.3.3.7.1.11.5n}$, b. 1856, d. 1930, m. Jacob Kraugh (1857-1929); Celestia$^{1.3.3.7.1.11.6n}$, b. 1859, d. 1876; William$^{1.3.3.7.1.11.7n}$, b. Jan., 1862; Willis McKey$^{1.3.3.7.1.11.8n}$, b. Jan., 1862, d. 1953, m. Mary Sabina (1864-1954), dau. of Joshua and Elmira (Medaugh) Wagers, July 4, 1888.

Elias Dull

Elias$^{1.3.3.7.1.12n}$ m. Jane Walters in Van Wert Co. Sept. 3, 1850 and Susannah Ream, widow of his brother, Lenhart, between 1900 and 1907. Jane was born Aug. 31, 1823, d. Wilshire Twp. April 25, 1900. Elias d. there Sept. 3, 1907. They had the following children in Wilshire Twp.:
Harriet Ellen$^{1.3.3.7.1.12.1n}$, b. July 1, 1853, m. John Lorenzo Hileman in Van Wert Co. May 5, 1870. He was b. 1848, d. 1918.
Hannah Lucretia$^{1.3.3.7.1.12.2n}$, b. Sept. 4, 1854, m. William Sylvania, son of Ephraim and Jane (Schlater) Medaugh, in Van Wert Co., Ohio Aug. 7, 1873. She d. Paulding Co., Paulding, Ohio Sept. 11, 1882. William d. Wilshire Twp. June 6, 1882.
John Wesley$^{1.3.3.7.1.12.3n}$, b. March 6, 1855, m. Mary Armand Bay in Van Wert Co. Dec. 2, 1875. She was b. 1855. He d. Wilshire Twp. in 1929.
William Walters$^{1.3.3.7.1.12.4n}$, b. March 4, 1857, m. Mary E. Shaffer. He d. Wilshire Twp. Nov. 19, 1909.
Rebecca Jane$^{1.3.3.7.1.12.5n}$, b. Feb. 4, 1860, m. Charley Blish in Van Wert Co. in 1882.
Mary Rosetta$^{1.3.3.7.1.12.6n}$, b. Nov. 11, 1865, m. Wirt A. Belden. Mary d. Wilshire Twp. July 9, 1890.

Catherine Dull

Catherine$^{1.3.3.7.1.13n}$ m. Peter Brubaker in Van Wert Co. Nov. 26, 1844. He was b. Franklin Co., Pennsylvania May 19, 1814, d. Van Wert Co., Liberty Twp., Ohio July 12, 1898. Catherine d. there July 28, 1909. They had the following children in Liberty Twp.:
George E.$^{1.3.3.7.1.13.1n}$, b. 1846.

Elizabeth$^{1.3.3.7.1.13.2n}$, b. 1847.
Naaman$^{1.3.3.7.1.13.3n}$, b. Dec. 12, 1849, m. Ellen Lintermoot. She was b. 1856.
Elmira$^{1.3.3.7.1.13.4n}$, b. Nov. 18, 1851, d. Sept. 2, 1853.
Eleanor$^{1.3.3.7.1.13.5n}$, b. 1854.
Willis$^{1.3.3.7.1.13.6n}$, b. 1857.
Annete$^{1.3.3.7.1.13.7n}$, b. 1859, m. ____ Smith.
Mary D.$^{1.3.3.7.1.13.8n}$, b. July, 1861, m. Solomon, son of Isaac and Sophia (Mihm) Putman$^{1.3.3.2.7.2.1n}$, in Van Wert Co., Ohio in 1880.
Hannah D.$^{1.3.3.7.1.13.9n}$, b. 1864.
William$^{1.3.3.7.1.13.10n}$, b. 1866.

Johan Georg Lenhart

Johan Georg$^{1.3.3.10n}$ m. Mary (possibly Berkey). She was b. 1799, d. 1875. Georg d. Somerset Co., Milford Twp., Pennsylvania in 1842. They had the following children in Milford Twp.: George$^{1.3.3.10.1n}$, b. c.1819, resided in Short Creek, West Virginia; Benjamin$^{1.3.3.10.2n}$, b. 1820, m. Elizabeth Ann Faust in 1847; Hannah$^{1.3.3.10.3n}$, b. 1823, m. Baltzer Walter (b. 1824); Monroe$^{1.3.3.10.4n}$, b. 1825, d. 1907, m. Rose Ann Coleman (1831-1900); Victorian$^{1.3.3.10.5n}$, b. c.1827; Mary$^{1.3.3.10.6n}$, b. c.1829, m. ____ Kiem; Useba$^{1.3.3.10.7n}$, b. 1833, m. ____ Shumaker; Elizabeth Ann$^{1.3.3.10.8n}$, b. 1837; Anna E.$^{1.3.3.10.9n}$, b. 1838.

Jon Christoph Lenhart

Jon Christoph$^{1.3.4n}$ m. Anna Maria. In 1780, he served as a Private in the Revolutionary War, and resided in York Co., Dover Twp., Pennsylvania. By 1790, he resided in Westmoreland Co., Unity Twp., Pennsylvania, d. there c.1813. Christoph and Anna Maria had the following children: Johan Christoffel$^{1.3.4.1n}$, bapt. at Strayer's Lutheran Church July 31, 1768, sponsored by Hans Georg and Christina Stauch; Johan Adam$^{1.3.4.2n}$, b. Sept. 6, 1770, bapt. at Strayer's Dec. 25, 1770, sponsored by Adam and Anna Margaretha Diehl; Peter$^{1.3.4.3n}$, b. c.1775; Johannes$^{1.3.4.4n}$, b. Sept. 30, 1779, bapt. at Strayer's March 26, 1780, sponsored by George and Barbara Richter; Frederick$^{1.3.4.5n}$, b. 1781; Heinrich$^{1.3.4.6n}$, b. c.1788.

Johan Christoffel Lenhart

Christoffel$^{1.3.4.1n}$ m. Catherine. Christoffel moved to Tuscarwas Co., Ohio with his brother Peter around 1809, in 1810, he was in Goshen Twp., and later settled in Muskingum Co., Newton Twp., Ohio, before 1816, where he d. June, 1848 (in 1819/20 he is on the census of Perry Co., Madison Twp., Ohio). Christoffel and Catherine had the following children:

John$^{1.3.4.1.1n}$, b. Unity Twp. in 1795, m. Eliza Fluke in Perry Co.,

Ohio April 29, 1824. He resided in Perry Co., Ohio in 1830, 40, 50.

Mary$^{1.3.4.1.2n}$, b. Westmoreland Co., Unity Twp., Pennsylvania c.1798, m. Adam Ramer, and resided in Tuscarwas Co., Wayne Twp., Ohio in 1820.

Elizabeth$^{1.3.4.1.3n}$, b. Unity Twp. in 1801, m. James Oatley in Muskingum Co., Ohio Feb. 19, 1824.

Joseph$^{1.3.4.1.4n}$, b. Unity Twp. c.1804, m. Nancy Vickers in Muskingum Co., Ohio Aug. 18, 1825. He resided in Perry Co. in 1830, d. before 1840.

David$^{1.3.4.1.5n}$, b. c.1806, m. Harriet Fluke in Perry Co., Ohio Feb. 28, 1828. He d. Perry Co., Ohio in 1850. His will was written June 18, 1850, and probated Sept. 30, 1850. He resided in Muskingum Co. in 1830 and 1840.

Isaac P.$^{1.3.4.1.6n}$, b. 1808, m. Ellen Rutledge in Perry Co. Dec. 28, 1848, and Sarah (b.1808) before 1850.

William M.$^{1.3.4.1.7n}$, b. c.1810, m. Mary Ann Emrey in Muskingum Co., Ohio July 29, 1830, Rachel Rambo in Muskingum Co. Oct. 2, 1834, Mary Ann Sylvester in Muskingum Co. Nov. 20, 1844, and Naomi J. Roberts in Muskingum Co. Sept. 15, 1859. He resided in Muskingum Co., Ohio in 1840.

Jacob$^{1.3.4.1.8n}$, b. c.1812, m. Hannah Griffith in Muskingum Co., Ohio May 27, 1834, and Polly (?Mary Ann Treesch in Stark Co., Ohio May 27, 1838), d. before 1848.

Peter Lenhart

Peter$^{1.3.4.3n}$ was in Tuscarwas Co., Dover Twp., Ohio from 1810-23. He is presumed to have d. c.1823. (A William Lenhart paid tax on a Dover Town Lot on Nov. 7, 1814) He came to Ohio with his brother, Christoffel c.1809/10. Peter had the following children: Daniel$^{1.3.4.3.1n}$, b. Westmoreland Co., Unity Twp., Pennsylvania c.1795, m. Elizabeth Shanks in Tuscarwas Co., Ohio Jan. 12, 1817; John$^{1.3.4.3.2n}$, b. Unity Twp. Feb. 24, 1797; David$^{1.3.4.3.3n}$, b. Unity Twp. in 1804; Margaret$^{1.3.4.3.4n}$, b. Unity Twp. c.1806, m. Anthony Fabra in Tuscarwas Co. Oct. 1, 1826; Peter$^{1.3.4.3.5n}$, b. Unity Twp. in 1807, m. Nancy Thomas in Tuscarwas Co. Sept. 18, 1823, d. 1872; Joseph$^{1.3.4.3.6n}$, b. Unity Twp. in 1809; Dalena$^{1.3.4.3.7n}$, b. Tuscarwas Co., Dover Twp., Ohio in 1812.

John Lenhart

John$^{1.3.4.3.2n}$ m. Rebecca, dau. of John Burrell, in Tuscarwas Co., Ohio c.1819. She was b. Washington Co., Maryland Sept. 22, 1801, d. Adams Co., Root Twp., Indiana May 20, 1873. They resided in Tuscarwas Co., Wayne Twp., Ohio from 1820 to the fall of 1839, and then moved to Adams Co., Indiana. From 1831-33, he had 60 acres in

Section 23, and 4 cattle. From 1842-43, John served as the Adams Co. Commissioner. He was a farmer in Section 34 of Root Twp., d. there May 18, 1877. John and Rebecca are buried in Alpha/Valley United Brethren cemetery. John's family also went by the spelling Linhard. They had the following children:

Lawson$^{1.3.4.3.2.1n}$, b. March 18, 1820, m. Lois, dau. of Josiah and Sarah (Warner) Brown, in Adams Co., Indiana May 3, 1847. She d. Root Twp. March 28, 1912. Lawson was a farmer, d. Root Twp. Dec. 18, 1894. They are buried in Alpha cemetery. Lawson had 54 acres in Section 40 of Root Twp.

Sarah$^{1.3.4.3.2.2n}$, b. June 9, 1822, m. John King in Adams Co., Indiana Jan. 31, 1841. He was b. March 26, 1820, d. Root Twp. Nov. 17, 1891. Sarah d. Adams Co., Decatur, Indiana Jan. 9, 1903.

Peter$^{1.3.4.3.2.3n}$, b. Aug. 14, 1824, m. Huldah, dau. of Josiah and Sarah (Warner) Brown, in Adams Co., Indiana March 25, 1849. About 1881, Huldah was committed to the Co. Home; she d. there April 13, 1888. She is buried in the Co. Home cemetery. Peter was a farmer in Root Twp., until 1893, when he moved to Allen Co., Madison Twp., Indiana. He d. Madison Twp. Feb. 19, 1902, and was buried in Alpha cemetery in Adams Co.

Catharine$^{1.3.4.3.2.4n}$, b. Dec. 14, 1826, m. Conrad Chronister in Adams Co., Indiana Nov. 28, 1850. He was b. Cumberland Co., Pennsylvania in 1827, d. Adams Co., Saint Mary's Twp., Indiana in 1905. Catherine d. Saint Mary's Twp. Oct. 6, 1917.

Elizabeth$^{1.3.4.3.2.5n}$, b. Oct. 24, 1830, m. Daniel Battenburg in Adams Co., Indiana Aug. 19, 1858. He was b. Butler Co., Ohio April 19, 1835, d. Allen Co., Monroe Twp., Indiana March 12, 1917. Elizabeth d. Monroe Twp. Feb. 5, 1922.

Mary$^{1.3.4.3.2.6n}$, b. Oct. 24, 1830, m. James Peterson in Adams Co., Indiana Jan. 1, 1852, d. c.1911.

John$^{1.3.4.3.2.7n}$, b. Sept. 8, 1832, d. Adams Co., Root Twp., Indiana July 28, 1872. He is buried in Alpha cemetery.

Joseph$^{1.3.4.3.2.8n}$, b. Dec. 31, 1835, m. Emma Bradley in Montgomery Co., Kansas Oct. 17, 1875, an unknown individual c.1881 (b. Missouri, d. before 1900), and Samantha D. before 1900. Emma was b. Illinois in 1857, d. c.1881. Joseph served in the Civil War from Adams Co., Indiana. He founded the town of Tyro, Kansas, had a general store there, d. there in 1923 (Montgomery Co., Fawn Creek Twp.).

Susannah$^{1.3.4.3.2.9n}$, b. Aug. 29, 1838, m. Phineas Shackley in Adams Co., Indiana Dec. 15, 1868. He was b. Massachusetts in 1829, d. Adams Co., Washington Twp., Indiana before 1880. Susannah d. Washington Twp. in 1917.

Rebecca$^{1.3.4.3.2.10n}$, b. 1841. She resided with her father until his death, and then remained on his farm.

William H.$^{1.3.4.3.2.11n}$, b. Jan. 20, 1844, d. Adams Co., Root Twp., Indiana May 24, 1904. He is buried in Alpha cemetery.

George Clinton$^{1.3.4.3.2.12n}$, b. June 1, 1849, d. Adams Co., Root Twp., Indiana in Feb., 1850. He is buried in Alpha cemetery.

David Lenhart

David$^{1.3.4.3.3.3n}$ m. Sarah Shoup in Tuscarwas Co., Ohio Sept. 3, 1823. She was b. Pennsylvania in 1805. They had the following children in Dover Twp.: Peter$^{1.3.4.3.3.1n}$, b. 1823 - He has not been confirmed as a son of David; Jacob$^{1.3.4.3.3.2n}$, b. 1832; Isaac$^{1.3.4.3.2.3.2.3.3.3n}$, b. 1833; William$^{1.3.4.3.3.4n}$, b. 1836; Susanna$^{1.3.4.3.3.5n}$, b. 1838; Sarah A.$^{1.3.4.3.3.6n}$, b. 1842; Elias$^{1.3.4.3.3.7n}$, b. 1844; Emily$^{1.3.4.3.3.8n}$, b. 1849.

Peter Lenhart

Peter$^{1.3.4.3.3.1n}$ m. Elizabeth (b. in Ohio in 1827). He was a shoemaker in Sugar Creek Twp. in 1850. They had the following children: Catherine$^{1.3.4.3.3.1.1n}$, b. 1846; William$^{1.3.4.3.3.1.2n}$, b. 1847; Mary M.$^{1.3.4.3.3.1.3n}$, b. 1849.

Joseph Lenhart

Joseph$^{1.3.4.3.6n}$ m. July Ann Stone in Tuscarwas Co., Ohio Dec. 17, 1829. She was b. Pennsylvania in 1813. They had the following children in Tuscarwas Co., Sugar Creek Twp.: Mahala$^{1.3.4.3.6.1n}$, b. 1832; Prudence$^{1.3.4.3.6.2n}$, b. 1834; John$^{1.3.4.3.6.3n}$, b. 1836; Peter$^{1.3.4.3.6.4n}$, b. 1838; Elizabeth$^{1.3.4.3.6.5n}$, b. 1840; William$^{1.3.4.3.6.6n}$, b. 1842; Hannah$^{1.3.4.3.2.3.6.7n}$, b. 1844; Hester A.$^{1.3.4.3.6.8n}$, b. 1846; Rebecca$^{1.3.4.3.6.9n}$, b. 1848.

Dalena Lenhart

Dalena$^{1.3.4.3.7n}$ m. Elijah Hawk in Tuscarwas Co., Ohio Nov. 16, 1834. He was b. Pennsylvania in 1806. They had the following children in Dover Twp.: Rebecca$^{1.3.4.3.7.1n}$, b. 1836; Elizabeth$^{1.3.4.3.7.2n}$, b. 1842; Edward$^{1.3.4.3.7.3n}$, b. 1848.

Johannes Lenhart

Johannes$^{1.3.4.4n}$ is presumed to have m. Anna, c.1793, and Eliza Morgan in Muskingum Co., Ohio May 11, 1809. He d. Muskingum Co., Ohio in 1822. Johannes had the following children in Westmoreland Co.: Johann Nichlaus$^{1.3.4.4.1n}$, b. Sept. 10, 1793, bapt. at Mount Zion Lutheran Church in Donegal Twp.; David$^{1.3.4.4.2n}$, b. Mount Pleasant Aug. 17, 1795, bapt. at St. John's Lutheran Church Dec. 13, 1795, sponsored by Frederick Mayer and Catharina Lavengeyer.

Frederick Lenhart

Frederick$^{1.3.4.5n}$ m. Mary M. (b. in Virginia in 1787), and resided in Tuscarwas Co., New Comer Twp., Ohio in 1850. They had a son in Ohio: Isaac$^{1.3.4.5.1n}$, b. 1822.

Heinrich Lenhart

Heinrich$^{1.3.4.6n}$ m. Catherine Munch in Muskingum Co., Ohio Feb. 20, 1816, d. Muskingum Co., Newton Twp., Ohio in 1840. He had the following son:
Frederick$^{1.3.4.6.1n}$, b. Feb. 19, 1819.

Wilhelm Lenhart

Wilhelm$^{1.3.6n}$ m. Anna Maria Rush. She was b. 1751, d. 1822. Wilhelm d. York Co., Dover Twp., Pennsylvania Oct. 27, 1819. They had the following children in Dover Twp.: Susanna$^{1.3.6.1n}$, b. c.1775, m. Samuel Close; Wilhelm$^{1.3.6.2n}$, b. March 3, 1777, bapt. at Strayer's April 20, 1777, and sponsored by Lorentz and Catharine Peitzel; Frederick$^{1.3.6.3n}$, b. 177(8), d. 1803; Catherine$^{1.3.6.4n}$, b. c.1780; John$^{1.3.6.5n}$, b. 1782, d. 1802; Johan George$^{1.3.6.5n}$, b. Sept. 26, 1784, bapt. at Strayer's Dec. 12, 1784, and sponsored by George and Barbara Stauch; Peter$^{1.3.6.6n}$, b. 1788; Lisabeth$^{1.3.6.7n}$, b. April 28, 1790, bapt. at Strayer's Aug. 2, 1790, m. Henry Miller; Heinrich$^{1.3.6.8n}$, b. c.1793.

Johan George Lenhart

Johan George$^{1.3.6.5n}$ m. Margareth (1783-1847), and Mary (1794-1864). George and Margareth bapt. the following children at Strayer's in Dover Twp.: Elisabeth$^{1.3.6.5.1n}$, bapt. April 5, 1807; Lidia$^{1.3.6.5.2n}$, bapt. May 1, 1808; Magdalena$^{1.3.6.5.3n}$, bapt. Aug. 11, 1816.

Peter Lenhart

Peter$^{1.3.6.6n}$ m. Elisabeth (1790-1859), d. 1868, and bapt. the following children at Strayer's in Dover Twp.: Catharina$^{1.3.6.6.1n}$, bapt. May 21, 1815; Elisabetha$^{1.3.6.6.2n}$, bapt. June 16, 1817; David$^{1.3.6.6.3n}$, bapt. April 27, 1819; Peter$^{1.3.6.6.4n}$, bapt. Nov. 4, 1821; Hanna$^{1.3.6.6.5n}$, bapt. March 21, 1824.

Heinrich Lenhart

Heinrich$^{1.3.6.6n}$ m. Christina, d. 1867, and bapt. the following child at Strayer's in Dover Twp.: Louisa$^{1.3.6.6.1n}$, bapt. Jan. 9, 1821.

Johan Peter Lenhart

Johan Peter$^{1.3.7n}$ m. Catherina Ogg c.1771. Peter d. Somerset Co., Addison Twp., Pennsylvania in May, 1814. Catharina was b. 1755, d. 1818. They moved to Bedford (now Somerset) Co., Pennsylvania in

1794. They had the following children:

Anna Maria$^{1.3.7.1n}$, bapt. at Strayer's in York Co., Dover Twp. Sept. 3, 1772, and sponsored by Christophel and Charlotha Kauffman.

Johan Peter$^{1.3.7.2n}$, b. Oct. 26, 1776, bapt. at Harold's Zion Church in Westmoreland Co., Pennsylvania Feb. 2, 1777, and sponsored by Peter and Catherine Klingensmith. He d. before 1813.

John$^{1.3.7.3n}$, b. c.1780.

Henry$^{1.3.7.4n}$, b. c.1782.

Eve$^{1.3.7.5n}$, b. c.1784.

Susannah$^{1.3.7.6n}$, b. Nov. 4, 1786.

Barbara$^{1.3.7.7n}$, b. c.1788, m. Thomas McMillan.

William F.$^{1.3.7.8n}$, b. 1793.

Jacob$^{1.3.7.9n}$, b. Jan. 2, 1793.

George$^{1.3.7.10n}$, b. April 10, 1794, d. Somerset Co., Lower Turkeyfoot Twp., Pennsylvania April 7, 1853.

Mary$^{1.3.7.11n}$, b. Somerset Co., Lower Turkeyfoot Twp., Pennsylvania in 1802.

Sarah$^{1.3.7.12n}$, b. Lower Turkeyfoot Twp. in 1803.

Susannah Lenhart

Susannah$^{1.3.7.6n}$ m. Jacob, son of Michael Schultz, and had the following children in Somerset Co., New Centerville, Pennsylvania: Peter$^{1.3.7.6.1n}$, b. 1806; John$^{1.3.7.6.2n}$, b. 1807; Catherine$^{1.3.7.6.3n}$, b. 1808; Elizabeth$^{1.3.7.6.4n}$, b. 1810; Barbara$^{1.3.7.6.5n}$, b. 1812; Jacob$^{1.3.7.6.6n}$, b. 1814; Jonas$^{1.3.7.6.7n}$, b. 1815; Susannah$^{1.3.7.6.8n}$, b. 1817; Mary$^{1.3.7.6.9n}$, b. 1818; Michael$^{1.3.7.6.10n}$, b. 1819; Phebe$^{1.3.7.6.11n}$, b. 1821; Lenhart$^{1.3.7.6.12n}$, b. 1823; Eva$^{1.3.7.6.13n}$, b. 1824.

William F. Lenhart

William F.$^{1.3.7.8n}$ m. Hulda, and had the following children in Lower Turkeyfoot Twp.: Zora$^{1.3.7.8.1n}$, b. 1830; George$^{1.3.7.8.2n}$, b. 1833; Jackson$^{1.3.7.8.3n}$, b. 1836; Millie$^{1.3.7.8.4n}$, b. 1839; Hiram$^{1.3.7.8.5n}$, b. 1843; Sarah$^{1.3.7.8.6n}$, b. 1844.

Jacob Lenhart

Jacob$^{1.3.7.9n}$ m. Diannah Christina Bowser. Jacob d. April 2, 1855. They had the following children: Elizabeth$^{1.3.7.9.1n}$, b. Sept. 4, 1818; Catherine A.$^{1.3.7.9.2n}$, b. c.1820, m. George W. Turney, d. Somerset Co., Addison Twp. March 14, 1885; Kiziah$^{1.3.7.9.3n}$, b. July 2, 1822, m. William Michael Wills, d. Somerset Co., Ursina Sept. 20, 1896; Susannah$^{1.3.7.9.4n}$, b. March 25, 1824, d. Addison Twp. Jan. 28, 1905; Peter J.$^{1.3.7.9.5n}$, b. Addison Twp. in 1828, m. Almira Hyatt in Lower

Turkeyfoot Twp. Dec. 1, 1853; Sarah M.$^{1\cdot3\cdot7\cdot9\cdot6n}$, b. Nov. 29, 1828, m. Daniel Herring, d. Jan. 12, 1908; Barbara$^{1\cdot3\cdot7\cdot9\cdot7n}$, b. Jan. 15, 1831, m. Samuel C. Wilhelm, d. Jan. 21, 1909; Levinia$^{1\cdot3\cdot7\cdot9\cdot8n}$, b. Feb. 13, 1833, d. Addison Twp. May 29, 1910; Diannah Christina$^{1\cdot3\cdot7\cdot9\cdot9n}$, b. July 22, 1834, m. William H. Bowser, d. May 17, 1879; Jacob Elogius$^{1\cdot3\cdot7\cdot9\cdot10n}$, b. June 25, 1838, m. Catherine Fike; William$^{1\cdot3\cdot7\cdot9\cdot11n}$, b. Jan. 29, 1845, d. Dec. 15, 1866.

Gottfried Lenhart

Gottfried$^{1\cdot3\cdot9n}$ m. Elizabeth Holtzinger in the First Reformed Church of York Nov. 14, 1778. She was b. 1753, d. 1824. Some sources say that he m. Maria Elisabetha, dau. of Yost and Maria Elisabetha Harbaugh, who was born on Good Friday, 1753, d. June 18, 1835. Possibly, Elizabeth Holtzinger was a widow, or Gottfried was m. twice. Gottfried was a clock maker in York, d. there Aug. 15, 1819. They bapt. the following children at the First Reformed Church of York: Margreda$^{1\cdot3\cdot9\cdot1n}$, b. Sept. 5, 1779, bapt. Dec. 19, 1779, m. Georg Adam Euntz (1777-1815), d. 1860; Elizabeth$^{1\cdot3\cdot9\cdot2n}$, b. Oct. 3, 1781, and bapt. Dec. 27, 1781; Heinrich$^{1\cdot3\cdot9\cdot3n}$, b. July 22, 1784, bapt. Aug. 30, 1784; William Jost$^{1\cdot3\cdot9\cdot4n}$, b. Jan. 19, 1787, d. July 10, 1840, a distinguished mathematician; Catharina$^{1\cdot3\cdot9\cdot5n}$, b. Oct. 10, 1791, bapt. Nov. 27, 1791.

Elizabeth Lenhart

Elizabeth$^{1\cdot3\cdot9\cdot2n}$ m. John Bayley in York April 30, 1803, d. 1845, and had a dau., Catherine$^{1\cdot3\cdot9\cdot2\cdot1n}$, m. Samuel Tyler.

Catharina Lenhart

Catharina$^{1\cdot3\cdot9\cdot5n}$ m. John Bayard McPhearson April 25, 1811, d. Jan. 25, 1859, and had a son, Edward$^{1\cdot3\cdot9\cdot5\cdot1n}$, resided in Gettysburg, Pennsylvania.

****

Hanss Peter Kessler

Hanss Peter^{1o} m. Anna Christina Peters in Horn Hunsrueck Oct. 13, 1663, and had the following children there: Anna Catharina$^{1\cdot1o}$, bapt. Aug. 28, 1664; Anna Gertraud$^{1\cdot2o}$, bapt. Oct. 18, 1666, m. Michael Schmidt in Horn Hunsrueck Oct. 31, 1683; Christophel$^{1\cdot3o}$, bapt. Feb. 25, 1671/72, m. Maria Gertruda Weutler in Horn Hunsrueck Nov. 10, 1693; Anna Eva$^{1\cdot4o}$, b. March 21, 1674/74, m. Johan Christopffel Leonhard^{1n}; Elisabeth Catharina$^{1\cdot5o}$, b. July 14, 1678.

****

Albinus Boyer

Albinus^{1p} was b. Germany in 1709, and arrived at Philadelphia in the ship Samuel Aug. 30, 1737. He m. Anna Maria Catarina (went by Anna Maria), dau. of Heinrich and Anna Maria Stentz, in York Co., Codorus Twp., Pennsylvania Sept. 23, 1740. She was born c.1722 in Germany. Albinus moved to Aug.a Co. (now Rockingham Co.) Virginia between 1751 and 1760. On Aug. 20, 1760, his dau., Barbara, age three, was bound out in Aug.a Co., because he could not afford to support and educate her. He purchased items from the Nicholas Null estate in Aug.a Co. March 16, 1770. Alvanious (Albinus) and Jacob Bowyer help to administer the estate of Conrad Bloze in Aug.a Co., Virginia Nov. 15, 1774. In 1787, He resided near his son, Johannes. Albinus d. Rockingham Co., Cub Run/McGaheysville, Virginia in Jan., 1789. Albinus had the following children:

Maria Sophia Margaretha[1·1P], b. York Co., Hellam Twp., Kreutz Creek, Pennsylvania Aug. 7, 1741, bapt. by Reverend John Stoever Sept. 27, 1741, and sponsored by Nicholas Kau and wife (at Christ Lutheran).

Jacob[1·2P], b. c.1742. He may have been a child of a previous marriage.

Adam[1·3P], b. York Co., Hellam Twp., Kreutz Creek, Pennsylvania Jan. 28, 1743/44, and bapt. at Christ Lutheran Church of York March 18, 1744. An Adam and Christina Boyer deeded land to James Hord in Rockingham Co.,Virginia Aug. 27, 1781 (this Adam 1740-1798 Monroe Co., Virginia, may have been a son of Michael Bowyer, m. Christona Lauderback (b. 1746)). In 1770, an Adam Bowyer purchased 200 acres on the North side of the Shanandore (delivered in Aug., 1781 from William Owler).

John Henry[1·4P], b. Dec. 1, 1750, and bapt. at Christ Lutheran Church of York Feb. 24, 1751.

Catherine[1·5P], b. c.1752, m. George Kissell in Shenandoah Co., Virginia June 9, 1773.

Johannes[1·6P], b. c.1754.

Barbara[1·7P], b. 1757.

Jacob Boyer

Jacob[1·2P] d. Rockingham Co., Cub Run, Virginia in Sept., 1798. On the 24th, his estate was administered by his son Lewis, witnessed by John Rush, George Carpenter (Zimmerman), George Keezle, John Koontz, and Jacob Cook, and valued at 7, 000 pounds. Jacob purchased 2 tracts on Cub Run on the west side of Peaked Mountain from William and Mary Beard Nov. 22, 1769, and sold a portion of this land to his brother-in-law, George Keisel in Rockingham Co. March 26, 1781. Jacob was too old and infirm to pay pole tax April 24, 1787. John, orphan of William Hammoke was bound to him Dec. 22, 1788. Jacob had the following children:

Ludwig[1·2·1P], b. c.1760 (1756).

Frederick$^{1.2.2p}$, b. c.1762, and was killed at the battle of Yorktown, at York Co., Virginia in Oct., 1781.

Eva$^{1.2.3p}$, b. c.1765, m. George Harmon before 1788.

Conrad$^{1.2.4p}$, b. c.1768, and was taxed in Rockingham Co. in 1787.

Hannah$^{1.2.5p}$, b. c.1771, m. Isaac Moore.

Elizabeth$^{1.2.6p}$, b. c.1777, m. George Carpenter in Rockingham Co., Virginia in 1801.

Susanna$^{1.2.7p}$, b. c.1780, m. Phillip Teter in Rockingham Co., Virginia in 1801.

Peggy$^{1.2.8p}$, b. c.1786.

Ludwig Boyer

Ludwig$^{1.2.1p}$ m. Polly Hildebrand on Jan. 21, 1785 in Washington Co., Maryland, and Ann Rosina, dau. of Adam and Elizabeth Kern, in Rockingham Co., Virginia in 1789. Rosina was bapt. in Shenandoah Co., Virginia, May 12, 1773, d. Miami Co., Spring Creek Twp., Ohio in June, 1846. Ludwig supposedly enlisted at age 22 to fight in the Revolutionary War. He was promoted March 27, 1781 by Governor Henry Lee to Private Dragoon of the Independent Troops, Light Dragoon of Pennsylvania, 2nd Battalion, 5th Virginia Regiment under command of Major Bartholomeus Van Herr. The Independent Troop of the Horse (Washington's Bodyguard), was under the command of Frederick the Great. They bodyguard consisted of 53 men, and 14 officers. All members were Germans (Pennsylvania Dutch) because of their reputation for patriotism and loyalty. His discharge was signed at Philadelphia by George Washington on Dec. 10(13), 1783, and his service ended on Dec. 31, 1783. He was also said to be a Lt. in the 2nd Battalion, 58th Regiment of the Virginia Militia for a time. He was pensioned (file S46370), and received 100 acres of land on March 7, 1805 (Warrant #187). He purchased 90 acres on Cub Run on July 29, 1785. In 1790, he was a Lieutenant in the Rockingham Co. Militia, and in 1793, he was a Captain. In Virginia, he operated a mill and iron furnace near Cub Run and Mine Run Furnace in one of the mountain gaps between Little Fort and Big Fort. On March 7, 1805, he was granted 100 acres in Miami Co., Ohio. Ludwig and Rosina resided in Virginia until 1810, when they moved to Miami Co., Ohio, and purchased 160 acres in Spring Creek Twp. Their cabin was near the east side of the farm on the south bluff overlooking a small branch of Rush Creek. While in Ohio, Ludwig operated a distillery (his neighbors said he manufactured an excellent article) located on the small branch of Rush Creek, at about the division line between his two 80 acre tracts. It was said that "His exterior was very uncouth, but he was one of those few men who are described as being diamonds in the rough, and it is said to have been an exceptional neighbor and valuable man in the community" (Beer's "History of Miami Co." published in 1880). In the late 1830s, Ludwig became a methodist circuit rider, and covered a radius of about 25 miles around Piqua, Ohio. When he was too old to ride a horse, he preached within a short distance of his home. He was pensioned on Aug. 3, 1829. Ludwig d. Spring Creek Twp. on Sept. 19, 1843. His funeral was held on the 25th, and the funeral procession was said to have extended more than a mile from his home to Wesley Chapel. He is buried in Wesley Chapel (now Washington's Bodyguard) cemetery. The inscription on the marker is as follows: "Sacred to the memory of Lewis Boyer who d. Sept. 19, 1843, aged 87 years. He was a soldier of the Revolution and by the side of the great Washington fought many a hard battle for his country's independence. Served as a lifeguard during the war and was honorably discharged Dec. 10, 1783 by special certificate signed by General Washington. Here Boyer lies, who Britain's arms withstood-Not for his own, but for his country's good.-The victor oft on famed Columbia's fields- To death the aged hero yields." Ludwig and Rosina had the following children:

Elizabeth[1.2.1.1P], b. July 10, 1790.

Catherine[1.2.1.2P], b. 1791.

Mary[1.2.1.3P], b. c.1793.

Margaret[1.2.1.4P], b. 1795.

Jacob[1.2.1.5P], b. July 12, 1796.

John[1.2.1.6P], b. 1801.

William[1.2.1.7P], b. 1807.

Lewis[1.2.1.8P], b. c.1811.

Nancy[1.2.1.9P], b. 1814, m. Israel Clawson in Shelby Co., Ohio March 21, 1830.

Rosina[1.2.1.10P], b. 1818, m. David Young in Miami Co., Ohio Nov. 27, 1836.

Elizabeth Boyer

Elizabeth[1.2.1.1P] m. Jonathan, son of James and Sophia (Pickel) Kiggins, in Miami Co., Ohio Oct. 21, 1813. She was b. Rockingham Co., Cub Run, Virginia July 10, 1790, d. Mercer Co., Dublin Twp., Ohio Oct. 8, 1840. Jonathan was a farmer, hunter, and hewer of timbers (woodcutter). After his brother James brought him and his other brother, Robert, to Ohio, Jonathan made his way to Fort Hamilton (Ohio), where he was employed in killing game for the army. Between 1810 and 1813, he moved to Miami Co., Ohio, and stayed there till 1816, when he moved to Shelby Co. He remained in Shelby Co. till 1824, and then moved to Mercer Co., Ohio. Jonathan d. Dublin Twp. Feb. 20, 1847. Jonathan and Elizabeth are buried in Mount Olive cemetery. They had the following children: Minerva Jane[1.2.1.1.1P], b. Miami Co., Spring Creek Twp., Ohio Dec. 25, 1810 (tombstone); Mary[1.2.1.1.2P], b. Spring Creek Twp. March 20, 1814; Lewis[1.2.1.1.3P], b. Spring Creek Twp. May 5, 1816; Rosina[1.2.1.1.4P], b. Spring Creek

Twp. May 5, 1816; Sophia$^{1.2.1.1.5p}$, b. Shelby Co., Perry Twp., Ohio c.1817, m. Joseph Crow in Mercer Co., Ohio Jan. 18, 1841; James$^{1.2.1.1.6p}$, b. Shelby Co., Orange Twp., Ohio March 25, 1819; Margaret$^{1.2.1.1.7p}$, b. Shelby Co., Orange Twp., Ohio Sept. 19, 1821; Elizabeth$^{1.2.1.1.8p}$, b. Shelby Co., Orange Twp., Ohio Sept. 19, 1821; Catherine$^{1.2.1.1.9p}$, b. Shelby Co., Orange Twp. in 1824; Harriet$^{1.2.1.1.10p}$, b. Shelby Co., Orange Twp. in 1826; Charlotte$^{1.2.1.1.11p}$, b. Mercer Co., Dublin Twp., Ohio in 1829, m. Thomas M. Elliot in Allen Co., Ohio April 11, 1848, and Michael Burns c.1849. Michael was b. Ireland in 1824.

Minerva Jane Kiggins

Minerva Jane$^{1.2.1.1.1p}$ m. Joseph Baltzell in Shelby Co., Ohio Aug. 8, 1826. He was b. 1806. Minerva d. Mercer Co., Dublin Twp., Ohio May 30, 1892. She is buried in Mount Olive cemetery. They had a son b. in Dublin Twp., Harrison$^{1.2.1.1.1.1p}$, b. 1833, m. Nancy Barton in Mercer Co. April 2, 1853. She was b. Ohio in 1830. Harrison d. Dublin Twp. June 20, 1909.

Mary Kiggins

Mary$^{1.2.1.1.2p}$ m. Andrew Clawson in Shelby Co., Ohio March 15, 1830. He was b. 1808. They had the following children: Jonathan$^{1.2.1.1.2.1p}$, b. Putnam Co., Ohio in 1833, m. Mary Clawson Oct. 12, 1856 in Allen Co., Ohio; Joseph$^{1.2.1.1.2.2p}$, b. Putnam Co. in 1835, m. Sarah Ann Brown in Allen Co., Ohio June 29, 1856; Franklin$^{1.2.1.1.2.3p}$, b. Putnam Co. in 1838, m. Elizabeth Brown in Allen Co., Ohio July 12, 1857; Harriet$^{1.2.1.1.2.4p}$, b. Putnam Co. in 1839, m. Samuel Patton in Allen Co., Ohio Oct. 21, 1858; Matthew$^{1.2.1.1.2.5p}$, b. Putnam Co. in 1841, m. Sarah Ann Moore in Allen Co., Ohio April 16, 1863; Aaron$^{1.2.1.1.2.6p}$, b. Putnam Co. in 1843; Thomas$^{1.2.1.1.2.7p}$, b. Allen Co., Ohio in 1845; Mary$^{1.2.1.1.2.8p}$, b. Allen Co. in 1848; Elizabeth$^{1.2.1.1.2.9p}$, b. Allen Co. in 1852; Andrew$^{1.2.1.1.2.10p}$, b. Allen Co. in 1855; Francis$^{1.2.1.1.2.11p}$, b. Allen Co. in 1858.

Lewis Kiggins

Lewis$^{1.2.1.1.3p}$ m. Mary Ellen Shindledecker in Mercer Co., Ohio Jan. 19, 1837. She was b. Ohio in 1815. Lewis d. Mercer Co., Dublin Twp., Ohio Feb. 26, 1887. He is buried in the New Frysinger cemetery. They had the following children in Dublin Twp.: Alfred$^{1.2.1.1.3.1p}$, b. 1838, m. Delinda Wiley in Mercer Co. Aug. 12, 1859, d. Dublin Twp. in 1907 (He is buried in Mount Olive cemetery; Luella$^{1.2.1.1.3.2p}$, b. 1840; Minerva J.$^{1.2.1.1.3.3p}$, b. 1842, m. Alfred Boroff; William$^{1.2.1.1.3.4p}$, b. 1844; Susan$^{1.2.1.1.3.5p}$, b. 1845; Ellis$^{1.2.1.1.3.6p}$, b. 1847.

Harrieta[1.2.1.1.3.7p], b. 1847; Armanda[1.2.1.1.3.8p], b. 1848; John[1.2.1.1.3.9p], b. 1849, m. Sarah J. (b.1860); Catherine[1.2.1.1.3.10p], b. 1849; Margaret[1.2.1.1.3.11p], b. c.1850, d. Sept. 22, 1851, buried in Mount Olive cemetery; Elizabeth[1.2.1.1.3.12p], b. Aug. 31, 1852, d. Sept. 7, 1852, buried in Mount Olive cemetery; Sarah[1.2.1.1.3.11p], b. Aug. 31, 1852; James[1.2.1.1.3.12p], b. 1854.

Rosina Kiggins

Rosina[1.2.1.1.4p] m. Cyrus, son of Abraham and Rebecca (Hoover) Shindledecker, and grandson of Jacob and Abigail (Longstreet) Shindledecker, in Mercer Co., Ohio Oct. 1, 1837. He was b. Ohio May 19, 1814, d. Dublin Twp. in 1894. Rosina d. Dublin Twp. in 1907. They are buried in Mount Olive cemetery. They had the following children in Dublin Twp.:
Clayborn[1.2.1.1.4.1p], b. 1844; Jeremiah[1.2.1.1.4.2p], b. March 3, 1846, m. Josophene Lehman in Van Wert Co., Ohio March 14, 1883, d. Van Wert Co. Feb. 21, 1935; Cyrus[1.2.1.1.4.3p], b. Feb., 1848, m. Celia A. (b.Oct. 1856); James[1.2.1.1.4.4p], b. 1851; Harriet[1.2.1.1.4.5p], b. 1853; Curtis[1.2.1.1.4.6p], b. 1854; Milton[1.2.1.1.4.7p], b. 1858; Mariah[1.2.1.1.4.8p], b. 1860; Alvin[1.2.1.1.4.9p], b. 1863.

James Kiggins

James[1.2.1.1.6p] m. Mercy Ann Clawson in Shelby Co., Ohio Nov. 19, 1837. She was b. Ohio Feb. 22, 1819, d. Allen Co., Marion Twp., Ohio July 16, 1884. James d. Marion Twp. Nov. 4, 1895. They are buried in Hartshorn cemetery. They had the following children in Allen Co., Marion Twp., Ohio (the first three may have been b. Shelby or Mercer Co.):
>   Elizabeth[1.2.1.1.6.1p], b. Feb. 23, 1839, m. Alexander Rayer, d. Marion Twp. July 6, 1904.
>   Josiah[1.2.1.1.6.2p], b. Oct. 8, 1840, m. Lucinda Bryan.
>   Lewis[1.2.1.1.6.3p], b. Oct. 2, 1842, m. Christina Alspaugh in Van Wert Co., Ohio July 11, 1863, d. Allen Co., Marion Twp. Nov. 19, 1871.
>   Alexander[1.2.1.1.6.4p], b. March 6, 1845, m. Rebecca Catherine Brown Dec. 4, 1866. She was born April 9, 1851, d. Feb. 4, 1932. Alexander d. Van Wert Co., Ohio Dec. 6, 1927
>   Louise Jane[1.2.1.1.6.5p], b. Jan. 9, 1847, m. James Belt.
>   Rosina[1.2.1.1.6.6p], b. April 23, 1849, m. Vincent Carey.
>   James[1.2.1.1.6.7p], b. Aug. 27, 1851, m. Ellen Bryan in Allen Co., Ohio May 11, 1872, d. Allen Co., Delphos, Ohio Feb. 8, 1939.

Margaret Kiggins

Margaret[1.2.1.1.7p] m. Ishmael, son of Ruel and Sarah (Jones) Roebuck, in Mercer Co., Ohio in Feb., 1835. She was b. Shelby Co.,

Orange Twp., Ohio Sept. 19, 1821, d. Dublin Twp. April 17, 1901. Ishmael was a farmer, d. Dublin Twp. Jan. 15, 1853. Ishmael and Margaret are buried in Roebuck cemetery. After Ishmael's death, Margaret m. Justice Wells in Mercer Co. Oct. 3, 1854. Justice was b. Huron Co., Ohio Aug. 23, 1826, d. Dublin Twp. June 18, 1893. Justice is buried in Roebuck cemetery. Ishmael and Margaret had the following children:

   Vincent[1.2.1.1.7.1p], b. 1836, and resided in Dublin Twp. in 1850.

   Mary[1.2.1.1.7.2p], b. Aug. 18, 1839, d. Oct. 30, 1851. She is buried in Roebuck cemetery.

   William Jasper[1.2.1.1.7.3p], b. July 3, 1841, m. Catherine, dau. of George and Margaret (Snyder) Shaffer, in Van Wert Co., Ohio Jan. 6, 1861, and Caroline Shindledecker in Mercer Co. March 27, 1870. Catherine was b. Van Wert Co., Liberty Twp., Ohio Nov. 5, 1842, d. Dublin Twp. Nov. 4, 1869. Caroline was b. 1847, d. c.1871. William was a farmer, d. Dublin Twp. Oct. 21, 1870. William and Catherine are buried in Roebuck cemetery.

   Harriet[1.2.1.1.7.4p], b. Nov. 9, 1842, d. May 31, 1849. She is buried in Roebuck cemetery.

   Garrison[1.2.1.1.7.5p], b. 1844, d. 1853.

   Eliza Jane[1.2.1.1.7.6p], b. March 20, 1847, m. Stephen Dysert in Mercer Co., Ohio Sept. 25, 1864. He was b. Mercer Co., Ohio Feb. 4, 1840.

   Sarah Ellen[1.2.1.1.7.7p], b. April 10, 1850, m. George W. Dysert in Mercer Co. Dec. 30, 1868, d. Dublin Twp. Sept. 13, 1874. She is buried in Roebuck cemetery. George was born Jan. 20, 1843, d. Dublin Twp. Sept. 9, 1912. After Sarah d., George m. Celia.

   Henry N.[1.2.1.1.7.8p], b. March 13, 1852, d. March 10, 1853. He is buried in Roebuck cemetery.

   Elizabeth C.[1.2.1.1.7.9p], b. March 13, 1852, d. Feb. 16, 1853. She is buried in Roebuck cemetery.

Margaret (Kiggins) Roebuck and Justice Wells had the following children:

   James Franklin[1.2.1.1.7.10p], b. 1856.

   Martha[1.2.1.1.7.11p], b. 1859.

   Florence[1.2.1.1.7.12p], b. 1861, m. David Archer.

Elizabeth Kiggins

Elizabeth[1.2.1.1.8p] m. Alexander F. Irick in Mercer Co., Ohio Feb. 10, 1839. He was b. Rockingham Co., Virginia Oct. 2, 1819. Elizabeth d. Allen Co., Marion Twp., Ohio in 1904. They had the following children in Allen Co., Marion Twp., Ohio (the first four in Mercer Co., Dublin Twp.): John F.[1.2.1.1.8.1p], b. 1839, d. in the Civil War Oct. 31, 1863;

William L.$^{1.2.1.1.8.2p}$, b. 1841, m. Mary Canada; Mary C.$^{1.2.1.1.8.3p}$, b. 1843, m. Sebastian Alspaugh; James Ishmael$^{1.2.1.1.8.4p}$, b. July 29, 1845, m. Melvina Ditto Nov. 6, 1866; Margaret$^{1.2.1.1.8.5p}$, b. c.1847, d. c.1849; Arminda$^{1.2.1.1.8.6p}$, b. 1850, m. Charles Peltier; Alexander F.$^{1.2.1.1.8.7p}$, b. 1852, m. Rebecca Holmes; Francis C.$^{1.2.1.1.8.8p}$, b. c.1854; Missouri$^{1.2.1.1.8.9p}$, b. 1855, m. John Ludwig; Dorisa/Denise$^{1.2.1.1.8.10p}$, b. 1858, m. David Hoffman; Jackson$^{1.2.1.1.8.11p}$, b. c.1860, m. Louise Hoffman; Eliza E.$^{1.2.1.1.8.12p}$, b. c.1862, m. Emanuel Tucker.

Catherine Kiggins

Catherine$^{1.2.1.1.9p}$ m. John Blackwell in Miami Co., Ohio April 15, 1847. He was b. 1824. They had the following children: George W.$^{1.2.1.1.9.1p}$, b. 1848; Elizabeth E.$^{1.2.1.1.9.2p}$, b. 1849.

Harriet Kiggins

Harriet$^{1.2.1.1.10p}$ m. Elijah Hooks in Mercer Co., Ohio Feb. 13, 1841. Elijah was b. Ohio in 1817. They moved to Grant Co., Lima, Wisconsin before 1843. They had the following children: Arminda$^{1.2.1.1.10.1p}$, b. 1843, m. William Redmond; Mary C.$^{1.2.1.1.10.2p}$, b. 1845, m. Hosea T. Mundon in Grant Co. Dec. 16, 1866; Minerva J.$^{1.2.1.1.10.3p}$, b. 1847, m. David Barrett in Grant Co. March 1, 1866; Calvin$^{1.2.1.1.10.4p}$, b. 1848, m. Mary Jane Walker Robinson in Grant Co. Jan. 26, 1878, and Elizabeth Clark nee Foot in Grant Co. May 13, 1899; Matilda$^{1.2.1.1.10.5p}$, b. c.1851, m. Reuben Green in Grant Co. Oct. 2, 1869; Emma$^{1.2.1.1.10.6p}$, b. c.1854, m. Charles C. Chesley in Grant Co. July 3, 1875; Albert$^{1.2.1.1.10.7p}$, b. c.1862, m. Caroline E. Bolzell in Grant Co. July 8, 1883; Laura$^{1.2.1.1.10.8p}$, b. c.1865, m. John Hutchcroft in Grant Co. March 10, 1886; Samuel$^{1.2.1.1.10.9m}$, b. c.1867, m. Emma Hutchcroft in Grant Co. Aug. 12, 1888; Julia$^{1.2.1.1.10.10p}$, b. c.1869, m. Isaac J. Hull in Grant Co. May 27, 1891.

Catherine Boyer

Catherine$^{1.2.1.2p}$ m. James Johnson in Miami Co., Ohio July 28, 1826. He was b. 1801. They had a son, Benjamin$^{1.2.1.2p}$, b. 1826, m. Isabell.

Mary Boyer

Mary$^{1.2.1.3p}$ m. Robert, son of James and Sophia (Pickel) Kiggins, in Miami Co., Ohio Nov. 24, 1814. She was b. Rockingham Co., Cub Run, Virginia c.1793, d. Mercer Co., Dublin Twp., Ohio before Sept., 1841. They had a son, John F.$^{1.2.1.3.1p}$, b. Miami Co., Ohio April 2, 1817.

John F. Kiggins

John F.$^{1.2.1.3.1p}$ m. Sarah Ann McCloskey in Shelby Co., Ohio Dec.

21, 1838. He d. Shelby Co., Sidney, Ohio Jan. 19, 1900, and is buried in Graceland cemetery. They had the following children: William$^{1.2.1.3.1.1p}$, b. c.1841, and served in the Civil War from Shelby Co. in the 20th OVI, Co. K from Jan., 1862 to July, 1862; John Charles Fremont$^{1.2.1.3.1.2p}$, b. Sep. 3, 1855 in Shelby Co., Orange Twp., Ohio.

Margaret Boyer

Margaret$^{1.2.1.4p}$ m. John, son of John and Margaret (Terfen-Rench) Millhouse, in Miami Co., Ohio Jan. 14, 1813. He was b. 1782, d. Miami Co., Ohio June 27, 1845. Margaret d. Miami Co., Ohio Aug. 27, 1866. They are buried in Millhouse cemetery. They had the following children in Spring Creek Twp.: Jacob$^{1.2.1.4.1p}$, b. May 8, 1814, m. Frances Johnson Dec. 3, 1840, d. June 20, 1871. David$^{1.2.1.4.2p}$, b. c.1815; John$^{1.2.1.4.3p}$, b. 1817, m. Susanna Nofsinger April 13, 1837; Joseph$^{1.2.1.4.4p}$, b. c.1819; Carlisle$^{1.2.1.4.5p}$, b. c.1821, m. ____ Love.

Jacob Boyer

Jacob$^{1.2.1.5p}$ m. Elizabeth Weeks McClerg in Miami Co., Ohio March 7, 1816. She was b. Athens Co., Ohio Oct. 7, 1794, d. Shelby Co., Orange Twp., Ohio Jan. 14, 1868. Jacob d. Shelby Co., Sidney, Ohio Nov. 12, 1881. They had the following children: Elizabeth$^{1.2.1.5.1p}$, b. c.1817, m. ____ McNeil; Charles$^{1.2.1.5.2p}$, b. 1819, m. Anna Valentine Oct. 30, 1839, d. Houston, Ohio Feb. 7, 1899; Susan$^{1.2.1.5.3p}$, b. Feb. 13, 1821, m. Henry B. Vandermark Jan. 17, 1844, d. Sept. 27, 1894; Lewis$^{1.2.1.5.4p}$, b. 1823, m. Sarah Fulton, d. Sept. 27, 1880; Rosana$^{1.2.1.5.5p}$, b. 1826, m. Francis Bailey in 1862, d. 1890; Cordelia$^{1.2.1.5.6p}$, b. 1828; Climelia$^{1.2.1.5.7p}$, b. 1831, m. Alexander Snodgrass in 1860, d. May, 1905; Frances V.$^{1.2.1.5.8p}$, b. 1834, m. Milton McNeil Jan. 18, 1853.

John Boyer

John$^{1.2.1.6p}$ m. Polly Jamison in Miami Co., Ohio Dec. 28, 1819, and had a dau., Rachel$^{1.2.1.6.1p}$, m. ____ Thorne.

William Boyer

William$^{1.2.1.7p}$ m. Elizabeth Bowersock in Miami Co., Ohio April 9, 1829. She was b. 1814, d. Oct. 4, 1850. William d. Mercer Co., Neptune, Ohio March 17, 1869. They had the following children: John$^{1.2.1.7.1p}$, b. 1830, and m. Minerva; David$^{1.2.1.7.2p}$, b. 1832, m. Lurena Buckmaster July 3, 1859; Isaac$^{1.2.1.7.3p}$, b. 1834; Mitchel$^{1.2.1.7.4p}$, b. 1836; Mary$^{1.2.1.7.5p}$, b. 1838; Robert$^{1.2.1.7.6p}$, b. 1840; Mary Jane$^{1.2.1.7.7p}$, b. 1841, m. Absalom Ashbaugh; William$^{1.2.1.7.8p}$, b. 1842, m. Ellen; Amos$^{1.2.1.7.9p}$, b. 1844; Samuel$^{1.2.1.7.10p}$, b. 1848.

Lewis Boyer

Lewis[1.2.1.8p] m. Nancy A. Bowersock in Miami Co., Ohio Feb. 3, 1831. She was b. 1811. They had the following children: Jonathan[1.2.1.8.1p], b. 1833; Mary[1.2.1.8.2p], b. 1838; Manun[1.2.1.8.3p], b. 1840; Autimus[1.2.1.8.4b], b. 1843; Jane[1.2.1.8.5p], b. 1845; Calvin[1.2.1.8.6p], b. 1847.

Johannes Boyer

Johannes[1.6p] m. Eva, and had the following children in Rockingham Co., Mcgaheysville, Virginia (bapt. at the Peaked Mountain Church): Barbara[1.6.1p], b. April 15, 1775; Maria Margaretha[1.6.2p], b. July 13, 1783; Johan Georg[1.6.3p], b. July 18, 1785; Johannes[1.6.4p], b. Aug. 18, 1793.

****

Lohr

unknown[1] was parent to the following Lohrs who arrived at Philadelphia, Pennsylvania on Sept. 30, 1754 on the ship Edinburgh (they are presumed to be brothers): Georg[1.1s]; Conrad[1.2s].

Georg Lohr

Georg[1.1s] m. Maria Margaretha. In 1755, they resided in York Co., York, Pennsylvania. They moved to Washington Co., Maryland sometime before 1776. They resided in Washington Co., Maryland in 1790. They had the following children:

  Johan Georg[1.1.1s], born at York on Sept. 13, 1755, bapt. at the First Moravian Church of York Sept. 16, 1755, sponsored by John and Catharina Heckedorn. He resided in Washington Co., Maryland in 1790. In 1800, he resided in Washington Co., Elizabeth Hundred.

  Johan Peter[1.1.2s], born at York Jan. 25, 1757, bapt. at the First Moravian Church on Feb. 7, 1757, and sponsored by Peter Binckele, John Heckedorn, Philip Rothrock, and John Daniel Votrin. In 1783, he resided in Washington Co., Marsh Hundred with 4 horses and 3 "bc". He m. Catherine, d. Aug.a Co., Virginia in 1841. He enlisted as a Private in the Revolutionary War at Hagerstown, Maryland in 1776. According to his pension, he marched to Fort Washington, New York, and fought in the battle of White Plains in Captain John Ronald's Company. His pension also stated that he was born within seven miles of Little York, Pennsylvania, and moved to Maryland when very young.

  Michael[1.1.3s], born at York Oct. 6, 1758, bapt. at the First Moravian Church on Oct. 9, 1758, and sponsored by Daniel Votring and wife, Adam Hoff and wife, and Melchior Schmidt.

121

Joseph[1.1.4s], b. Berks Co., Tulpehocken Twp., Stouchburg, Pennsylvania, Nov. 26, 1759, while his parents were visiting his uncle. Joseph was bapt. at Stouchburg on Dec. 2, 1759. He stated that he was born within 7 or 8 miles of Lebanon, Pennsylvania.

Anna Magdalen[1.1.5s], b. Aug. 24, 1760, and bapt. at Christ Evangelical Lutheran of York on March 24, 1761.

Jacob[1.1.6s], b. c.1762, and resided in Washington Co., Maryland in 1783.

John[1.1.7s], b. c.1762, and had 2 horses and 3 "bc" in Washington Co., Maryland in 1783.

Anna Maria[1.1.8s], bapt. by Reverend Jacob Lischy at York on July 28, 1765.

Michael Lohr

Michael[1.1.3s] m. Catharine Schriner in Washington Co., Maryland. Michael enlisted as a Private in the Revolutionary War in Washington Co., Maryland in 1778. He was residing in Washington Co., Maryland in 1783. Michael moved to Rockingham Co., Virginia, d. there in 1835. They had a son at Hagerstown, Maryland, Michael[1.1.3.1s], b. Dec. 15, 1787.

Joseph Lohr

Joseph[1.1.4s] enlisted in the Revolutionary War with his cousin, Baltasar Lohr, at Lebanon, Pennsylvania in Nov., 1775 (possibly 1776). He spent the first year as a Private in Captain Soull's Company, Colonel Shee and Cadwalder's Pennsylvania Regiment. They marched to Reading, Pennsylvania, thence to Philadelphia, thence to Fort Washington to help construct the fort, thence to New York, where they fought in the battle of Long Island. After the battle, they returned to Fort Washington where they were taken prisoner at the fort's surrender. They were released after about nine weeks, and then went to Philadelphia, where Balthasar was honorably discharged on Jan. 21, 1777. On Jan. 16, 1777, Joseph reenlisted, and served three years as a sergeant in the 4th Pennsylvania Line under Lieutenant Colonel Butler, in Captain John Connelly's Company. Joseph fought in the battles of Brandywine, Germantown, and Monmouth, and was honorably discharged in 1781. After the war, Joseph returned to York Co. (now Adams Co.), Pennsylvania, where he appears on the tax list of Germany Twp., Littletown as a single man in 1782. He m. Anna Maria c.1782/83. She was b. 1756, d. Aug., 1822. Joseph moved to York Co., Heidelberg Twp., Pennsylvania, where he appears on the tax lists from 1795-99. From 1800-10, he resided in Frederick Co., Pipe Creek, Taneytown, Maryland, from 1811-15 in Frederick Co., Monocacy, Maryland, and from 1816 till his death on Jan. 5, 1837, he resided in

Frederick Co., Emmitsburg, Maryland. Joseph was allowed pension in Emmitsburg, Maryland on July 15, 1828. Joseph and Anna Maria are buried in Emmitsburg Lutheran cemetery. They had the following children:

Margaretha[1.1.4.1s], b. c.1783.

John[1.1.4.2s], born at Littletown on May 8, 1794, bapt. at Christ's Church of Littletown, and sponsored by Baltasar and Elisabeth Lohr. He m. Christina Overholtzer in Frederick Co., Maryland on Feb. 19, 1820, d. Frederick Co., Thurmont, Maryland on Dec. 13, 1863.

Maria[1.1.4.3s], b. c.1796 (1799).

George[1.1.4.4s], b. 1798, d. Frederick Co., Emmitsburg, Maryland on May 12, 1817.

Margaretha Lohr

Margaretha[1.1.4.1s] m. Joseph, son of Jonathan Thomas and Hannah (Pittinger) Braun, in Frederick Co., Taneytown, Maryland on March 23, 1802. Margaretha was b. York Co., Germany Twp., Littletown, Pennsylvania c.1783, d. Mercer Co., Dublin Twp., Ohio in Sept., 1846. In her will she left her land to her dau., Margaret Harp. Joseph purchased 110 acres in Section 33, Miami Co., Monroe Twp., Ohio on Feb. 8, 1826. He had 2 horses, 1 cattle, and 100 acres RTS 6/4/33 in 1829, 110 acres in Section 33 in 1830, and 100 acres in 1831; 100 acres in 1832; 110 acres in 1835. He d. there Aug. 21, 1836, and is buried in Loy cemetery. They had the following children:

Elizabeth[1.1.4.1.1s], b. Frederick Co., Taneytown, Maryland c.1804. She m. John Campbell in Miami Co., Ohio on Jan. 8, 1825, and ____ Beach before 1846. Elizabeth d. 1858. John Campbell d. Miami Co., Ohio in 1838.

Isaac[1.1.4.1.2s], b. c.1806, m. Susan Crowder in Miami Co. on Sept. 20, 1827, and resided besides Joseph in Monroe Twp. in 1840. He has not been confirmed as a son.

Margaret[1.1.4.1.3s], b. Taneytown in 1808, m. Amos, son of Johan Peter and Elisabetha (Hillegas) Harp/Herb, in Miami Co., Ohio on Aug. 19, 1830. Margaret d. Auglaize Co., Noble Twp./Mercer Co., Dublin Twp., Ohio between 1860 and 1865. Amos was a farmer. He was b. Berks Co., District Twp., Pennsylvania in 1807, d. Mercer Co., Dublin Twp., Ohio between 1870 and 1880. He is buried in Stringtown cemetery.

Abraham[1.1.4.1.4s], b. Taneytown c.1812, m. Cynah Skinner in Miami Co. Oct. 28, 1836, and was residing there in Oct. 1849. On Oct. 12, 1844, he deeded part of his land in Miami Co. to Jacob Studebaker, and Oct. 26, 1849, he deeded the remainder to Susanna Pence.

John Lohr

John[1.1.4.2s] m. Christina Overholtzer in Frederick Co., Maryland on Feb. 19, 1820. Christina was born Oct. 31, 1800, d. April 11, 1879. John d. Frederick Co., Thurmont, Maryland Dec. 13, 1863. They are buried at Apples Lutheran Church. They had the following children: J. Nicholas[1.1.4.2.1s], b. June 30, 1822, d. in Thurmont Dec. 3, 1894, buried Apples Lutheran cemetery, m. Margaret; David[1.1.4.2.2s], b. 1828; Simon[1.1.4.2.3s], bapt. at Apples Dec. 12, 1830; Margaret[1.1.4.2.4s], b. 1830; Samuel[1.1.4.2.5s], b. 1831; Elizabeth[1.1.4.2.6s], b. Dec. 23, 1832, d. April 14, 1852, buried at Apples Lutheran Church; William[1.1.4.2.7s], b. April 7, 1836, d. Feb. 22, 1837, buried in Emmitsburg Lutheran cemetery; James[1.1.4.2.8s], b. 1839; John[1.1.4.2.9s], b. 1843.

Maria Lohr

Maria[1.1.4.3s] m. Isaac, son of Johan Georg and Anna Elisabetha (Frey) Gump, in Frederick Co., Graceham Moravian Church, Maryland on June 2, 1816. Isaac was b. Maryland on Feb. 28, 1795. They resided in Miami Co., Monroe Twp., Ohio in 1830, and Shelby Co., Salem Twp., Ohio in 1850. They had the following children in Ohio: George[1.1.4.3.1s], b. 1831; Jeremiah[1.1.4.3.2s], b. 1834; O.[1.1.4.3.3s], b. 1837; Isaac[1.1.4.3.4s], b. 1840; Levi[1.1.4.3.5s], b. 1843.

Conrad Lohr

Conrad[1.2s] m. Elisabetha Catharina, and resided in Berks Co., Stouchburg, Pennsylvania in 1757. He received a land warrent for 50 acres of land in Lebanon Co., Bethel Twp., Pennsylvania on Jan. 28, 1771. From 1769-1771, Conrad appears in Lancaster Co., Donegal Twp., Pennsylvania, and in 1778-82, he appears on the tax lists for Cumberland Co., Letterkenny Twp., Pennsylvania. Conrad and Elisabetha Catharina had the following children: Baltasar[1.2.1s], b. Stouchburg on Sept. 9, 1757 (according to pension); Anna Elisabetha[1.2.2s], born at Stouchburg on Nov. 5, 1757.

Baltasar Lohr

Baltasar[1.2.1s] enlisted in the Revolutionary War with his cousin, Joseph Lohr, at Lebanon, Pennsylvania in Nov., 1775. They marched to Reading, Pennsylvania, thence to Philadelphia, thence to Fort Washington to help construct the fort, thence to New York, where they fought in the battle of Long Island. After the battle, they returned to Fort Washington where they were taken prisoner at the fort's surrender. They were released after about nine weeks, and then went to Philadelphia, where Baltasar was honorably discharged on Jan. 21, 1777. He appeared on the tax lists of Cumberland Co., Letterkenny Twp., Pennsylvania from 1778-82. In 1780, he reenlisted in the war in

the 6th Class, 3rd Company, 4th Battalion, Cumberland Co., Militia.
From 1781-92 (1781-82 he was single), he appears on the tax list of
York Co., Germany Twp., Littletown, Pennsylvania. In 1799-1800, he
was taxed in York Co., Mount Joy Twp., and in 1810, he resided in
Franklin Co., Fannet Twp., Pennsylvania. In 1819, he resided in
Montgomery Co., Maryland, d. Frederick Co., Maryland on March 4,
1827. He m. Lena Elisabetha Knauf (b. Aug. 15, 1763, d. on March 20,
1841) on March 15, 1787, and had the following children (bapt. at
Christ's Church of Littletown):
Anna Maria[1.2.1.1s], b. Nov. 6, 1788, and sponsored by Anna Maria
Knauf. She resided with her brothers, David and Jacob, in Frederick
Co., Maryland in March, 1855. She m. ___ Beidel, who d. before 1850.
Johan Jacob[1.2.1.2s], b. Aug. 1, 1790, and sponsored by Jacob and
Susanna Schyly. He d. Frederick Co., Maryland on Nov. 1, 1851. He
resided with his siblings in 1850.
David[1.2.1.3s], b. Jan. 2, 1796, and sponsored by Joseph and Anna
Maria Lohr. He resided with his sister and brother in Frederick Co.,
Maryland in March, 1855.
****

Heinrich Stentz

Heinrich[1t], son of Rudolp and Eva Barbara Stentz, was b. Germany in
Sept., 1694. He m. Anna Maria c.1718, and Maria Dorothea Bosserth
in 1732. Anna Maria d. Germany c.1731. Dorothea was alive in 1758.
Heinrich arrived at Philadelphia on the ship Elizabeth on Aug. 27,
1733. Heinrich d. York Co., Hellam Twp., Kreutz Creek, Pennsylvania
on Oct. 14, 1758, after being ill for eight days, and was buried at the
Reformed Church of Kreutz Creek on Oct. 16, 1758. They had the
following children: infant[1.1t], b. c.1719, d. before 1758; Anna Maria
Catrina (Anna Maria)[1.2t], b. Germany c.1722, m. Albinus Boyer[1p];
Maria Catharina (Dorothea)[1.3t], b. c.1724; Maria Catharina?[1.4t], b.
c.1726.
Johan Jacob[1.5t], b. c.1731; Philip Daniel[1.6t], b. Feb. 1, 1735, and bapt.
at Christ Evangelical Church of York on Feb. 23, 1735; John
Leonard[1.7t], b. May 26, 1736, and bapt. at Christ's Lutheran Church
of York on July 3, 1736, m. Anna Catharine (d. 1807); Judith[1.8t], b.
c.1738; Anna Maria Catharina Elisabeth[1.9t], b. Jan. 28,
1739.Juliana[1.10t], b. 1741, m. Johan Martin Schultz in York Co. on
July 28, 1760; Anna Maria?[1.11t], b. 1743; Maria Catharina[1.12t], bapt.
by Reverend Jacob Lischy on Dec. 11, 1748, and sponsored by Heinrich
and Maria Catharina Liebhardt.

Maria Catharina Stentz

Maria Catharina[1.3t] m. Abraham, son of Johann Nickel and Liebstahl
Hol/Holl in York Co. on May 7, 1745, and had the following children:

Johan Heinrich$^{1.3.1t}$, bapt. at Kreutz Creek on Jan. 19, 1746, and sponsored by Heinrich and Maria Dorothea Stentz; Peter$^{1.3.2t}$, bapt. by Reverend Jacob Lischy on Feb. 25, 1759, sponsored by Peter Schneider and Catharina Stentzin; Emanuel$^{1.3.3t}$, bapt. by Reverend Jacob Lischy on May 16, 1765, and sponsored by Phill and Eva Morgenstern.

Philip Daniel Stentz
Philip Daniel$^{1.6t}$ m. Catharina Elisabetha Hertzog in York Co. on Aug. 11, 1761. He d. 1807. They had the following children:
Catharina$^{1.6.1t}$, b. May 15, 1762, and bapt. at Christ's Lutheran Church of York on May 23, 1762.
Anna Maria$^{1.6.2t}$, b. Oct. 10, 1763, bapt. at Kreutz Creek on Oct. 16, 1763, and sponsored by George Hertzog Sr. and wife.
Daniel$^{1.6.3t}$, b. May 19, 1779, bapt. at the First Reformed Church of York on June 17, 1779, and sponsored by Daniel and Maria Wagner.

Judith Stentz
Judith$^{1.8t}$ m. Johann Georg Hertzog Jr. in York Co. on June 17, 1759, and bapt. the following children at Christ's Lutheran Church of York:
Catharine Elisabeth$^{1.8.1t}$, b. March 16, 1760, and bapt. March 23, 1760.
Georg$^{1.8.2t}$, b. Dec. 16, 1761, bapt. Jan. 1, 1762, and sponsored by Georg and Anna Maria Hertzog.
Anna Maria$^{1.8.3t}$, b. Feb. 1, 1764, and bapt. Feb. 12, 1764.

Anna Maria Catharina Elisabeth Stentz
Anna Maria Catharina Elisabeth$^{1.9t}$ m. John Peter Schneider in York Co. on April 15, 1759. She d. 1782. They had the following children: Henry$^{1.9.1t}$, b. Jan. 10, 1760, bapt. at Christ's Lutheran on May 29, 1760; Anna Barbara$^{1.9.2t}$, bapt. by Reverend Jacob Lischy on April 12, 1761, and sponsored by Adam Michel and Anna Maria Imlerin.

Johan Jacob Stentz
Johan Jacob$^{1.11t}$ m. Anna Lehman in 1761, and had a son, Johan Jacob$^{1.11.1t}$, b. Feb. 22, 1766, bapt. at Kreutz Creek on March 23, 1766, and sponsored by Philip and Catharina Stentz.
****

Jacob Jauler
Jacob^{1u} m. Maria C., and had the following children: Jacob$^{1.1u}$, b. c.1740; Isaac$^{1.2u}$, b. c.1743; Anna Dorothea$^{1.3u}$, bapt. by Reverend Jacob Lischy in York Co., West Manchester /Dover Twp., Pennsylvania on May 16, 1756, sponsored by Adam and Anna Dorothea Bartmesser.

Jacob Jauler

Jacob[1.1u] m. Barbara, and had the following children (all bapt. at Frederick Co., Middletown Lutheran Church except the first):

Anna Maria[1.1.1u], bapt. by Reverend Jacob Lischy in York Co., Pennsylvania on Aug. 28, 1765, and sponsored by Jacob Bohrech and Appolonia Pfeifferin. She m. Nicholas Schaeffer in Frederick Co., Maryland on May 9, 1786.

Catharina[1.1.2u], b. Frederick Co., Middletown, Maryland on Oct. 29, 1771.

Eve[1.1.3u], b. Middletown c.1772, m. Nicholas Neihoff in Frederick Co., Maryland on Jan. 8, 1793.

Jacob[1.1.4u], b. Middletown on Feb. 27, 1774, and sponsored by Conrad and Margaret Gedultig.

Magdalena[1.1.5u], b. Middletown on Sept. 29, 1776, and sponsored by Johannes and Magdalena Link.

Elisabetha Margaretha[1.1.6u], b. Middletown in March, 1779, and sponsored by Frederick and Margaret Schonholtz.

Eleonora[1.1.7u], b. Middletown on April 20, 1780, sponsored by Leonora Bucher, m. Daniel Staufer in Frederick Co., Maryland on April 11, 1803.

Michael[1.1.8u], b. Middletown on Oct. 9, 1781, and sponsored by Michael and Magdalena Storm.

Johan Georg[1.1.9u], b. Middletown on July 14, 1785, and sponsored by Nicholas Shafer.

Michael Jauler

Michael[1.1.8u] m. Catharine Shafer in Frederick Co., Maryland on Sept. 17, 1809, and had a son in Middletown, Johannes[1.1.8.1u], b. 1809.

Johan Georg Jauler

Johan Georg[1.1.9u] m. Maria Lambrecht in Frederick Co., Maryland on Aug. 30, 1809, and had the following children in Middletown: Elenora[1.1.9.1u], b. Oct. 1, 1809; Marianne[1.1.9.2u], b. Jan. 12, 1812.

Isaac Jauler

Isaac[1.2u] m. Anna Eva. They moved from York Co. West Manchester Twp., Pennsylvania to Frederick Co., Middletown, Maryland between 1767 and 1771, and from Maryland to Bedford (now Somerset) Co., Elk Lick Twp., Pennsylvania between 1775 and 1778. The name Jauler evolved to Youler and finally Yowler. In 1787, Isaac was taxed with 100 acres 2 horses and 3 cattle in Elk Lick Twp., and served in the Twp. Militia on Feb. 7, 1789. He d. Aug., 1798, and his wife survived him. Isaac and Anna Eva had the following children:

Anna Maria[1.2.1u], bapt. York Co., West Manchester Twp., Wolf's (St. Paul's) Reformed Church on July 26, 1767, and sponsored by Michael and Anna Eva Lau.

Maria Eve$^{1.2.2u}$, b. c.1770.

Adam$^{1.2.3u}$, b. Middletown, Maryland on April 20, 1772, and bapt. at Middletown Lutheran Church.

Peter$^{1.2.4u}$, b. April 20, 1772, and bapt. at Middletown Lutheran Church.

Johan Jacob$^{1.2.5u}$, b. March 10, 1775, and bapt. at Middletown Lutheran Church.

Isaac$^{1.2.6u}$, b. Bedford Co., Elk Lick Twp., Pennsylvania on March 1, 1778, bapt. Berlin Lutheran Church in Brother's Valley Twp. in 1779, and sponsored by Clement Engle.

Margaretha$^{1.2.7u}$, b. May 5, 1781, and bapt. at Berlin Lutheran Church, m. George Newman.

Elisabetha$^{1.2.8u}$, b. March 3, 1785, bapt. at Berlin Lutheran Church, d. before 1798.

Anna Maria Jauler

Anna Maria$^{1.2.1u}$ m. James Boyd in Bedford Co., Pennsylvania on Aug. 3, 1790. He was b. Scotland c.1760. According to family tradition, James and two brothers ran away from Scotland via Ireland to Americ. James was in Elk Lick Twp. in 1785, and had 50 acres there in 1798. He moved to Greenville Twp. between 1810 and 1813. Anna Maria d. Somerset Co., Greenville Twp., Pennsylvania in 1814, and James d. there in May, 1828. James had the following children: Adam$^{1.2.1.1u}$, b. Bedford Co., Elk Lick Twp. on May 13, 1791, bapt. at Sailsbury (St. John's) Reformed Church on July 16, 1791; John$^{1.2.1.2u}$, b. Elk Lick Twp. on Aug. 10, 1794, and bapt. at Sailsbury on Oct. 18, 1794; Isaac$^{1.2.1.3u}$, b. 1795; Hannah$^{1.2.1.4u}$, b. Somerset Co., Elk Lick Twp. on April 19, 1799, and bapt. at Sailsbury on July 13, 1799; James$^{1.2.1.5u}$, b. Elk Lick Twp. on May 17, 1801; Douglas B.$^{1.2.1.6u}$, b. Elk Lick Twp. on Oct. 6, 1803, and bapt. at Sailsbury on Sept. 2, 1804; Elizabeth$^{1.2.1.7u}$, b. Elk Lick Twp. in 1806, m. George Shultz; Mary Ann$^{1.2.1.8u}$, b. Elk Lick Twp. on Dec. 22, 1810, m. Peter Shock.

Adam Boyd

Adam$^{1.2.1.1u}$ m. Eve Catherine, dau. of Clement and Margaretta (Weimer) Engle, in Somerset Co., Pennsylvania on May 18, 1818, d. Clay Co., Missouri c.1839. She was b. Somerset Co., Pennsylvania on Sept. 22, 1800, and resided in Bates Co., Missouri in 1850. They had the following children in Somerset Co., Greenville Twp.:

Eliza Sarah$^{1.2.1.1.1u}$, b. 1820, m. John Martin Lindeman in Somerset Co., Pennsylvania on Feb. 19, 1838, d. on Oct. 6, 1895; Michael$^{1.2.1.1.2u}$, b. Dec. 9, 1822, m. Nancy Ann Gibson on Oct. 11, 1846, d. Oregon on Nov. 3, 1907; Catherine$^{1.2.1.1.3u}$, b. 1826, m. John Barns; Adam$^{1.2.1.1.4u}$, b. May 15, 1830, m. Mary Crowthers;

Reuben$^{1.2.1.1.5u}$, b. Feb. 26, 1832; Levi$^{1.2.1.1.6u}$, b. Feb. 17, 1834;
Solomon$^{1.2.1.1.7u}$, b. Aug. 21, 1836, m. Nanie, d. on May 8, 1908;
Sarah$^{1.2.1.1.8u}$, b. 1837; Henry$^{1.2.1.1.9u}$, b. Sept. 15, 1838.

Isaac Boyd

Isaac$^{1.2.1.3u}$ resided in Somerset Co., Greenville Twp. in 1830 and
Addison Twp. in 1850. He m. Magdalena (b. 1792) and had the
following children: Mary$^{1.2.1.3.1u}$, b. 1827; Solomon$^{1.2.1.3.2u}$, b. 1829;
Adam$^{1.2.1.3.3u}$, b. 1834.

Hannah Boyd

Hannah$^{1.2.1.4u}$ m. Solomon Hutzell, d. Somerset Co., Greenville Twp.,
Pennsylvania on April 15, 1836. He was b. Frederick Co., Maryland on
April 10, 1800, d. Greenville Twp. on July 10, 1863. They had the
following children in Greenville Twp.: Margaret$^{1.2.1.4.1u}$, b. 1827, m.
Daniel Garletz (1820-1858), d. July, 1888; LaFayette$^{1.2.1.4.2u}$, b. 1829,
d. on May 2, 1887; Susannah$^{1.2.1.4.3u}$, b. 1831, m. Daniel
Swarner/Suarner, and resided in Elmhurst, Illinois; Mary$^{1.2.1.4.4u}$, b.
1834, m. Solomon Weimer on June 4, 1854; Matilda$^{1.2.1.4.5u}$, b. 1837,
m. Adam Caton and William Patton, resided in Illinois in 1876;
Catherine$^{1.2.1.4.6u}$, b. 1840, m. Christian Steinley, d. La Grange Co.,
Indiana; Dinah$^{1.2.1.4.7u}$, b. 1843, d. Greenville Twp. in 1864;
Harriet$^{1.2.1.4.8u}$, b. c.1845, m. George Weaver.

James Boyd

James$^{1.2.1.5u}$ m. Catherine, dau. of Peter and Barbara (Garletts)
Engle, in Somerset Co., Pennsylvania on March 20, 1831, d. Noble Co.,
Cosperville, Indiana on Sept. 1, 1889. She was b. Somerset Co. on
Feb. 22, 1815, d. LaGrange Co., Clay Twp., Indiana on Feb. 6, 1881.
They had the following children:

Delilah$^{1.2.1.5.1u}$, b. Somerset Co., Greenville Twp. on Dec. 2, 1831,
m. John Frick in 1852, d. on March 18, 1913. He was b. 1819,
d. on Feb. 21, 1872.

Eston$^{1.2.1.5.2u}$, b. Greenville Twp. on Dec. 9, 1832, m. Sarah E.
Frisbey on Feb. 10, 1855, Ann Guann Gindlesparger on Aug.
19, 1866, and Magdalene Gindlesparger on Sept. 25, 1879.
Eston d. LaGrange Co., Indiana on Nov. 2, 1899. Sarah was
born on March 2, 1837, d. LaGrange Co., Clay Twp., Indiana on
Dec. 30, 1865.

Arion$^{1.2.1.5.3u}$, b. Greenville Twp. on Feb. 7, 1834, m. Nancy
Carnaham in 1855, d. on March 26, 1873. She was b. June 8,
1836, d. on March 11, 1897.

Harrison H.$^{1.2.1.5.4u}$, b. Greenville Twp. on Aug. 14, 1835, m.
Emily Landis, d. Noble Co., Elkhart/Albion Twp., Indiana on
March 8, 1914. She was born July, 1838, d. on June 24, 1907.

Edward$^{1.2.1.5.5u}$, b. Tuscarwas Co., Ohio on Dec. 23, 1836, m.
Lucinda A. Sayler in 1858, Eva Baumgarten on July 27, 1865,
Mary Jane McBeth on Nov. 1, 1874, and Ellen Schoyer after
1891. Lucinda was born on Jan. 18, 1840, d. on June 19, 1863.
Eva was born on Aug. 20, 1846, d. on April 9, 1872. Mary was
b. 1842, d. on Nov. 27, 1891. Ellen was born on Nov. 18, 1854,
d. on Aug. 16, 1918.

John$^{1.2.1.5.6u}$, b. Tuscarwas Co. on June 24, 1838, m. Amanda
Landis in Noble Co., Albion, Indiana on March 2, 1865, d.
LaGrange Co., Indiana in 1909. She was b. Noble Co., Eden
Twp., Indiana on Sept. 15, 1846, d. LaGrange Co. on Dec. 20,
1931.

Charles$^{1.2.1.5.7u}$, b. Tuscarwas Co. in 1840, d. Noble Co., Indiana in
1851.

Elizabeth$^{1.2.1.5.8u}$, b. Noble Co., Indiana on Nov. 21, 1841, m. Cory
Roger Frisbey on Oct. 27, 1867, d. on Aug. 9, 1933. He was
born on Feb. 21, 1836, d. on May 13, 1925.

James V.$^{1.2.1.5.9u}$, b. Noble Co. in 1843, m. Sarah Cherry and
Ruth, d. on March 21, 1891.

Mary$^{1.2.1.5.10u}$, b. Noble Co. on Sept. 5, 1845, m. Andrew McBeth
on April 7, 1868, d. on Oct. 3, 1926. He was born on Dec. 10,
1845, d. on Sept. 10, 1924.

Peter$^{1.2.1.5.11u}$, b. Noble Co. on June 14, 1848, m. Adelaide Fish in
Tama Co., Iowa on Dec. 5, 1871, d. Clay Co., Clay Center,
Nebraska on Dec. 28, 1928. She was born on Jan. 26, 1854, d.
on May 11, 1924.

Jacob$^{1.2.1.5.12u}$, b. Noble Co. on June 22, 1850, m. Julia Bell Saum,
d. on Oct. 9, 1926. She was born on April 4, 1865, d. on May 6,
1923.

Douglas$^{1.2.1.5.13u}$, b. Noble Co. on April 11, 1852, m. Susan Ann
Korn in June, 1873 and Molly Moose. Susan was born on June
7, 1852, d. on March 14, 1876.

Urias$^{1.2.1.5.14u}$, b. LaGrange Co., Indiana on Aug. 5, 1853, m. Ida
May Clark on Oct. 30, 1880, d. on April 18, 1941. She was
born on Aug. 22, 1862, d. on Oct. 8, 1951.

Phillip$^{1.2.1.5.16u}$, b. LaGrange Co. on July 14, 1856, m. Henrietta
Fleck on June 11, 1878, Elizabeth Malone on July 28, 1886,
and Christine Sodquest in April, 1925. Phillip d. on March 6,
1932. Henrietta was born on April 5, 1858, d. on March 18,
1880. Elizabeth was b. 1860, d. on october 29, 1922. Christine
d. 1931.

Samuel$^{1.2.1.5.17u}$, b. LaGrange Co. in Jan., 1860, d. June, 1860.

Daniel$^{1.2.1.5.18u}$, b. Jan., 1860, d. Nov., 1860.

Corinda$^{1.2.1.5.19u}$, b. LaGrange Co. on March 10, 1862, m. George
Albert Coger on Aug. 14, 1879, d. on May 7, 1950. He was

born on Nov. 11, 1856, d. on June 27, 1938.

Douglas B. Boyd

Douglas B.[1.2.1.6u] m. Susanna, dau. of John and Elizabeth (Miller) Lichty, in Somerset Co., Pennsylvania in Sept., 1830, d. Marshall Co., Iowa on July 26, 1878. She was b. Somerset Co., Pennsylvania on May 26, 1813, d. Marshall Co., Iowa on Sept. 3, 1896. They had the following children in Somerset Co., Greenville Twp., Pennsylvania:

Samuel Douglas[1.2.1.6.1u], b. Sept. 11, 1832, m. Catherine Bueghley, d. Glaen Rock, Nebraska in 1917. She was b. Somerset Co., Summit Mills, Pennsylvania on June 26, 1835, d. Rock Co., Nebraska on April 19, 1892.

Manasses[1.2.1.6.2u], b. April 13, 1834, d. 1840.

John D.[1.2.1.6.3u], b. May 7, 1836, m. Sarah Jane Wright on Dec. 1, 1861, d. Liscomb, Iowa on Feb. 17, 1918. She was b. Pennsylvania on May 20, 1838, d. Liscomb on Feb. 25, 1913.

William Douglas[1.2.1.6.4u], b. May 23, 1839, m. Barbara Engle in Somerset Co., Elk Lick Twp. on Dec. 25, 1860, d. Liscomb, Iowa on Dec. 2, 1922. She was b. Somerset Co. on Oct. 26, 1840, d. Liscomb on May 28, 1926.

Matilda[1.2.1.6.5u], b. Oct. 3, 1841, m. Jacob R. Johnson in Marshalltown, Iowa on Feb. 20, 1869, d. Liscomb, Iowa on Dec. 20, 1928. He was b. Berks Co., Reading, Pennsylvania, d. Liscomb, Iowa on Dec. 22, 1924.

Francis[1.2.1.6.6u], b. Jan. 8, 1844, d. on Nov. 28, 1851.

James D.[1.2.1.6.7u], b. Feb. 20, 1847, m. Elizabeth Bueghley in Liscomb, Iowa on March 10, 1870, d. Liscomb on July 26, 1938. She was b. Somerset Co., Pennsylvania on May 10, 1841, d. on July 23, 1916.

Mary Ann Boyd

Mary Ann[1.2.1.8u] m. Peter, son of George and Elizabeth (Schultz) Shock, in Somerset Co., Pennsylvania on April 22, 1827. About 1829, Peter moved from Elk Lick/Greenville Twp. to Addison Twp., where he farmed 40 acres of government land. In April, 1832, he sold some of his land in Greenville Twp. to his brother-in-law, Solomon Hutzell, and in Nov., 1835, sold the remainder to John Walker. On June 6, 1837, Peter purchased land in Coshocton Co., Ohio, but did not make the move to Ohio until 1840. In 1846, he moved to Allen Co., Amanda Twp., where he farmed 50 acres in section 34. In 1886, he moved to Mercer Co., Black Creek Twp., Ohio, and purchased 80 acres. while They resided in Black Creek Twp., Peter and Mary lived with their son, Levi, and in 1892, moved in with their dau., Sarah. Peter and Mary were members of the Dunkard Church until 1855, when they converted to the United Brethren Church. In their old age, both lost their sight. Peter d. Mercer Co., Black Creek Twp., Ohio on Nov. 13, 1895, and Mary Ann on Oct. 1, 1895. They are buried in Fountain Chapel cemetery. They had the following children:

Levi[1.2.1.8.1u], b. May 9, 1828, m. Mary Jane Carr in Allen Co., Ohio on Feb. 8, 1851 and Mary Albert in Coshocton Co., Ohio on March 30, 1869. Mary Carr was b. Ohio in 1831, d. Mercer Co., Black Creek Twp., Ohio on Dec. 31, 1868. Mary Albert was b. Coshocton Co., Ohio on Nov. 27, 1822, d. Black Creek Twp. on July 30, 1905. Levi d. Mercer Co., Rockford, Ohio on July 3, 1912.

Elizabeth[1.2.1.8.2u], b. Dec. 25, 1829, m. David Eaton Baxter in Allen Co., Ohio on Jan. 30, 1848, d. Allen Co. on July 4, 1927. He was b. Ross Co., Ohio on April 28, 1828.

Huldah Ann[1.2.1.8.3u], b. Sept. 1, 1832, m. Reuben R. Carr in Allen Co., Ohio on Dec. 4, 1852, d. Lucas Co., Toledo, Ohio on July 2, 1909. He was b. Ohio on May 2, 1832, d. Mercer Co., Black Creek Twp., Ohio on June 16, 1909.

Carlisle[1.2.1.8.4u], b. Jan. 1, 1835, m. Amos Crites in Allen Co., Ohio on Aug. 17, 1854, d. Allen Co. on May 18, 1918. He was b. Fairfield Co., Ohio on Nov. 18, 1832, d. Buckland, Ohio on March 4, 1919.

Catherine[1.2.1.8.5u], b. May 21, 1837, m. Joseph Daniel Allen in Allen Co., Ohio on Dec. 31, 1859, d. Allen Co., Allentown, Ohio on July 4, 1927. He was born on Dec. 6, 1838, d. Allen Co. on Oct. 29, 1918.

George[1.2.1.8.6u], b. Oct. 14, 1839, m. Nancy[1.2.7.7.2.3v], dau. of Lewis and Elizabeth (Shope) Herring, in Allen Co., Ohio on Oct. 7, 1862, d. Mercer Co., Black Creek Twp., Ohio on Nov. 28, 1892. George farmed 20 acres in section 34 in Allen Co., Amanda Twp., Ohio until 1886, when he moved to Mercer Co., Black Creek Twp., Ohio where he took up 20 acres in section 24. George died from a heart attack suffered while clearing this land. Nancy d. Paulding Co., Payne, Ohio c.1894, while residing with her sons, that were laboring, clearing trees. George is buried in Fountain Chapel cemetery, and Nancy's grave has not been located.

Sarah[1.2.1.8.7u], b. March 16, 1842, m. Hiram Baxter in Allen Co., Ohio on Dec. 10, 1863 and William C. Wagoner in Allen Co. on July 29, 1866. She d. Mercer Co., Rockford, Ohio on March 19, 1913. William was b. Allen Co., Ohio on April 26, 1845, d. Mercer Co., Black Creek Twp., Ohio on Aug. 11, 1926.

Mary Ann[1.2.1.8.8u], b. Aug. 17, 1845, had a illegitimate son by Louis McBride, m. William T. Rumple in Allen Co., Ohio on April 11, 1877. Mary Ann d. Mercer Co., Ohio on June 13, 1922. William was b. Carroll Co., Ohio n Jan. 18, 1839, d.

Mercer Co. on Dec. 6, 1912.

Elvina$^{1.2.1.8.9u}$, b. Dec. 11, 1847, m. Asa Binkley in Allen Co., Ohio on Dec. 24, 1871, d. Van Wert Co., Jackson Twp., Ohio on Aug. 10, 1914. He was b. Allen Co., Ohio on Dec. 8, 1850, d. Van Wert Co., Jackson Twp., Ohio.

William$^{1.2.1.8.10u}$, b. Aug. 22, 1850, m. Margaret Elizabeth Kiracoff in Allen Co., Ohio on April 25, 1872, d. Allen Co., Amanda Twp., Ohio on Nov. 26, 1933. She was b. Aug.a Co., Virginia on April 22, 1951, d. Van Wert Co., Van Wert, Ohio on Feb. 1, 1919.

Peter$^{1.2.1.8.11u}$, b. May 12, 1852, m. Melinda Shope in Allen Co., Ohio on Dec. 7, 1876, d. Isabella Co., Blanchard, Michigan on March 5, 1932. She d. Defiance Co., Ney, Ohio on Oct. 17, 1918.

Maria Eve Jauler

Maria Eve$^{1.2.2u}$ m. Johan Adam Fadley in Bedford Co., Elk Lick Twp. in 1787, d. Somerset Co., Elk Lick Twp., Sailsbury, Pennsylvania c.1792. Johan Adam was b. Montgomery Co., New Hanover Twp., Pennsylvania on June 15, 1765. After Maria Eve's death, he m. Anna Maria, dau. of Solomon and Maria Eva (Frensch) Glatfelter. Adam and Maria Eve had the following children: John William$^{1.2.2.1u}$, b. Dec. 20, 1788, m. Barbara Krieder in 1811; Susanna$^{1.2.2.2u}$, b. 1790.

Adam Jauler

Adam$^{1.2.3m}$ had 137 acres in Elk Lick Twp. in 1798, and was on the 1830 census on Somerset Co., Milford Twp., Pennsylvania. In 1850, he resided in Somerset Co., Henry Twp. He m. Salla, and had the following children: Israel$^{1.2.3.1m}$, b. 1813; Hannah$^{1.2.3.2m}$, b. April 20, 1817, and bapt. at Berlin Lutheran Church on May 9, 1819; Josiah$^{1.2.3.3m}$, b. 1822.

Israel Jauler

Israel$^{1.2.3.1m}$ m. Margaret (b. 1816), resided in Milford Twp. in 1860, and had the following children: John$^{1.2.3.1.1m}$, b. 1838; Cyrus$^{1.2.3.1.2m}$, b. 1839; Sarah$^{1.2.3.1.3m}$, b. 1841; Lucinda$^{1.2.3.1.4m}$, b. 1843; Adam$^{1.2.3.1.5m}$, b. 1845, m. Anna Catharina Denney; Peter$^{1.2.3.1.6m}$, b. 1847; Lydia$^{1.2.3.1.7m}$, b. 1849; Phebe$^{1.2.3.1.8m}$, b. 1850, m. William Mickley; Henry$^{1.2.3.1.9m}$, b. 1852; William$^{1.2.3.1.10m}$, b. 1852; Elizabeth$^{1.2.3.1.11m}$, b. 1855; Susanna$^{1.2.3.1.12m}$, b. 1857; Margaret$^{1.2.3.1.13m}$, b. 1857.

Josiah Jauler

Josiah$^{1.2.3.3m}$ m. Elizabeth Nedrow (b. 1826) in Somerset Co. on Nov. 16, 1845, resided in Milford Twp. in 1860, and had the following children: Christina[1.2.3.3.1m], b. 1846; Jonathan[1.2.3.3.2m], b. 1847; Sullena[1.2.3.3.3m], b. 1851; Susanna[1.2.3.3.4m], b. 1854; Louisa[1.2.3.3.5m], b. 1856.

****

Johannes Herring

Johannes[1v] m. Anna Margaretha, and immigrated to Pennsylvania on the ship, Neptune, on Sept. 24, 1751. In 1754, 56, 58, they were communicants at Trinity Lutheran Church in Bucks Co., Springfield Twp., Pennsylvania. They had the following children: Johann[1.1v]. Johann Ludwig[1.2v]; Anna Margaretha[1.3v], was a communicant at Trinity Lutheran Church in Bucks Co., Springfield Twp., Pennsylvania in 1757; Margaretha Barbara[1.4v], was a communicant at Trinity Lutheran Church in Bucks Co., Springfield Twp., Pennsylvania in 1757; Maria Elisabeth[1.5v], confirmed on Good Friday, 1753, at Ne Goshenhoppen Lutheran Church in Upper Hanover Twp.; Johann Jacob[1.6v]; Johann Phillip[1.7v].

Johann Herring

Johann[1.1v] immigrated to America on the ship, Neptune, on Sept. 24, 1751, m. Anna Elisabeth. Johann d. Berks Co., Pennsylvania before 1790, and his widow d. Bucks Co. after 1800. They had the following children:

Margareth Elisabetha[1.1.1v], bapt. at St. Paul's Lutheran Church in Montgomery Co., Upper Hanover Twp., Pennsylvania on Feb. 8, 1752, and sponsored by Michael and Elisabeth Kabel.

Johann Henrich[1.1.2v], b. Feb. 23, 1755, bapt. at St. Paul's (Blue) Church, Northampton (now Lehigh) Co., Upper Sauccon Twp., Pennsylvania on March 30, 1755. He took the Oath of Allegiance in Berks Co. on June 7, 1778, and resided in Bucks Co. in 1800.

Johannes[1.1.3v], bapt. York (now Adams) Co., Pennsylvania at Littletown Christ's Reformed Lutheran Church on Oct. 16, 1763 (this has not been confirmed as the same Johannes and Anna Elisabeth).

Johann Ludwig Herring

Johann Ludwig[1.2v] immigrated to America on the ship, Neptune, on Sept. 24, 1751, m. Maria Catharina, d. Montgomery Co., Upper Hanover Twp., Pennsylvania between 1765 and 1769. They bapt. the following children at St. Paul's Lutheran Church in Upper Hanover Twp. (except the last in Old Goshenhoppen in Upper Salford Twp.):

Johann Georg[1.2.1v], b. Nov. 13, 1753, d. on April 25, 1776. He is buried at Goshenhoppen Church in Upper Salford Twp.

Anna Christina[1.2.2v], b. Jan. 14, 1756, and confirmed at Indian

Creek Reformed Church in 1770.

Jacob$^{1.2.3v}$, b. Montgomery Co., Marlborough Twp. on Oct. 28, 1758.

Eva Catharina$^{1.2.4v}$, b. Jan. 8, 1761, and confirmed at St. Paul's on Feb. 14, 1774.

Johan Nickel$^{1.2.5v}$, b. Feb. 16, 1763, d. 1839.

Johann Luttwig$^{1.2.6v}$, b. Feb. 1, 1764, d. 1815.

Jacob Herring

Jacob$^{1.2.3v}$ m. Magdalena, dau. of Henry and Barbara (Nees) Guttelman, at St. John's on May 27, 1783, d. Bucks Co., Rockhill Twp., Pennsylvania Feb. 10, 1817. She was born on Nov. 23, 1757, d. on April 26, 1842. They are buried in St. John's Lutheran Church, Ridge Valley. They had the following children in Montgomery Co., Franconia Twp.: Johan Georg$^{1.2.3.1v}$, bapt. Jan. 31, 1785; Johannes$^{1.2.3.2v}$, bapt. 1790; Johan Jacob$^{1.2.3.3v}$, bapt. Feb. 7, 1792; Maria Catharina$^{1.2.3.4v}$, bapt. May 10, 1795; Samuel$^{1.2.3.5v}$, bapt. April 17, 1797.

Johan Nickel Herring

Johan Nickel$^{1.2.5v}$ m. Maria, d. 1839. They had a son in Montgomery Co., Franconia Twp., Johannes$^{1.2.5.1v}$, bapt. Dec. 19, 1790; and a dau. Maria$^{1.2.5.2v}$, bapt. Dec. 1, 1793.

Johann Jacob Herring

Johann Jacob$^{1.6v}$ m. Maria Catharina Hackmann in Montgomery Co., Upper Hanover Twp., Pennsylvania on Oct. 31, 1758. He resided in Northampton Co., Hanover Twp., Pennsylvania in 1800. They bapt. the following children in St. Paul's Lutheran Church: Johann Ludwig$^{1.6.1v}$, b. May 1, 1759; Anna Elisabetha$^{1.6.2v}$, b. March 27, 1760; Anna Maria$^{1.6.3v}$, b. Feb. 3, 1761; Maria Catharina$^{1.6.4v}$, b. Feb. 3, 1761.

Johann Phillip Herring

Johann Phillip$^{1.7v}$ m. Anna, d. Fairfield Co., Amanda Twp., Ohio in 1821. She d. Amanda Twp. after 1800. Phillip was naturalized on Aug. 8, 1765. He was taxed in Bucks Co., Richland Twp., Pennsylvania until 1769, when he appears on the tax list of York Co., Paradise Twp., Pennsylvania with two horses, and 46 acres. This was part of John Brady's Warrant on the North Side of Pidgeon Hills. The other portion of this Warrant had been purchased by Philip's presumed uncle, Henry Herring, on Jan. 2, 1759. Phillip was taxed in Paradise Twp. until 1783. Around 1784, he moved to Dover Twp. He served in the Revolutionary War as a Corporal in the York Co., Militia in 1780 and 1782. In 1786,87,88, he served in the York Co., Militia in the 3rd Company of Foot, 3rd Battalion. Around 1803/04, he moved to

Fairfield Co., Amanda Twp., Ohio. Phillip and Anna had the following children:

dau.[1.7.1v], b. c.1763. Possibly, Magdalena, wife of Michael Seiffert. They had Philip in Dover Twp. on March 22, 1787, bapt. at Strayer's on Nov. 14, 1791, and sponsored by Philip and Anna Herring; Catherine, b. March 25, 1776, bapt. at Strayer's on April 21, 1776, and sponsored by Adam and Maria Seiffert; Maria Elizabeth, b. Dec. 21, 1781, bapt. at Strayer's, and sponsored by Valentine and Maria Elizabeth Wild; George Michael, b. Aug. 14, 1777, bapt. at Strayer's on Sept. 14, 1777, and sponsored by Herman and Magdalena Helman; John, b. Dec. 22, 1783, bapt. at Strayer's on Nov. 14, 1791, and sponsored by Andrew and Catherine Honz; John George, b. Oct. 13 (1791), bapt. at Strayer's on March 14, (1792), and sponsored by George and Catherine Fliger; Daniel, b. Dec. 28, 1798, bapt. at Strayer's on April 9, 1798, and sponsored by Jacob and Anna Maria Zin.

Heinrich[1.7.2v], b. Bucks Co., Richland Twp., Pennsylvania c.1765.

Elizabeth[1.7.3v], b. c.1769.

dau.[1.7.4v], b. c.1771. Possibly, Barbara, wife of Johan Nicholaus Lichte. They had a dau., Barbara, in Dover Twp. on Dec. 6, 1794 (bapt. at Strayer's, and sponsored by Eve Haren and Philip Hering). They also had Joseph, b. March 4, 1796, bapt. at Strayer's on May 15, 1796, and sponsored by Joseph and Gred Beigler.

Philip[1.7.5v], b. c.1773, m. Maria Eva, dau. of Jeremias and Maria Elizabeth Beer, before 1807. She was born on Oct. 28, 1774, bapt. at Strayer's on Nov. 26, 1774, and sponsored by Michael and Maria Eva Spaar.

dau.[1.7.6v], b. c.1774.

John[1.7.7v], b. c.1775.

Eva[1.7.8v], b. c.1777, m. Peter Stuckey in Fairfield Co., Ohio on Oct. 6, 1805.

dau.[1.7.9v], b. c.1779.

son[1.7.10v], b. c.1782. Possibly the David Herron that m. Elizabeth Hornett in Fairfield Co., Ohio on July 8, 1804 and Mary Wilson in Fairfield Co. on June 4, 1807.

dau.[1.7.11v], b. c.1784. Possibly, Anna Maria, wife of Philip Wollet. They had Georg Michael in Dover Twp. in 1803.

dau.[1.7.12v], b. c.1786.

Heinrich Herring

Heinrich[1.7.2v] m. Margaret, dau. of Samuel and Margaretha Wildasin, of York Co., Manheim Twp. She was b. 1771, d. Adams Co., Straban Twp., Pennsylvania on Oct. 5, 1846. Heinrich served in the York Co.

Militia in Captain John Sharp's 3 rd Company of Foot, 3rd Battalion in 1786, 87, 88. He d. Dover Twp. in Aug., 1825. He was a farmer and weaver. They had the following children: Malli$^{1.2.7.2.1v}$, b. c.1788, m. Jacob, son of Charles and Barbara Mitman, in York Co. Oct. 19, 1809; Johannes$^{1.2.7.2.2v}$, b. March 3, 1790, bapt. at Strayer's on Aug. 2, 1790, sponsored by Mattheis Mayer and Lizabeth Haring; Georg Michael$^{1.2.7.2.3v}$, b. Feb. 12, 1792, bapt. at Strayer's on April 6, 1792, sponsored by Michael and Magdalena Seifert; John Philip$^{1.2.7.2.4v}$, b. Nov. 7 (Sept. 17), 1793, bapt. at Strayer's on March 31, 1794, sponsored by John Philip and Anna Hering; Henry$^{1.2.7.2.5v}$, b. Aug. 15, 1796; Elizabeth$^{1.2.7.2.6v}$, b. 1800; Catharine$^{1.2.7.2.7v}$, b. April 3, 1802, m. Henry Bierbrauer in York Co. on Jan. 31, 1832; Salome$^{1.2.7.2.8v}$, b. 1805; Isarah$^{1.2.7.2.9v}$, b. c.1807; Jacob$^{1.2.7.2.10v}$, b. Oct. 17, 1810.

Johannes Herring

Johannes$^{1.2.7.2.2v}$ m. Catharina (and possibly Catharina Kring in Fairfield Co., Ohio on April 6, 1825). Catharina d. Ohio before 1825. Johannes had the following children: Salome$^{1.2.7.2.2.1v}$, b. March 2, 1816, m. Henry J. King in Guernsey Co., Ohio on Feb. 9, 1840; Benjamin S.$^{1.2.7.2.2.2v}$, b. Oct. 6, 1817, m. Sarah E., d. Guernsey Co., Ohio on July 4, 1894; Louise$^{1.2.7.2.2.3v}$, b. Dover Twp. on July 15, 1821.

Philip Herring

Philip$^{1.2.7.2.4v}$ m. Elizabeth Rupert in York Co. in 1817 and Elizabeth Hartman in Allen Co., Ohio on July 21, 1833. Elizabeth Rupert was b. 1799, d. Allen Co., German Twp., Ohio on May 22, 1833. Elizabeth Hartman was b. 1814, d. Allen Co., German Twp. in 1896. Philip inherited his father's land in Fairfield Co., Amanda Twp., Ohio, and moved there after his father's death. After spending a short time in Fairfield Co., Philip and his uncle, John Herring, moved to Allen Co., Ohio. Philip had the following children:

Emanuel$^{1.2.7.2.4.1v}$, b. York Co., Dover Twp. on Nov. 30, 1818, m. Julia Ann Crites in Allen Co., Ohio on Dec. 27, 1849, d. Allen Co., German Twp. on May 15, 1852. After Emanuel's death, Julia m. Abraham Kesler in Allen Co. on Jan. 3, 1857.

Cassandra$^{1.2.7.2.4.2v}$, b. July 16, 1820.

Rebecca$^{1.2.7.2.4.3v}$, b. c.1822, m. Charles Miller in Allen Co., Ohio on May 28, 1843.

John Andrew$^{1.2.7.2.4.4v}$, b. Oct. 8, 1824, d. Fairfield Co., Amanda Twp., Ohio on Nov. 17, 1831.

Penrose R.$^{1.2.7.2.4.5v}$, b. Fairfield Co., Amanda Twp., Ohio on Aug. 24, 1829, m. Lydia Hunsaker in Allen Co., Ohio on Feb. 11, 1855, d. Allen Co., German Twp. on April 7, 1874.

Gideon$^{1.2.7.2.4.6v}$, b. Amanda Twp. on Aug. 11, 1832, m. Mary
Bowsher in Allen Co., Ohio on Dec. 7, 1856, d. Allen Co.,
German Twp. on Dec. 9, 1915.

Saloma$^{1.2.7.2.4.7v}$, b. c.1834, m. William Wurt in Allen Co., Ohio on
Jan. 15, 1853.

William$^{1.2.7.2.4.8v}$, b. c.1836, m. Phebe Jacobs in Allen Co., Ohio
on Aug. 9, 1858.

Sarah$^{1.2.7.2.4.9v}$, b. c.1837, m. David Piper in Allen Co., Ohio on
Sept. 23, 1858.

Henry Herring

Henry$^{1.2.7.2.5v}$ m. Salome Bailey, d. York Co., Fairview Twp. on Dec.
14, 1861. She was born on Jan. 12, 1806, d. Fairview Twp. on May 19,
1885. Henry was a Private in the War of 1812. They had the
following children: George Frederick$^{1.2.7.2.5.1v}$, b. 1827, d. 1910;
Caroline$^{1.2.7.2.5.2v}$, b. 1830, m. ____ Boyer, d. 1920; Eliza$^{1.2.7.2.5.3v}$,
b. 1832, m. ____ Smyser, d. 1861; Susanna$^{1.2.7.2.5.4v}$, b. 1835, d. on
June 12, 1843; Sarah Jane$^{1.2.7.2.5.5v}$, b. 1838, m. ____ Gray, d. 1921;
Levi$^{1.2.7.2.5.6v}$, b. 1840, d. 1916; Rebecca$^{1.2.7.2.5.7v}$, b. Dec. 25, 1842,
d. on May 31, 1890; Henry B.$^{1.2.7.2.5.8v}$, b. May 31, 1847, d. on March
20, 1848; Malinda$^{1.2.7.2.5.9v}$, b. 1850, m. ____ Hale, d. 1929.

Jacob Herring

Jacob$^{1.2.7.2.10v}$ m. Sarah Strayer in York Co. on Jan. 24, 1833, d.
Greene Co., Osborn (now Fairborn) Ohio. He was a Second
Lieutenant in the York Co., Militia. They had the following children:
Catherine$^{1.2.7.2.10.1v}$, b. Dover Twp. on April 2, 1834, m. William
Bentzel in Adams Co., Hanover, St. Matthew's Lutheran
Church, Pennsylvania on Aug. 24, 1862, d. York Co., West
Manchester Twp., Pennsylvania in 1892.

Lydia$^{1.2.7.2.10.2v}$.

Alvin$^{1.2.7.2.10.3v}$.

Jack$^{1.2.7.2.10.4v}$, b. 1839, m. Maggie, d. Holmes Co., Ohio on Feb.
17, 1909. She d. Holmes Co. July 29, 1919.

Samuel Edward$^{1.2.7.2.10.5v}$, b. Jan. 22, 1840, m. Catharine, dau. of
Henry H. and Elizabeth (Peterman) Atticks, d. York,
Pennsylvania on April 20, 1922. She was b. Fairview Twp. on
Jan. 13, 1840, d. York on July 2, 1926.

John Herring

John$^{1.2.7.7v}$ m. Jane "Ginney" Poole in Fairfield Co., Ohio on June 16,
1807, d. Allen Co., German Twp., Ohio in June, 1847. She was b.
Maryland in 1775, and was residing in German Twp. in 1850. John
moved his family from Fairfield Co., Amanda Twp. to Allen Co.,
German Twp., Ohio in 1833. John and Jane had the following children

in Amanda Twp.: Mary Jane$^{1.2.7.7.1v}$, b. 1807; Lewis$^{1.2.7.7.2v}$, b. 1808; David$^{1.2.7.7.3v}$, b. 1810; John$^{1.2.7.7.4v}$, b. Sept. 10, 1811; Henry$^{1.2.7.7.5v}$, b. 1813; Elizabeth$^{1.2.7.7.6v}$, b. 1814; Harriet$^{1.2.7.7.7v}$, b. c.1819, m. Jacob Sours in Allen Co., Ohio, Feb. 1, 1849; Susan$^{1.2.7.7.8v}$, b. 1823, unmarried, living with her mother in 1850.

Mary Jane Herring

Mary Jane$^{1.2.7.7.1v}$ m. John/Jacob Stemen in Allen Co., Ohio on July 4, 1837. He d. Allen Co. on Aug. 30, 1866. They had the following children: Magdalene$^{1.2.7.7.1.1v}$, b. c.1838, m. ____ Ditto; Judith$^{1.2.7.7.1.2v}$, b. c.1840, m. Eli Stevick in Allen Co. on Jan. 27, 1859; Elizabeth$^{1.2.7.7.1.3v}$, b. c.1842, m. F. D. Judkins in Allen Co. on Sept. 15, 1861; John H.$^{1.2.7.7.1.4v}$, b. c.1844, m. Emilene Leist in Allen Co. on July 15, 1866; Enos M.$^{1.2.7.7.1.5v}$, b. c.1847, m. Rachel A. Baxter in Allen Co. on Oct. 29, 1860; Benjamin F.$^{1.2.7.7.1.6v}$, b. c.1850, m. Sarah A. Bumgardner in Allen Co. on Feb. 17, 1876; William A.$^{1.2.7.7.1.7v}$, b. c.1852, m. Rachael John in Allen Co. on Dec. 21, 1871; ary Evaline$^{1.2.7.7.1.8v}$, b. c.1854, m. Jacob J. Boggs in Allen Co. on July 8, 1875; Noah S.$^{1.2.7.7.1.9v}$, b. c.1856.

Lewis Herring

Lewis$^{1.2.7.7.2v}$ m. Elizabeth, dau. of William and Elizabeth (Tester) Shope, in Allen Co., Ohio on April 28, 1835. She was b. Fairfield Co., Greenfield Twp., Ohio on Aug. 18, 1816. In 1850, Lewis was a farmer in German Twp., and on Jan. 20, 1851, he purchased land in the southwest quarter of section thirty-four in Allen Co., Amanda Twp. He moved there between 1860 and 1870, and he and Elizabeth d. between 1870 and 1875. They had the following children:

Mary Ann$^{1.2.7.7.2.1v}$, b. April, 1836, m. Jacob Little in Allen Co. on Dec. 30, 1860, and resided in Amanda Twp. in 1900. He was b. Ohio in 1833.

John$^{1.2.7.7.2.2v}$, b. 1840.

Nancy$^{1.2.7.7.2.3v}$, b. 1842, m. George Shock$^{1.2.1.7.6u}$.

William$^{1.2.7.7.2.4v}$, b. 1844.

Lavina$^{1.2.7.7.2.5v}$, b. 1846, m. Peter Allard in Allen Co. on March 5, 1871, and resided in Amanda Twp. in 1880. He was b. Ohio in 1846.

Samuel S.$^{1.2.7.7.2.6v}$, b. 1849, m. Elizabeth A. Raines in Allen Co. on Jan. 9, 1868 and Kitturah Miller in Allen Co. on June 4, 1874. He d. Allen Co., Amanda Twp. in 1917. Kitturah was b. 1848, d. 1920.

Lewis J.$^{1.2.7.7.2.7v}$, b. Oct., 1852, m. Ida A. Highland in 1890, d. Allen Co., Amanda Twp. in 1928. She was b. 1862, d. 1925.

George$^{1.2.7.7.2.8v}$, b. 1855, m. Mary E. Miller c.1885, d. Allen Co.,

Amanda Twp. in 1936. She was b. 1867, d. 1943.
Henry $^{1.2.7.7.2.9v}$, b. 1858.

David Herring

David$^{1.2.7.7.3v}$ m. Susannah Van Wey in Allen Co., Ohio on Aug. 1, 1841, d. Shelby Co., Shelbyville, Illinois before 1870. She was b. Ohio in 1825, and was alive in 1870. They had the following children: Nancy Jane$^{1.2.7.7.3.1v}$, b. Allen Co. in 1845, m. Jacob (Isaac) Rysacker in Allen Co. on Nov. 10, 1866; Jacob Van Wey$^{1.2.7.7.3.2v}$, b. Aug., 1847, m. Minerva Swisher in Allen Co. on Sept. 1, 1866, d. Leavenworth Co., Leavenworth, Kansas on Dec. 23, 1909; Henry S.$^{1.2.7.7.3.3v}$, b. Allen Co., Bath Twp. in 1849; Manuel W.$^{1.2.7.7.3.4v}$, b. Bath Twp. in 1851; Abraham A.$^{1.2.7.7.3.5v}$, b. Bath Twp. in 1852; John$^{1.2.7.7.3.6v}$, b. Bath Twp. in 1856; William A.$^{1.2.7.7.3.7v}$, b. Bath Twp. in 1858; George$^{1.2.7.7.3.8v}$, b. Shelby Co., Shelbyville, Illinois in 1863.

John Herring

John$^{1.2.7.7.4v}$ m. Catherine Bressler, widow of ____ Stuckey, in Allen Co., Ohio on Nov. 2, 1848, d. Allen Co., German Twp. on Sept. 23, 1873. She was b. 1816, d. on March 30, 1881. They had the following children: Isaac$^{1.2.7.7.4.1v}$, b. July 21, 1849, d. on Sept. 17, 1863; John W.$^{1.2.7.7.4.2v}$, b. 1853, m. Susanna Porter in Allen Co. March 14, 1873; Charles$^{1.2.7.7.4.3v}$, b. 1856, m. Catherine Bowersock in Allen Co. on March 27, 1879.

Henry Herring

Henry$^{1.2.7.7.5v}$ m. Nancy, dau. of William and Elizabeth (Tester) Shope, in Allen Co., Ohio on Nov. 2, 1842 and Rachel Lowrey c.1854. Nancy was b. Fairfield Co., Greenfield Twp., Ohio on Nov. 2, 1820, d. German Twp. c.1853. Henry d. German Twp. in Jan., 1886. He had the following children in German Twp.:

Rebecca$^{1.2.7.7.5.1v}$, b. 1844.

David$^{1.2.7.7.5.2v}$, b. June 15, 1845, m. Mary M. Cremean in Allen Co. on Jan. 16, 1868 and Nanna Lowrey in Allen Co. on March 27, 1884. He d. Allen Co., American Twp., Ohio on June 4, 1933.

Elizabeth$^{1.2.7.7.5.3v}$, b. 1846, m. Moses Thomas in Allen Co. on May 28, 1868.

Lewis$^{1.2.7.7.5.4v}$, b. 1847, d. before 1885.

Jeremiah$^{1.2.7.7.5.5v}$, b. 1848.

June$^{1.2.7.7.5.6v}$, b. 1852.

Hiram$^{1.2.7.7.5.7v}$, b. 1855, m. Isabele Johnson in Allen Co. on Jan. 3, 1878.

William$^{1.2.7.7.5.8v}$, b. 1856, m. Mary Collins in Allen Co. on Oct. 10, 1878, d. Allen Co., American Twp., Ohio in 1944. She was

b. 1856, d. 1942.

Henry E.[1.2.7.7.5.9v], b. 1858, m. Mary M. Miller in Allen Co. on
Dec. 19, 1878, d. Allen Co., German Twp., Ohio on March 11,
1880. She was b. 1845, d. German Twp. Aug. 30, 1881. This
may be Henry, son of Lewis Herring.

Jane/Jennie[1.2.7.7.5.10v], b. 1861, m. John A. Burget in Allen Co. on
April 26, 1883, d. before 1885.

Nancy[1.2.7.7.5.11v], b. c.1862, d. German Twp. on Feb. 4, 1869.

Eleanor[1.2.7.7.5.12v], b. c.1864, d. German Twp. on Feb. 26, 1869.

Elizabeth Herring

Elizabeth[1.2.7.7.6v] m. Jacob Bressler in Allen Co., Ohio on Aug. 16,
1840, d. Allen Co. in 1896. He was b. Pennsylvania in 1802. They had
the following children: Sarah Elling[1.2.7.7.6.1v], b. 1838, m. Samuel
Crider in Allen Co. May 11, 1856; Henry[1.2.7.7.6.2v], b. 1842, m. Lavey
Wallet in Allen Co. on Aug. 31, 1865; William[1.2.7.7.6.3v], b. 1844, m.
Hester A. Fisher in Allen Co. Nov. 5, 1866; Catherine L.[1.2.7.7.6.4v], b.
1846, m. John Thomas in Allen Co. Dec. 15, 1870;
Marriann[1.2.7.7.6.5v], b. 1848; Daniel[1.2.7.7.6.6v], b. 1849.

INDEX

-A-

Adam, 22
Adams, 97
Agler, 95
Agler, 97, 105
Albrecht, 24
Allard, 139
Allen, 32, 132,
Allison, 35, 62
Alspauch, 119
Alspaugh, 117
Anderson, 102
Anstine, 22
Antony, 85
Archer, 118
Arechtler, 1, 10
Arford, 102
Arnold, 40
Arntz, 72
Ash, 96
Ashbaugh, 120
Atticks, 138
Attig, 68
Augustine, 66
Ault, 103
Austin, 81

-B-

Bader, 41
Baehli, 24, 36, 77,
78, 79, 80, 81, 82,
83, 84, 86, 87, 89,
90, 91
Bahm, 15
Bahn, 13, 16, 81,
82
Bailey, 120, 138
Baker, 78
Baltzell, 100, 101,
116
Balyeat, 102
Barbee, 32

Baringer, 7
Barker, 44, 62
Barnes, 43
Barns, 128
Barr, 40
Barrett, 119
Barsinger, 65
Bartmesser, 126
Barton, 116
Bartruff, 96
Batt, 59
Battenburg, 108
Baugh, 64
Baughman, 20
Baumann, 5, 6, 7
Baumgarten, 130
Baxter, 132, 139
Bay, 105
Bayley, 112
Beach, 123
Beard, 113
Bechley, 16
Becker, 2, 64
Beer, 136
Beery, 17, 18, 19,
20, 38, 29, 42, 43,
52, 53
Behler, 90
Beidel, 125
Beidler, 96
Belden, 105
Bell, 36
Belt, 117
Beltz, 28
Bender, 77
Benkiser, 5, 6, 7,
8
Benner, 80
Benss, 56
Bentzel, 138
Berebile, 60

Berkebeil, 27
Berkey, 99, 106
Biber, 21
Bierbrauer, 137
Bieri, 51
Binckele, 121
Binfert, 94, 98
Binkley, 133
Black, 32
Blackwell, 119
Blake, 32
Blish, 105
Block, 32
Blokes, 42
Bloper, 42
Blosser, 53
Blossner, 85
Bloze, 113
Boggs, 139
Bohrech, 127
Bollinger, 62, 87
Bolzell, 119
Bomberger, 58
Bope, 11
Boroff, 116
Bortner, 14, 84
Bosserth, 125
Boudemont, 94,
99
Boudemount, 98
Bourgey, 94
Bowersock, 120,
121, 140
Bowman, 40
Bowser, 111, 112
Bowyer, 113
Boyce, 59, 88
Boyd, 128, 129,
131
Boyer, 20, 112,
113, 114, 115, 119,

143

144

Edson, 103
Eger, 48
Ehrhardt, 41, 42,
44-49, 55, 68
Ehrhart, 17, 21,
22, 61, 62, 64, 75
Ehrman, 12, 25,
26, 64, 79
Einsel, 33, 34
Elling, 141
Elliot, 116
Encill, 103
Engel, 4, 18
Engle, 40, 128,
129, 131
Ensign, 41
Erman, 31
Esch, 57
Estell, 104
Evans, 20
Everding, 69
Everett, 100
Ewing, 18
Exline, 104

-F-
Fabra, 107
Fadley, 133
Fast, 17, 18, 53
Fate, 83
Fauley, 32
Faust, 60, 106
Ferree, 12, 23, 60,
66
Fields, 64
Fies, 7
Fike, 112
Fischel, 61
Fish, 130
Fisher, 32, 80
Fissel, 59, 60, 61
Fister, 93
Fitzgerald, 61
Flauer, 57
Fleck, 130

Fletcher, 20
Fliger, 136
Flinchbaugh, 67
Flowers, 60, 65
Fluke, 106, 107
Folk, 79
Foot, 119
Fortney, 97, 103
Frank, 52
Frederick, 78
Frensch, 133
Frey, 33, 60, 72,
73, 124
Friedline, 94
Friesner, 4, 17-19,
39-44, 46, 40, 54
Frisbey, 130
Frysinger, 100,
101
Fulton, 120
Funk, 53
Furry, 81

-G-
Gable, 30
Gaertner, 70
Gaier, 97
Gail, 33
Gallagher, 43
Gantz, 14, 24, 88
Garber, 53
Gardner, 20, 95
Garletts, 129
Garletz, 129
Gebel, 69
Geckler, 28, 29,
43
Gedultig, 127
Geil, 42, 52
Geilelman, 61
Geiselman, 11, 12,
14
Geisselman, 75
Gerberich, 22, 80,
82, 84, 85, 89

Gibson, 128
Giesey, 35
Gilespie, 37
Gindlesparger,
129
Ginter, 29
Gladfelter, 63
Glatfelder, 12, 74
Glatfelter, 15, 75,
76, 90, 133
Gochenour, 52
Godfrey, 72
Good, 55
Gorshuch, 36
Grau, 45
Graut, 76
Graves, 44
Gray, 51
Green, 119
Greiner, 2
Griffith, 96, 107
Grim, 6, 66, 93
Grimes, 4
Grimm, 39, 40, 50,
51
Groff, 51
Groh, 80
Gross, 74, 94
Grove, 67, 82, 87
Groves, 55
Gudling, 56
Guentner, 1
Gump, 124
Gunsett, 104
Guttelman, 135

-H-
Hackmann, 135
Hagenbuch, 78
Hahl, 93
Hahnawaldt, 84
Hall, 94
Hamann, 9
Hamen, 92
Hamilton, 8, 19,

145

40

1059118

Made in the USA